A LIGHTHOUSE FOR ALEXANDRIA:

PHAROS
ANCIENT WONDER OF THE WORLD

Thomas C. Clarie

A Lighthouse for Alexandria:
Pharos, Ancient Wonder of the World
Copyright © 2008 by Thomas C. Clarie
ISBN 13: 978-1-934582-12-1
ISBN 10: 1-934582-12-3

All rights reserved. No part of this book may be reproduced or utilized in any form or by any means, electronic or mechanical, including photocopying, scanning, recording or by any information storage and retrieval system now known or hereafter invented, without permission in writing from the publisher. Inquiries should be addressed to:

BACK CHANNEL PRESS
170 Mechanic Street
Portsmouth, NH 03801
www.backchannelpress.com
Printed in the United States of America

Design and layout by Nancy Grossman
Library of Congress PCN 2008935758

DEDICATED TO

Agustinus Manek Tae of Indonesia
August 20, 1991 – April 2, 2008
Christian Children's Fund Sponsor Child

Boy raised in a land of volcanoes,
Painted blue surf, and seething tsunamis –
You are suddenly sitting quietly
Under a tall waterfall
Holding rubies and diamonds.
I wrote to you of life
But forgot to tell you about death.
You always teased that
You would pray for me endlessly.
Now, that promise is forever.

The Hand that directs the evolution of worlds
always leaves one monument as a lighthouse.
Louis Charpentier, in his
Mysteries of Chartres Cathedral, p. 206.

The city had no need of sun or moon,
for the glory of God gave it light,
and its lamp was the Lamb.
Revelation 21:22-23.

Jesus was leaving the temple when his disciples came
and pointed to the temple buildings.
He answered, "Yes, look at it all.
I tell you this: not one stone will be left upon another;
all will be thrown down."
Matthew 24:1-2.

THE FOUNDER OF ALEXANDRIA

After his stinging defeat by Alexander the Great, Persian ruler Darius abandoned his mother on the battlefield and fled for his life. Alexander paid a personal visit to Sisygambis, to assure her that her son was still alive. On the visit, he brought with him his lifelong best friend, Hephaestion. As both walked in side by side, Sisygambis took one look at the handsome, polished, and taller Hephaestion and then prostrated herself before him. Shocked murmurs from those gathered caused the Queen Mother to become confused and stumble. Alexander smiled, rushed forward and helped her up, saying, "Never mind, Mother. You made no mistake; he too is Alexander."

Alexander and Hephaestion enter Darius family tent. Curtius, 1696 edition.

Ancient door in Alexandria's Fort Qaitbay

TABLE OF CONTENTS

xiii	Acknowledgments
xv	Introduction
xix	Prologue
xxi	Chronology
xxiii	Examples of Variant Spellings
1	Chapter 1—As It Might Have Been
5	Chapter 2—Alexander Chooses the Site
19	Chapter 3—The Desert Oracle at Siwa
25	Chapter 4—A Famous City is Born
37	Chapter 5—Ptolemy I, Builder of the Pharos
43	Chapter 6—Sostratus and the Inscription
51	Chapter 7—High Enough to Touch the Stars?
57	Chapter 8—Square, Octagon, and Globe
67	Chapter 9—A Mirror of Light
73	Chapter 10—Top Statue Ruling Alexandria
77	Chapter 11—The Alexandria of Ancient Rome
85	Chapter 12—Religious Fever Hits the City
91	Chapter 13—The Lighthouse During Islamic Times
103	Chapter 14—Napoleon Comes to Alexandria
119	Chapter 15—The Weathering of Stone
129	Chapter 16—Clues: Abusir, Coins, Mosaics
137	Chapter 17—Fort Qaitbay
141	Chapter 18—Modern-Day Alexandria: Beauty and Hope vs. Chaos
159	Chapter 19—Empereur, Goddio, and UNESCO Go Underwater
181	Chapter 20—Pierre Cardin's Dream
185	Chapter 21—Mile-High Skyscrapers
193	Color Plates 1-26
213	Chapter 22—Legacy: Wonder of the World and More
225	Bibliography
235	Index
248	Illustration Credits
249	About the Author

ILLUSTRATIONS

vii	Alexander and Hephaestion enter Darius family tent by Curtius
viii	Ancient door in Fort Qaitbay
xvii	Bibliotheca Alexandrina letter to Clarie
xviii	Pyramids, lure of Mother Egypt
xx	Osiris and Isis and four children of Horus
4	Alexander by Ludwig Burger
6	Map of ancient Mediterranean
13	Map of ancient Alexandria
16	Alexander laying out the city by Castaigne printed 1899
18	Alexandria 1893 outside city
20	Shearing camels by Gentz printed 1879
22	Oasis of Siwa
24	Coat of arms, city of Alexandria
27	Ancient Alexandria by Grauth printed 1879
29	Rosetta Gate in Alexandria printed 1801
31	Map of ancient Alexandria by Botti
34	Alexandria's Mahmudiya Canal in 1900
35	Banks of the Mahmudiya Canal by Gentz printed 1879
39	Pharos from 1938 book by Halliburton
40	Gem portraits of Ptolemy II Philadelphus and Arsinoe
44	Pharos in 1870 book by Adams
46	Pharos close-up in 1938 book by Halliburton
50	Pharos, 1630 atlas of Jansson Jansonius
52	Tall twisting Pharos fantasy printed 1879
53	Trading card depiction of Pharos printed 1880
54	Pharos depiction by Ehrlach printed 1721
58	Thiersch 1909 book frontispiece
59	Thiersch detailed version 1909 book
64	Pharos by Heemskerck printed 1550
68	Pharos magazine ad published 1938
74	Begram vase third-fourth century B.C.
74	Pharos mosaic sixth century church floor
75	Poseidon at Virginia Beach
78	Cleopatra carried into palace; by Keller printed 1879
81	Map of Alexandria as Roman provincial town

ILLUSTRATIONS

84	St. Menas marble relief, fifth century A.D.
86	St. Mark sermon in Alexandria by Bellini 1504-7
88	Arab cemetery by Welsch printed 1879
90	Maiden of Coptic faith by Richter printed 1879
93	Pharos in Arab period by Thiersch printed 1909
96	Pharos Arab period
98	Sais or footman by Muller printed 1879
100	Alexandria and New Harbor 1762
102	Map of Alexandria by Bellin 1764
103	Bonaparte Before the Sphinx by Gerome printed 1867-8
105	Sea battle near Alexandria
107	Alexandria April 1, 1813 by Pinkerton
108	Meeting with Mehemet Ali by Roberts 1839
109	Alexandria Harbor by Bartlett 1846
110	Pompey's Pillar 1848
111	Alexandria by Ramage and Brandard 1860
112	Cleopatra's Needles by Roberts 1839
113	Cleopatra's Needles by Bonfils 1878
114	Place Mohamed Ali by Strassberger 1879
117	Alexandria Grand Square after attack by British 1882
120	Sphinx
128	Roman coin illustration
130	Abusir Tower at Taposiris Magna
131	Coin 150 by Donaldson
133	Thirteenth Century mosaic, Zen Chapel, St. Marks, Venice
136	Caesarea 2007
137	Fort Qaitbay 1798
138	Fort Qaitbay 1886
139	Fort Qaitbay Citadel sign
139	Fort Qaitbay Main Tower sign
142	Modern map of Alexandria's eastern area
144	Refugees leave Alexandria 1882
145	Flying boat Caledonia over Alexandria 1937
149	Carl Sagan's Ancient Library of Alexandria, Cosmos series
154	Port of Alexandria 1920
155	Quay of the Grands Couriers Alexandria
158	Alexandria's breakwater from Fort Qaitbay

ILLUSTRATIONS

161	Honor Frost triangulating sixteenth century wreck
162	Stephen Schwartz psychic investigator
164	Empereur teaching at Fort Qaitbay
165	Pharos block 1027 ID sheet
168	Drawing of underwater wreck site 1963 Frost book
170	U.S.A.I.D.'s Andrew Natsios and Pope Shenouda
178	Goddio exhibit at Grand Palais in Paris 2006
184	Cairo minaret after Pharos
188	Frank Lloyd Wright's mile-high proposed skyscraper
193	Color Plate 1 – Chicago spire September 2007
194	Color Plate 2 – Burj Dubai at over 160 floors June 2008
195	Color Plate 3 – Burj Dubai March 2008
196	Color Plate 4 – Louisiana State Capitol Building
197	Color Plate 5 – Washington Masonic National Memorial Alexandria, Virginia
198	Color Plate 6 – Traveler's Tower Hartford, Connecticut
199	Color Plate 7 – Luxor light Las Vegas
200	Color Plate 8 – 911 Tribute in Lights September 11, 2006
200	Color Plate 9 – Alexandria planetarium
201	Color Plate 10 – Bibliotheca Alexandrina back view
201	Color Plate 11 – Bibliotheca Alexandrina dome
202	Color Plate 12 – Bibliotheca Alexandrina letter wall
203	Color Plate 13 – Bibliotheca Alexandrina from across harbor
204	Color Plate 14 – Logo of the Baltimore Friends of Bibliotheca Alexandrina
204	Color Plate 15 – Bibliotheca Alexandrina interior
205	Color Plate 16 – Google satellite view of Pharos location
206	Color Plate 17 – Tom and Rose at Montazah Palace
206	Color Plate 18 – Maze of commercial signs in Alexandria
207	Color Plate 19 – Marketplace in Alexandria
207	Color Plate 20 – Fort Qaitbay women and surf
208	Color Plate 21 – Our Saviour's Church Copenhagen
209	Color Plate 22 – Pharos reconstruction Changsha, China
209	Color Plate 23 – Eilean Glas, Scotland and Pharos by Grimsdale
210	Color Plate 24 – Pharos Harbor in Roman times by Grimsdale
211	Color Plate 25 – Arab astronomers atop Pharos by Grimsdale
212	Color Plate 26 – Fort Qaitbay surf by Limber
214	Seven Wonders, Magyar Posta by Dudas and Janas
216	Seven wonders certificate www.new7wonders.com
249	Author Thomas C. Clarie at Fort Qaitbay

ACKNOWLEDGMENTS

I want to thank many of my colleagues—faculty and librarians at Southern Connecticut State University—for steadily encouraging me over the years in my research for this book. My close friend at Southern, Research Librarian Claire Bennett, whose recent passing I view as a tragedy, never let me get discouraged. She and her husband, former Quinnipiac College President Harry Bennett, always inspired me both by their high competence and by the loving way they treated people.

Former Library Director Richard Hegel, among many things the Treasurer of the Yale University Graduate Club, encouraged me to apply both for my job at Southern and for promotion. I owe him a great debt. Former Library School Director Emanuel Prostano always encouraged me, both as board member at a public library where I worked and later at my university. His wink, smile, and powerful look proved to be my great allies. Southern librarian Ananda Pandiri, who has just published two massive bibliographies on Gandhi, never let me abandon my lighthouse research. I will also be forever grateful to my colleague, German professor Gary Gesmonde, for translating two crucial German texts as a personal favor to me.

My parents, Federal Judge T. Emmet Clarie and his wife, Gertrude, now both deceased, were always the perfect parents, asking questions, laughing at my worries, and watching my golden retriever while I researched. My wife's parents, U.S. Fish and Wildlife hiring officer Mary Dorr and her husband, John Dorr, were always highly supportive.

I want to thank my longtime Connecticut friends, Joe Ogle and Edward Moore, and my New Hampshire SPCA friends, Betty Brigham, Lisa DiBerardinis, Nick Ruse, Don Tucker, Kelly LaBossiere, and Angie Brintle. University of Southern New Hampshire department chairperson Betsy Gunzelmann and her son, Matthew, have been great friends and neighbors. Whenever my inspiration dried up, Matt would say, "Let me know if you want my help." His confidence and kindness immediately made me again creative.

My chief acknowledgment of appreciation is addressed to my wife Rosemary, who had to endure countless statements that everything was hopeless, as she dared ask me once a month, "Why do you *need* to do a book on the Pharos?" I always made up a different answer, and she never laughed at my replies. Her heroic attempts to wear her yoke gracefully will forever be appreciated by her husband.

I also want to thank the United Nations Educational, Scientific, and Cultural Organization. In a fierce, daily, often unappreciated fight, UNESCO is working to preserve the world's cultural history, not just structures, but ideas, language, art, dance, and music. UNESCO's

ACKNOWLEDGMENTS

World Heritage Committee and its Committee for the Safeguarding of Intangible Cultural Heritage get gold stars from me for their patient courage.

It is an honor to thank Nancy and John Grossman, the owners of Backchannel Press, who edited and published this book. Their skill and creativity have quickly become known throughout New England. To all those colleagues and friends from my past whom my exhausted mind has forgotten to mention, let me just say, you know who you are, and you know I could not have done either this book or my life without you.

INTRODUCTION

This work takes a fresh look at the Lighthouse of Alexandria, one of the Seven Ancient Wonders of the World, and along the way explores both the modern and ancient city of Alexandria, Egypt. Built in 279 B.C. to proclaim Alexandria the Pearl of the Mediterranean, the Pharos served as a beacon of freedom, acceptance, and intellectual fervor for centuries.

Many famous rulers passed through the light of this magnificent tower that was, perhaps, planned by the city's founder, Alexander the Great. Julius Caesar, Mark Antony, Cleopatra, and Napoleon all saw it cast its beacon of both welcome and warning. Weakened by earthquakes, wind, and waves, it was finally destroyed in 1349 A.D.

In the past few decades, stubborn divers have sought to find the lighthouse underwater and have exhorted the Egyptian government to make its rediscovery a priority. UNESCO and two noted divers are making exciting finds. Jean-Yves Empereur has found massive underwater blocks near the ancient lighthouse site. Franck Goddio has dived further east and found first Cleopatra's Palace and then, still further east, the lost cities of Herakleion and Canopus.

This book explores these questions, among others: Why was the Pharos on the Ancient Wonders list? What happened to the Pharos? What was so special about the lighthouse site and the city of Alexandria? Would the Pharos be considered a wonder in today's modern era?

I have written this work because there continues to be no book currently available just about the Pharos, though huge interest in the topic of the Lighthouse of Alexandria persists. The only work marginally close is a self-published work titled *The Electric Mirror on the Pharos*, a highly opinionated book on ancient batteries and occultism. UNESCO and universities with money and expertise are studying the Alexandrian harbor area now. Also, a New Seven Wonders list, compiled from 100 million Internet votes, was announced in the summer of 2007.

I have long regretted that most books on Alexandria are coffee table books filled mostly with diving photos. One goal of this publication has been to include a nice balance of detailed text and high-quality images on many topics. Secondly, I have attempted to show the iconography of the Pharos by including illustrations of the many different ways in which it has been depicted. A third goal has been to create a very readable and exciting text while carefully documenting each statement. Following my first draft 20 years ago that contained 532 endnotes, I added still more sources, then removed numbered references and instead cited

INTRODUCTION

them directly in the body of the work. The references remain in this version of the text, but hopefully in a more convenient form for the reader.

Of particular delight to me was funding the translation of two German books published in 1901 and 1909, both classics. The German words of Johann Heinrich Friedrich Adler and Hermann Thiersch have never been extensively referred to in an English-language book until my work. Twenty-first century researchers still refer to Thiersch constantly, and it is a special pleasure to present his thoughts here in detail.

I believe strongly in the concept of "value-added," not just addressing a specific topic but discussing over, under, and around that topic to enrich it and augment it. This book makes a strong effort to discuss such related and highly interesting topics as Wonders of the World in general, lighthouse flames and lights, ancient Egypt, the Nile River and canals, Alexander the Great, Julius Caesar, Mark Antony, Cleopatra, Napoleon, the new Library of Alexandria which opened in 2002, underwater diving, worldwide monument preservation efforts, obelisks, skyscrapers, attempts to save a declining city, and Arab culture.

This is a time when Alexandria's new library, the Bibliotheca Alexandria, heralds the hope of a new era of greatness for the city. Therefore it is an exciting and highly appropriate time to contemplate both the past and possible future of the Pharos, Lighthouse of Alexandria.

Thomas C. Clarie
Hampton, New Hampshire

The Executive Secretariat
Shallalat Bldg. 116, El Horreya Av.
Bab Sharqi, Alexandria, Egypt
Tel. : (203) 4836024/28/52
Fax. : (203) 4836001
P . O . Box : 138 El Mansheya

الإمــانــة التنفيذيــة
١١٦ طريق الحرية - عمارة الشلالات
باب شرقـى - الاسكندريـة - مصــر
تليفون : ٥٢ / ٢٨ / ٤٨٣٦.٢٤ (٢.٣)
فاكس : ٤٨٣٦..١ (٢.٣)
ص . ب : ١٣٨ المنشية

Mr. Thomas Clarie
64 Long Hill Road
Clinton, CT. 06413
USA

Ref.:   PM/96/084   18 February, 1996

Dear Mr. Clarie,

    We have recently received a notice from Dr. Mohammed Aman, Dean of the University of Wisconsin School of Library and Information Science, and the Friends of the Bibliotheca Alexandrina, about your generous contribution to the Bibliotheca Alexandrina Project. ($100).

    The Bibliotheca Alexandrina Project is now proceeding very quickly. As you may know already, Phase #1 of the Project (TP1: Foundations and Ground Engineering) will be completed in the Summer, 1996. The Tender Action for Phase #2 (TP2: Structure, Finishing, Fit-Out, and Services) will also be completed by the Summer and work on the building is foreseen to begin at that time.

    In the meantime, our Library Services Department has arranged two successful international Symposiums on the "Intellectual Contents of the Library". Work in that Department is also continuing on training the future librarians, acquisition of books and other materials, and bibliographic format and automation for the new library.

    The project needs in the next 2 and 1/2 years has risen dramatically, and we are looking forward to increased activities from the Friends groups around the world and the supporters of the project to help us bring the project to completion.

    Thank you again for your interest and continuing support of the Project.

                               Sincerely yours,
                               Project Manager a.i.

                               Prof. Dr. Mohsen Zahran

cc. Dr. M. Aman with best regards
              001-414-2204848

Bibliotheca Alexandrina letter to Clarie February 18, 1996

Pyramids, lure of Mother Egypt, National Geographic 1917

PROLOGUE

What is it about Egyptian history? The sand, desert storms, heat, pyramids, mummies, the large red sun, a massive moon hanging out of the sky over Alexandria Harbor? Thoughts of ancient Egypt stir the blood and make adventurers of us all. My wife and I journeyed there in April 1988. Six years earlier, Egyptian president Anwar Sadat, whom I had long revered as my secret mentor, had been assassinated. Strange that the first site our guide took us to on our initial day in Cairo was Sadat's tomb and eternal flame. The guide had no idea how much that meant to me, for I had Alexandrian flames on my mind as well—the flames from the ancient Pharos.

My wife and I hired a driver and assistant in Cairo for the trip to Alexandria. Coincidence found us visiting during Ramadan. While we ate spaghetti in an "Italian" restaurant overlooking the ancient Pharos harbor, our guides patiently waited outside with no thought of food for the entire day. We loved it that they were calm, reverent, intelligent men. They were what we hoped we had always been—unassuming. Why did they treat us with such respect? That was a question for the Sphinx. We felt our ignorance made us undeserving of that respect.

We had long pictured in our fiery imaginings an Alexandria of Greek columns gracing ancient, huge-blocked Roman roads, with pedestrians from every nation waving grandly to us as we passed by majestically. Instead, our eyes found irregular roads covered with sand, and endless bazaars. We did find the pedestrians, but they were all unsmiling Arabs in local dress. There were no waves at the passing car. Was that because we were intentionally no longer looking out the windows?

My hope, and my wife's, as we present this book for your enjoyment, is that a bewitching Alexandria of columned, wide-avenued roads will someday be born again, and that people of all races will someday visit Alexandria just to wave at each other and love each other. That is the promise of Alexandria's past beauty, the promise of which Alexander the Great dreamed, the promise for which his ancient lighthouse burned so brightly.

Osiris and Isis and four children of Horus, book by Rappoport

CHRONOLOGY

B.C.

332 – Alexandria, Egypt founded by Alexander the Great.
299 – Construction of Pharos begins.
279 – Pharos dedicated.
47 – Caesar's Alexandrian War damages dam leading to lighthouse.

A.D.

312 – Earthquake hits Alexandria.
358 – Earthquake hits Alexandria.
365 – Disastrous earthquake and tidal wave hits area, undoubtedly damaging base area of Pharos.
396 – Earthquake hits Alexandria.
500 – Considerable repairs to foundation accomplished under Emperor Anastasius I from 491-518; planner Ammonios designs surf breakers in form of curve on north side and fixes tower underpinnings.
641 – Arab conquest of Alexandria after 14-month siege by Arabian General Amr.
705 – Greek Emperor Masoudi tricks Calif Walid ben Abd el-Melik into dismantling upper half of lighthouse watchtower by telling him Alexander the Great's treasure lies buried there. Mirror destroyed in moving process.
796 – Top of tower destroyed by earthquake or windstorm.
850 – Mohammedans from Arabia occupy Egypt.
880 – Ibn Tulun renovates upper two stories with brick faced with stucco; octagon restored; wooden cupola built on top becomes a minaret.
890 – Chamarya, Ibn Tulun's son, repairs west side.
956 – Fifty feet of tower (upper half of upper story) falls due to earthquake felt in Egypt, Syria and Magreb.
969 – Cairo built; Alexandria falls into neglect.
1100 – Octagon falls, due to earthquake.
1182 – Domed mosque built on top of remains.
1193 – Extensive restoration begins.

CHRONOLOGY

1274 – One side of Pharos repaired, and cupola/mosque reinstalled under Sultan Melik Zaher Beibars, who sends men to Alexandria to rebuild structure.

1302 – Earthquake ravages north coast of Africa, and hits Alexandria especially hard; mosque destroyed.

1303 – Mosque reconstructed under Rokn el din Beibar El Gaschenkir.

1326 – Another quake strikes; traveler Batuta says one face in ruins.

1349 – Pharos now completely ruined.

1365 – A second lighthouse is completed to replace the old one.

1435 – Another earthquake leaves that lighthouse just a pile of stones.

1477 – Sultan Qaitbay visits Alexandria and sees remains of the ancient lighthouse.

1479 – Fort Qaitbay is inaugurated personally by the sultan.

1519 – Turkish invasion of Alexandria.

1798 – Conquest of fort by General Bonaparte.

1805 – Fort is repaired.

1882 – Bombardment of Alexandria by the British fighting Arabi destroys fort.

1898 – German expedition looks for foundation of Pharos in sea; no luck.

1910 – Engineer Gaston Jondet discovers Old Port of Pharos.

1961 – Egyptian diver finds large statues on sea bed at entrance to Alexandria Harbor.

1968 – Divers study remains of 36-foot statues.

1994 – Jean-Yves Empereur finds Pharos remains underwater.

1998 – Pierre Cardin's plan for new 480-foot Pharos is rejected.

1998 – Franck Goddio finds Cleopatra's Palace underwater in Eastern Harbor across the harbor from Pharos site.

2002 – New library of Alexandria, the Bibliotheca Alexandrina, opens across the harbor from Pharos site.

EXAMPLES OF VARIANT SPELLINGS

Many words in this book are of Greek, Roman, and Arabic origin. Over the years they have been filtered through German, French, and English before appearing once again, often changing their spelling. An attempt has been made to choose one spelling out of several, even many, for a word. That choice has been a spelling widely used and accepted by modern institutions and experts. The following list presents just some of these problem words.

Abukir (also Aboukir, Abu Qir, Abu Kir)
Abusir (also Abu Sir)
Alexandria (also Al Iskandariya, Iskandariyah)
Amr (also Amru)
Anastasius (also Anastasios)
Caesar Augustus (instead of Augustus Caesar)
Chersonesus Fortress (also Chersonese)
Cnidos (also Cnidus, Knidos)
Canopic Branch (also Canobian Branch)
Demetrius I Poliorcetes (also Demetrios Poliorkete, Demetrios Poliorcetes)
Dinocrates (also Deinocrates)
Domitian (also Domitius)
El-Dekheila Port (also El-Dekhila Port)
Epiphanius (also Epiphanus)
Fort Agami (also Fort Agame)
Gerasa (also Jerash, Gerash)
Greco (also Graeco)
Heptastadium (also Heptastadion)
Heracles (also Herakles)
Heracleion (also Herakleion)
Hosni Mubarak (also Hosny Mubarak)
Ismail Pasha (also Isma'il Pasha, Ismael Pasha)
Kibotos (also Kobotos)
Magreb (also Maghrib)

VARIANT SPELLINGS

Mahmudiya (also Mahmoudieh, Mahmoudia, Mahmoudeyeh)
Mameluke (also Mamluk, Mamluke)
Mareotis Lake (also Mariout Lake, Mariyut Lake).
Mohammed Ali (also Mohamed Ali, Mohmaid Ali, Mehemet Ali)
Montazah (also Montazzah)
Naukratis (also Naucratis)
Nebuchadnezzar (also Nebuchodonossa)
Octavian (also Octavius)
Paraetonia (also Paraetonium)
Pompey's Pillar (also Pompeii Pillar, Pompeii's Pillar, Pillar of Pompey, Pillar of Pompeii)
Posedeion (also Posideum, Poseideim)
Ptolemy I (also Ptolemaeus)
Ptolemy II Philadelphus (also Ptolemaeus Philadelphus)
Qaitbay (also Qait Bay, Qait Bey, Qait-Bay, Qaitbey, Quaitbey, Quait Bey, Quay-Bay, Qaytbey, Kait Bay, Kait-Bay, Kait Bey);
Ras-el-Tin (also Ras el Tin)
Rhacotis (also Rhakotis)
Serapeum (also Serapion, Serpeion)
Sostratus (also Sostratos)
Strabo (also Strabon)
Taposiris Magna (also Tabusiris Magna)
Tutankhamen (also Tutankhamon, Tutankhamun)
Tuthmosis (also Thothmes, Thutmose)
Wadi el Natrun (also Wadi Natron, Wadi Natroun)

A LIGHTHOUSE FOR ALEXANDRIA:

PHAROS
ANCIENT WONDER OF THE WORLD

CHAPTER 1
AS IT MIGHT HAVE BEEN

A flash of light! There—it happened again! His eyes weren't making it up! It wasn't just sunlight striking the water! Or, was it? The boy turned to his uncle.

"Sir, did you see that flash of light? I think I've seen others in the last few minutes. What is it?"

The uncle did not turn toward the boy, nor did the corner of his mouth twist up into a patronizing smile. Instead, the well-dressed merchant kept his gaze on the horizon line, to see another flash of light, this one still longer and more brilliant.

"That's Alexandria, boy."

"But, sir, we're still more than a half-day's sail away! How can we be seeing the great city?"

"Boy, it's the lighthouse—the great lighthouse of Pharos."

"But, Uncle, how can you say that? The light wouldn't be on during the day—would it?"

"No, Ammonios, that is the huge statue on top of the lighthouse that you see. It holds a translucent sword that glistens like diamonds in the sun. As soon as you see it out here on the ocean, you know that the gods give special protection to Alexandria. Can you feel it? Some say they see the sword's glint even a whole day's sail away. Imagine—seeing a city's glory while one day removed from it!"

2 | A LIGHTHOUSE FOR ALEXANDRIA

The boy was unable to fully follow his uncle's line of thought. But, yes, he could feel Alexandria's unique glory burning into his heart over and over, as the powerful glint pierced all time and space to illuminate his face in amazing ways as the merchant ship plowed steadily onward towards port.

Three hours from Alexandria, the boy and his uncle noticed another ship a few hundred yards away. They and some crew members waved from time to time to the other ship, but received no gestures back.

"Unfriendly cusses!" murmured the uncle.

A few minutes later, a bit closer to Alexandria, Ammonios was startled to see a huge steam geyser rise out of the ocean, a bit to the right of the unfriendly ship.

"Did you see that, Uncle? What was it? A sea serpent? An angry god? A storm under the waters?"

Before the man could answer, another seething, steamy circle exploded on the waters, this one just to the left and slightly behind the strange ship. And, as they gaped in wonder and shock, they beheld yet another marvel. The entire sail area of that ship became encircled in an intensely bright glow, causing the sails to begin steaming and then warp. In seconds, the sails exploded in flames, just as the masts began to vibrate and split from the sheer intensity of the glow. The rest of the vessel shuddered and then burst into violent flames within seconds. It sank in no time at all. Only a few pitiful screams broke the ensuing, eerie silence. The boy and his uncle stared at each other for what seemed like an eternity. Ammonios suddenly burst into horrible sobs.

"They're dead—all dead. Scorched! The flames came so fast. Do you think they felt it? Uncle, I think I'm going to faint. The pain—I feel their pain! Am I on fire? Uncle, are we to die next? Tell me from where it will come. I must face it and be brave. If we too have offended the gods, I want to die well."

The uncle answered none of Ammonios' questions, and yet answered them all, uttering one word as he shook the boy hard to fight off his hysteria—"Pharos."

The boy jolted loose from his uncle's hard grasp and ran to the ship rail. He now saw nothing but empty sea and the occasional glint of the Pharos' tip. "Uncle—was that an enemy ship? And how did they know?"

The uncle continued to stare in the direction of the ever-closer lighthouse and murmured, "Yes, it was a bad ship. They know everything in Alexandria."

Later, they arrived in the port of Alexandria, with the looming lighthouse sliding by on their right as they stared up and up in wonder at its glistening tower. Its sounding horns and strange singing statues cast melodies over sail after sail in the busy harbor. To their left, opposite the Pharos, magnificent palaces and rich emporia slipped by.

Ammonios breathlessly panted, "This Alexandria, Uncle—it must be heaven, and the Pharos the very top of heaven."

The boy's uncle laughed gently but long, nodding all the while, "It just could be, boy—it just could be."

4 | A LIGHTHOUSE FOR ALEXANDRIA

Alexander by Ludwig Burger, 1879
book by G. Ebers

CHAPTER 2
ALEXANDER CHOOSES THE SITE

Napoleon has said that Alexander rendered himself more illustrious by founding Alexandria, and perhaps making it the seat of his Empire, than by his most brilliant tactical victories. Napoleon felt that Alexandria should become the capital of the world. It was located near one of the ancient mouths of the Nile. It was situated between Asia and Africa within reach of India and Europe. Its harbor afforded the only safe anchorage from the coastline of Tunis or ancient Carthage to Alexandretta. The Old Port sheltered ships from wind and attack. Its proportions were such that Napoleon marveled that all the navies of the world could moor in Alexandria's harbor.

While honoring the genius of Alexander in choosing the site, one might note that the spot he chose was not barren desert wilderness with no previous development, history, or trade. The area had a long history prior to this period, and was undoubtedly better-watered and fairly green with vegetation 2,000 years ago. When Alexander the Great arrived in the area in 332 B.C. and took control of Egypt from the Persians, the countryside near the future city of Alexandria probably was viewed by many civilized Greeks as being occupied by wild herdsmen. But in reality, the area was cultivated with olives, grape vines, and figs, and enjoyed an active if slightly disorganized trade.

Three thousand years before Alexander the Great, there existed an area in Egypt known as the petty kingdom of Marea, also known as the "Kingdom of the Harpoon," perhaps because this was a common weapon for killing fish in nearby Lake Mareotis. In ancient times, this great, deep, freshwater body had an eastern arm extending thirty

6 | A LIGHTHOUSE FOR ALEXANDRIA

miles southeast of Alexandria, reaching all the way to the Canopic branch of the Nile River. The very ancient Egyptian port of "The Great Door" is assumed by some to have been near the mouth of the now-extinct Canopic Nile.

Lake Mareotis also had a long, finger-like arm stretching 40 miles west of Alexandria called Lake Maryut. It was separated from the sea by the Abusir ridge, a narrow, well-cultivated piece of land. In ancient days this area was known as the Taenia or Taposiris. Along it ran the only road from Alexandria to the western

Map of ancient Mediterranean

provinces. The olive trees that grew in profusion west of the city caused the area to be known as "Olive Land."

Dr. Salah A. Tahoun, of the University of El-Zagazig's Soil Science Department, today refers to this area as the Northwestern Coastal Zone (NWCZ) of Egypt, running along the Mediterranean coast at the northern extremities of the Western Desert from Alexandria west 300 miles to El-Salloum on the Libyan border.

Libyans on the western borders of Egypt continuously infiltrated the Egyptian Nile Delta in ancient times, causing such a threat that Seti I (1313-1292 B.C.) attacked them, defeating the Libyan forces during two fierce battles in the Delta. His son, Ramses II, had to fight them off again in later years. Outpost positions in the western Egyptian frontier called "Mount of the Horns of the Earth" and "Fortress of the West" were always the first to see Libyan intruders. West of Alexandria, Marsa Matruh in ancient times was the principal port of the important kingdom of Siwa. The harbor there was known as Ammonia.

In 637 B.C., Greeks arrived in Libya and founded Cyrene. After numerous fights between the Greeks and Egypt, Amasis of Egypt invited Greek merchants into his country, assigning to them the Western Delta city of Naukratis. This old border city was situated on a highly advantageous canal leading from the Canopic Nile to Lake Mareotis. Naukratis quickly became the most important commercial town in the empire. After the founding of Alexandria, Greek residents moved quickly into the new city, leaving Naukratis to fall into ruin behind them.

In 332 B.C., Alexander left Gaza, marched along the coast, and in seven days reached Pelusium. At this frontier fortress of Egypt, his friend Hephaestion waited with the fleet. He now marched south to Memphis. There, Satrap Mazaces surrendered the city to him, together with its garrison and treasury, without struggle.

Alexander now journeyed from Memphis on the Canopian Nile tributary to the western mouth of the Nile Delta. He then turned to the west and eventually reached the area of Pharos Island. After examining the locale, Alexander quickly decided to found the new city of Alexandria at the site.

Plutarch was born about 46 A.D. at Chaeronea in Boeotia, where he later had a school and years later took up the priesthood at nearby Delphi. He was one of the last of the classical Greek historians, writing essays and dialogues on all sorts of scientific, literary, and philosophical subjects. He traveled in Egypt and traveled to Rome, where he had many influential friends. Emperor Hadrian granted him a government appointment in Greece. His *Parallel Lives* on prominent Greeks and Romans was written late in life and is his best-known and most influential work.

Plutarch says that Alexander had chosen a previous site on the advice of his architects, and was on the point of measuring and marking it out. But as he lay asleep Alexander dreamed that a grey-haired man of regal appearance stood by his side and recited lines from the *Odyssey*: "Out of the tossing sea where it breaks on the beaches of Egypt, rises an isle from the waters; the name that men give it is Pharos."

Alexander rose the next morning and immediately visited Pharos, at that time still an island. What he saw was a place with wonderful natural advantages, a strip of land resembling a broad isthmus stretching between the sea and a great lagoon with a spacious harbor at its end. Alexander immediately ordered that the plan of the city be designed to conform to this site.

The area of Pharos that Alexander viewed contained the old, wretched fishing village of Rhacotis. In fact, the name of Alexandria remained "Rakoti" in Coptic. This village on the northeastern shore of Lake Mareotis was already in existence in 1300 B.C. The long, narrow, flat island of Pharos was well-known as the spot where all the Greeks out of Homer had camped. Its northern coast was fringed with small islets. A deep bay on the northern side was called Pirate's Haven because it had been a place of refuge for Greek, Phoenician, Carian and Samian sea rovers in earlier times.

Legends told of Helen of Troy coming to Egypt with Paris. She became bored with the island of Pharos and left, complaining that there was nothing to see and that its only residents were seals. She returned to the island ten years later with her husband Menelaus when they were blown off course while returning home from Troy. In Homer's *Odyssey*, Book 4, Menelaus wrote:

> There is an island washed by the open sea lying off Nile mouth—seamen call it Pharos—distant a day's sail in a clean hull with a brisk land breeze behind. It has a harbor, a sheltered bay, where shipmasters take on dark water for the outward voyage. Here the gods held me twenty days becalmed.

Menelaus asked an old man there, "What island is this?" and the man answered, "Pharaoh's," but with a pronunciation that made it sound like "Prouti's." Menelaus misinterpreted this as "Proteus," the name of the sea deity to whom Poseidon had granted the gift of prophecy. Pharos as the name for the island passed down in history, as did that of Proteus as a patron diety. The word "pharos" was not formed from any Greek word meaning "light" or "to see," as some have claimed. Also incorrect is the guess by some that the word served as a Hellenic form of *Phrah*, the Egyptian name for the sun.

The island was a strip of white, dazzling, calcareous rock, much larger than it is today. Houses and the Temple of Poseidon were built on the western part of the island. This section was named Point Ras-el-Tin, that is, Head of the Fig, because of the point's resemblance to that fruit. At the island's end stood a temple to Hephaestion and at the other stood the great Gate of the Moon.

At the eastern end of the island stood a rock that was washed all around by the sea and had upon it a tower of many stories that was admirably constructed of white stone, perhaps marble. It bore the same name as the island. The coastline in that area was harborless and low on either side, with numerous reefs and shallows. Those sailing from the open sea needed some lofty and conspicuous sign to direct their course straight to the entrance of the harbor.

The lighthouse site has been disputed as being between Fort Qaitbay at the extreme end of the island and a small submerged rock just east of the fort called The Diamond. Historian Peter Fraser and others feel that this rock, at 80 feet in length, is much too small to have been the foundation of the Pharos. Most researchers accept the theory that the present-day remains of Fort Qaitbay rest on the old foundation footprint of the Pharos.

As Fraser will be referred to often in this volume, it is useful to provide some information on his career. Peter Marshall Fraser, a Highland Scot who died in September 2007, was the pre-eminent historian of the Hellenistic Age and lecturer in Hellenistic history at Oxford University. He had great expertise reading Greek inscriptions on stone, but also loved current-day Greek language, literature, and culture. Fraser spoke perfect Greek and could read Arabic as well. In 1943, at age 25, he was parachuted into Greece. After surviving a long Gestapo interrogation that failed to expose the fact that he was a British officer, he blew up the airport at Argos. Fraser published a major study on the cult of Serapis in 1960, followed by his highly respected massive, three-volume work in 1972 titled *Ptolemaic Alexandria*. In the 1970s and 1980s, he masterminded British excavations in Old Kandahar in southern Afghanistan. His *Cities of Alexander* was published in 1996 when Fraser was 78.

Johann Heinrich Friedrich Adler, in his classic 1901 work, *Der Pharos von Alexandria*, theorizes that the lighthouse probably connected with The Diamond and other rocks or reefs by means of a long wall or fort to form Diabathra, a heavy entrance gate to the large harbor that could be locked by iron chains in case of war.

Adler, also referred to often in this work, was a German architect, architectural historian, and archaeologist specializing in ancient excavations and medieval German architecture. He was also responsible for the construction of several churches in Prussia. Adler worked on the Olympia excavations under Ernst Curtius and was responsible for the design of the original museum at Olympia in 1883. He co-authored with Curtius a book on Olympia in 1882 and later in the 1890s wrote a five-volume work on excavations at the site. Adler wrote a study on the Mausoleum at Halicarnassus in 1900 and followed it a year later with his study on the Pharos.

A map of Alexandria drawn in the early 1840s by M. Metter gives the exact coordinates of the Pharos as 31 degrees 13 minutes 5 seconds North Latitude by 29 degrees 55 minutes 44 seconds East Longitude. One can find many variations of latitude/longitude for Alexandria in current sources, but many use 31 degrees 13 minutes North by 29 degrees 55 minutes East.

From the Pharos to the city was one mile by sea and three miles by land. Hermann Thiersch noted that a few Arab writers believed the Pharos had been built at a point far removed from the sea. In 326 A.D., the sea encroached and had steadily come in further since then. These ancient Arabs mentioned it as being in the middle of Alexandria, saying the sea ate away the land until it ended up in the middle of the ocean. These legends are not believable after viewing the site.

Hermann Thiersch's classic 1909 work *Pharos; Antike Islam und Occident* or *Pharos, Antiquity, Islam and Occident: A Contribution to Architectural History* is referred to often in this volume, and an explanation is due the reader as to his credentials. He was a German professor of classical archaeology and the son of August Thiersch, a professor of architectural history. Thiersch's first book was published at age 25, concerning black-painted amphorae figures from sixth century B.C. Etruscan tombs.

In 1902, Thiersch and American archaeologist and theologian John Punnett Peters were alerted to Hellenistic paintings just found in a pair of tombs at Marisa in Israel. They published a book on the painted tombs illustrated with hand-drawn copies, which has recently been republished for modern readers. Born in 1852, Dr.

Peters, professor of Hebrew at the University of Pennsylvania and later Rector of St. Michael's Church in New York City, led an expedition in 1888 to excavate at Nuffar, sixty miles southeast of Babylon in modern-day Turkey. Part of the ancient city of Nippur and many inscribed tablets were uncovered, and G. P. Putnam's Sons published a book on Peters' expedition in 1897.

In 1903, a party of German archaeologists led by Thiersch stumbled upon the ancient remains of Shechem, the main settlement of the Samaritans, about 35 miles north of Jerusalem. It is also the location of Jacob's Well, where Jesus met the Samaritan woman. In 1904, Hermann Thiersch published a book on two ancient Alexandrian grave sites. It was soon followed, in 1909, by his masterpiece on the Pharos. That work included an appendix on his research at Taposiris Magna to the west of Alexandria.

Pharos; Antike Islam und Occident was quickly accepted as the definitive description of the ancient lighthouse, even though Thiersch had to rely on conflicting, weak and sometimes questionable sources. Twenty-first century depictions of the Pharos continue to be based closely on drawings provided in the 1909 publication. Thiersch was a man of wide interests, even publishing a book on Russian Christianity in 1932, just a few years before his death.

In ancient times, an artificial mound or causeway called the Heptastadium served as both a bridge and an aqueduct from the mainland to the western part of the island. This causeway was the only connection from the island to the mainland until intervening land formed in the ninth century A.D. It was called Heptastadium due to its length, seven stadia, 4,270 feet, or three-quarters of a mile. Two special bridgeheads, one on the city side, the other on the island side, protected Heptastadium, the lifeline upon which hung the success or failure of the entire layout.

Writing just a few years after the death of Christ, Strabo (Strabon in Greek) provided an excellent description of the area. He compiled his famed 17-volume *Geographica* after studying under Aristodemus and geography expert Tyrannion. The set was meant to be a sequel to a 43-book history that no longer exists except for one fragment of papyrus. He traveled widely, including a trip in Egypt in 25-24 B.C. to explore the country and the Nile. He wrote in part to educate rulers of the Roman Empire, but his geographical writings were ignored until the late fifth century. He died shortly after 23 A.D.

In Strabo's time, the city's two harbors held more ships than were to be seen in any other port in the world, and carried on a huge export trade. Geographer Strabo wrote a long and famous description of Alexandria's harbor site when it was under Roman rule. Adler considered it the oldest and most valuable period account of the harbor.

Between the Heptastadium and Lochias was the eastern Great Harbor or Great Port. Strabo described it as being a narrow passage with rocks, some under the water and others projecting out of it, which were continually struck hard by waves from the open sea. This passage was so deep close to shore that even the largest ship could be moored at the steps of the docks. Entering the Great Harbor, a merchant vessel would pass through the opening in the breakwater, seeing the Pharos on its right and the Ptolemies' Palace Quarter on its left. The large east basin eventually became a naval base, home to the Royal Fleet. Straight ahead were the colonnaded buildings of the Emporium, where most vessels unloaded and loaded cargo. Goods were shipped to and from these docks to the lake that connected with the Nile.

Well-known British travel writer and novelist Colin Thubron reports in his 1981 Time-Life book, *The Ancient Mariners,* that traffic in the port was so heavy that a vessel might spend days waiting in designated anchorages before reaching the Emporium unloading area. Born 1939 in London and a distant relative of the writer John Dryden, Thubron attended Eton College from 1953-57, joined the publishing staff of Hutchinson and Company in 1959, did freelance travel documentaries for the BBC, and worked for the publisher Macmillan Company in New York. His first travel book, the 1968 *Mirror to Damascus,* was shortly followed by a book on Lebanon. Among his novels, his *To the Last City* in 2002 about a group exploring an Inca city in Peru has been well-received. His latest travel book, *Shadow of the Silk Road* in 2006, is an account of a 7,000-mile journey revisiting the sites of his previous books.

Strabo noted that the western harbor on the other side of the Heptastadium was difficult to enter, although it did not require as much caution as the eastern entrance. A smaller port, Eunostos, the Haven of Happy Return or the Port of Safe Return, was named after a Cypriot king and relative of Ptolemy I. Eunostos fronted the Rhacotis quarter of the city. On the western horn of Eunostos were public granaries. This smaller western harbor later became the commercial port, connected by a canal with sluices to Lake Mareotis, from which products and wares came.

ALEXANDER CHOOSES THE SITE | 13

To the south of the Harbor of Eunostos, surrounded by a city wall, was a basin-like extension called Kibotos, meaning "The Chest." This inner harbor was used for shipping the most expensive merchandise, via two canals, one going to Lake Mareotis and a separate branch going east to the Canopic mouth of the Nile.

An empty ship seeking grain, a high-priority cargo, would pass through the eastern harbor and continue through a dike opening into Alexandria's inner harbor. There it met barges bringing Egypt's inland harvest to the city by means of a short canal connecting to Lake Mareotis. Colin Thubron says that between income from Egypt's sale of grain and other commodities plus revenues from ship toll collections, the Ptolemies became rich. Ptolemy IV, who ruled Egypt in the 3rd century B.C., built a huge 300-foot-long, 45-foot-wide royal barge that towered 60 feet above the waterline.

Map of ancient Alexandria

Alexandria was a fine spot for a commercial city. The headland of Lochias sheltered its harbors to the east, while the body of water between Rhacotis and the island of Pharos was larger and deeper than what Alexander had just experienced while conquering Tyre. The city was strategically placed near the southeastern corner of the Mediterranean.

Ulrich Wilcken has stated, "down to the foundation of Constantinople, no city was founded which had such world-wide importance as Alexandria in Egypt." Born in 1862, Wilcken was a German historian and papyrologist who studied ancient history and Oriental studies in Leipzig, Tubingen, and Berlin. He was a disciple of the famous historian Theodor Mommsen, who encouraged Wilcken to take the position of cataloguer of papyri after his graduation. He became professor of history in Leipzig, Bonn, Munich, and finally Berlin. Wilcken was a pioneer in Greco-Roman papyrology in Germany, creating a large archive of Ptolemaic papyrus documents. Among his written works was a 1931 book on Alexander the Great.

Strabo commented that the advantages of the city's site were many. It was washed by two bodies of water, on the north by the so-called Aegyptian Sea, and on the south by Lake Mareotis, with Mareotis serving as an inland harbor for Nile Valley commerce. The lake's long western arm going to Abusir also strongly encouraged travelers from early times to go by water as far as Taposiris when traveling to Libya or Cyrenaica from Alexandria. This accounts for the large size of the lake harbor and the jetties that are now under water at this western branch.

Alexandria also became a natural transfer point for merchandise traveling to and from the East by way of the Nile, with only a short overland route to the Red Sea. Many canals from the river brought inland imports and exports to the area in much larger quantities than from the sea, so that harbor structures on Lake Mareotis were much richer than those facing seaward. During one period the canal of Darius provided Alexandria direct water communication with the Red Sea.

In an article appearing in *World Heritage*'s March 2007 issue, John Lawton drew a picture of Alexandria as the glittering western terminal of the Spice Route for more than a thousand years, receiving goods via Red Sea ports from Arabia, India, Africa and Southeast Asia to ship throughout the Mediterranean.

Most of the export trade of Egypt arrived via Lake Mareotis through Alexandria. Besides serving as a trade route, Lake Mareotis was used by the Alexandrian population for holiday excursions and relaxing. They sailed in boats with cabins and stopped at lake towns such as Nicium, Mareotis, Plinthing, and Taposiris or at little inns on lake islands for good local wine and beer. People of that day also vacationed at a rocky spot near Abusir very close to the sea, where numerous resorts were located.

Anthony DeCosson mentions that Lake Mareotis was not always a gentle holiday destination. The level of its waters was controlled by both the level of the Nile and the channels connecting lake and river. DeCosson, whose research is often referred to by writers, was a government official working for the railway system in Northern Egypt and a friend of noted desert traveler Wilfred Jennings-Bramly. He cites records of ancient flooding. For example, Sozomen, writing about the year 380 A.D., told of the Nile overflowing its banks to such an extent that it was feared that the city of Alexandria and land bordering the lake would be destroyed by the inundation.

Even when Alexandria had been built and become prosperous, the fortified town of Marea was still the chief port on the south side of the lake. As late as 1400 A.D., when Lake Mareotis had begun receding from Marea and trade declined there, Maqrizi considered Marea to be a market of some importance to Alexandria.

The quality of the air at Alexandria was also considered remarkable, because the area was washed from two different sides by ocean and lake. Also, the Nile in ancient days was full in the summer, which kept the lake at a high level. While other Egyptian cities situated on lakes had to contend with marshland and heavy, stifling air of summer, Alexandria offered relatively pleasant breezes. The Etesian winds, also called by Strabo the "Aegyptian Monsoons" or "Annual Winds," blew from the north and northwest across a vast sea, so that Alexandrians passed their time most agreeably in summer.

The city of Alexandria was founded by Alexander the Great as perhaps the first known city to bear the name of its founder rather than that of a god or mythical hero. Plutarch states that Alexander was anxious after conquering Egypt to found a great and populous Greek city there to be named after him. While nearly all ancient rulers built cities to serve a strategic purpose, Alexander appears to have built cities largely to transplant Greek culture, importing colonists from the Greek homeland to form the populations. He believed that a city created from and sustained by Greek culture would make him stronger yet. Founding a city contributed to a ruler's fame and ability to rule effectively.

Many scholars feel that it was the eye of a brilliant man that saw in the tiny village of Rhacotis a perfect site for the great city of Alexandria. Ancients such as Vitruvius describe the selection of the site by Alexander as a stroke of genius. Alexander recognized that a well-protected harbor could be created here to serve as both commercial port and military base.

Writing a few decades before Christ, Vitruvius was famous for his *De Architectura,* today known as *The Ten Books on Architecture,* the only surviving major work on architecture from classical antiquity. He believed architecture was an imitation of nature, and that a structure should exhibit durability, usefulness, and beauty. His last three volumes review Roman technology, including machines, aqueducts, and construction materials.

Researcher Colin Thubron emphasized that Alexandria was to become the capital of Egypt for over 1,000 years and the grandest port in the world during the last three centuries before Christ. On the other hand, the traditional view of Alexander's brilliance in selecting the site is contradicted by some scholars, who feel this city meant nothing more to Alexander than many others he built. These writers feel he chose the site quickly, perhaps based on advice obtained locally, with little to differentiate it from many similar locations. Some theorize that traders of the ancient Greek city of Naukratis, which had a long tradition of trade looking westward, convinced Alexander to build near their city.

Alexander laying out the city by A. Castaigne, engraved by S. G. Putnam, 1899

Plutarch provides us with an interesting account of early construction at the site. There was no chalk to mark the ground plan, so they took barley meal that Strabo says had been prepared for the workmen, sprinkled it on the dark earth, and marked out a semi-circle. It was divided into equal segments by lines radiating from the inner arc to the circumference, similar in shape to that of the *chlamys* or military cloak worn by the Macedonian cavalry. As those present were enjoying the symmetry of the design, suddenly huge flocks of birds appearing from the river and lagoon descended on the site and devoured every grain of the barley.

Alexander was greatly disturbed by this omen, but his diviners urged him to take heart. They interpreted the event as a sign that the city would not only have abundant resources of its own, but would be provider to innumerable nations. He ordered those in charge of the work to proceed at once. His architect, Dinocrates of Rhodes, immediately began to gather data and draw up plans. Justin says that Cleomenes of Naukratis, appointed the financial administrator of Egypt by Alexander, was one of the architects, along with Dinocrates. As the city was being planned, Alexander set out westward to visit the oasis oracle of Siwa and find his divinity.

18 | A LIGHTHOUSE FOR ALEXANDRIA

Alexandria 1893 outside city

CHAPTER 3
THE DESERT ORACLE AT SIWA

Ulrich Wilcken stated in 1931, "This mysterious excursion to the oracle of Ammon in the oasis of Siwa is one of the most remarkable episodes in Alexander's life." Historians have always been confused as to exactly what Alexander's motives might have been for this trip.

Arrian says that Alexander was gripped by a *pothos*, a word Greeks of the period used to describe a violent, extremely passionate desire, which today might be referred to as a severe mood swing or even manic tendency.

Born Flavius Arrianus Xenophon to well-to-do parents a few years before 90 A.D., Arrian studied philosophy under Epictetus, became consul, and then was appointed governor of the border province of Cappadocia by Emperor Hadrian a year later. Under his command were two Roman legions and other troops. He wrote a tactical manual on cavalry and also an account of his trip around the Black Sea. He retired to Athens, where he devoted the rest of his life to writing. His surviving works include an account on the voyage of Alexander's fleet from India to the Persian Gulf, and also *The Campaigns of Alexander* in seven volumes.

Alexander set out for the oracle of Zeus at Ammon, sometimes referred to as the Temple of Jupiter Ammon, which sat in the oasis of Siwa near the Libyan border. The Sun god Ammon-Ra or Kneph-Ra, the god of Thebes, was essentially an Egyptian deity, although his cult had been carried by traders and sailors throughout the

Mediterranean and had somehow become associated with the Greek god Zeus. Every Egyptian king had called himself "son of the Sun," or "beloved by Ammon-Ra."

While Alexander undoubtedly would have wanted to make an offering to this god at the temple at Thebes, that would have required a 500-mile march. Alexander therefore chose the closer, less-known temple in the oasis of Siwa, 180 miles from the coast.

Alexander journeyed along the coast to Paraetonium, about 200 miles from Rhacotis. The early part of the trip, sailing along the western arm of Lake Mareotis, was not particularly demanding. However, the trip became exceedingly difficult when he and his party headed south-west on camels on the old caravan road from Paraetonium. Here he began to encounter true desert conditions.

It is said that Alexander and his men ran out of water and nearly died on this journey. Alexander would encounter similar conditions years later when he nearly died in the Gedrosian Desert after leaving India. In 1805, a caravan of 2,000 people on camels vanished during an extremely powerful sandstorm in the Siwa area.

Shearing camels by William Gentz, 1879 book by G. Ebers

One cannot help but wonder if Alexander on his trip to Siwa came close to the fate of the Lost Army of Cambyses. This ancient tale may have come into Alexander's mind as he thirsted in the desert. The story of this lost army is considered one of the great mysteries of Egypt's 7,000-year-old civilization. Cambyses, son of Cyrus the Great, conquered Egypt's Pharaonic dynasty in 525 B.C., and then sent an army from Thebes and Luxor. They headed 625 miles northwest towards their destination, the temple and oracle of Ammon at Siwa Oasis.

Using the people of Siwa as his source, Greek historian Herodotus says that a southerly wind of extreme violence, known as the *khamsin*, came up, a powerful, dry, hot storm that sweeps across the Sahara desert annually in March and April. The gale drove the sand over Cambyses and his men in heaps as they were taking their midday meal. Cambyses and his army disappeared forever.

A February 9, 1984, wire service article reported that remains of the mysterious lost army's bones had perhaps been found in an area 53 miles south of Siwa. American Gary Chafetz found several hundred graves that some experts felt could be the army. Just south of the area were 125 strange large rock piles or cairns erected to mark paths in this wilderness area. They were built in parallel rows pointing toward Siwa. Dunes in that area are sometimes over 300 feet high.

As they now struggled through the desert towards the oracle at Siwa, legends say that Alexander and his men were saved only by a rare desert shower; a great downpour suddenly burst from the heavens. Alexander took this miracle as yet another sign of his divinity.

Diodorus Siculus adds that, a few days later, a southern sandstorm called a *simoon* totally wiped out the trail. Observant guides noticed that two crows seemed to be cawing on their right, as if calling attention to a specific spot. The group moved to the area and found the route leading to the temple.

Born at Agyrium in Sicily, Diodorus was a Greek historian who wrote a 40-volume world history titled *Bibliotheke* covering 1,138 years, not counting the mythology section. He compiled his work from 60 to 30 B.C. Only books 1-5 and 11-20 still exist, the largest surviving body of work of any Greek historian; books 11-20 are the only surviving continuous account of the Greek classical age. Diodorus traveled to Egypt during the 180th Olympiad in 59 B.C. and is the only source on the rise of

22 | A LIGHTHOUSE FOR ALEXANDRIA

Philip of Macedon. His description of Alexander's last few weeks in Babylon is riveting material.

Legend has it that the priest at Siwa attempted to address Alexander in Greek as *O, paidion*, meaning *O, my son*. It came out instead as *O pai Dios*, meaning *O, son of Zeus*. The prophet was pronouncing Alexander to be a son of Ammon-Ra or Ammon-Zeus. Alexander had not just received some special blessing from Ammon. Rather, he was now viewed as an incarnation of the god.

Some writers say that Alexander was astounded and excited by this unexpected announcement. Word of this startling event spread across much of the then-known world. From this time on, Alexander viewed himself as both a pharaoh and the son of a god. On coins issued after this date, Alexander is shown wearing rams' horns over his Macedonian royal diadem. This was to symbolize Zeus-Ammon, to whom the ram was especially sacred. The oracle must have made a deep impression on Alexander. When the Macedonian was near death years later, he gave orders that he be buried near his father Ammon in Siwa. The order, however, was ignored.

Some, such as the aforementioned Diodorus, say that Alexander chose the site for Alexandria only *after* visiting the oracle at Ammon. Professor A. Hoyt Hobbs says that, after visiting the temple of Ammon at the oasis of Siwa, Alexander then marched along the Mediterranean coast to establish the city of Alexandria. If so, it would have been fortunate for the city and the lighthouse that Alexander did not suffer the same fate as the Lost Army of Cambyses.

Oasis of Siwa in modern times
egypt.travel-photo.org

Son of a well-known conservative sociologist and professor at the University of Pennsylvania, A. Hoyt Hobbs graduated from the University of Pennsylvania and earned a Ph.D. in philosophy from Brandeis University. Currently chairman of the Philosophy Department at the C. W. Post campus of Long Island University with an emphasis in epistemology, he has co-authored four travel guides on Egypt, Spain, and Portugal, one of them part of the Fielding's series. He has also conducted research in Egyptology and published books and papers on the subject, including *Daily Life of the Ancient Egyptians.*

However, we discount Hobbs' theory and instead accept the traditional view reported by Arrian and Plutarch in the early second century A.D., that Alexander first visited the Alexandria site, chose it, and made his decision to build. Only then did he go off to the oasis of Siwa to consult the oracle.

After leaving Siwa, Alexander returned to Memphis along trails through the Nitrian desert. He viewed city plans drawn up by Dinocrates several months earlier. After approving them, he ordered the construction of Alexandria. He then took some time to organize Egypt's affairs, finally leaving the country in the spring of 331 B.C., now headed for Phoenicia and Tyre. As Alexander marched east, the priests of Persia began calling him *Ahuramazda,* "The Great Sight."

24 | A LIGHTHOUSE FOR ALEXANDRIA

Coat of arms, City of Alexandria

CHAPTER 4
A FAMOUS CITY IS BORN

It is not known for sure whether the construction of a lighthouse was provided for in the original plan for Alexandria. However, it seems very probable. There certainly was a need for one. The west coast of Egypt is flat, making it difficult to see from the ocean. Alexandria is situated at the extremity of a gulf, surrounded by plains and vast deserts where neither mountains nor other objects exist to serve as reference points. Most other Mediterranean ports, constructed on mountainous coasts, could be distinguished by a nearby peak. Also, a lighthouse was needed to guide vessels through the numerous limestone reefs near the shore. Pliny the Younger, also named Gaius Plinius Caecilius Secundus, tells us that owing to treacherous shoals, Alexandria could only be reached by three channels of the sea, those of Steganus, Poseideion and Taurus.

Pliny was an author, philosopher, and lawyer in ancient Rome, prosecuting many cases against provincial governors. He was also a noted orator, but only one oration still survives. He witnessed the eruption of Mount Vesuvius in 79 A.D., during which his uncle Pliny the Elder died. He was taught rhetoric by the great teacher Quintilian and had as friends the famous historian Tacitus, the poet Martial, and the biographer Suetonius. His main surviving work is *Epistulae* or *Letters*, an important record of Roman administrative history and everyday first century A.D. life. At age 38, he became a Roman senator. He is one of the few people from ancient times about whom we have a great deal of information.

26 | A LIGHTHOUSE FOR ALEXANDRIA

As for reefs near the shore, modern-day underwater research is proving that the harbor entrance to Alexandria was indeed dangerous. Explorer Jean-Yves Empereur has recently discovered numerous Greek and Roman shipwrecks a mile off the coast. There will be extensive mention of Empereur later. A French archaeologist and Egyptologist, he studied classical literature at the Sorbonne in Paris, receiving his doctorate in archaeology in 1977. At one time general secretary of the Ecole Francaise d'Athenes, he conducted excavations, some underwater, in Greece, Cyprus, and Turkey, especially at the sites of Thasos and Amathus. He founded the Center d'Etudes Alexandrines in 1990 and is currently director of that group.

Well-known novelist E. M. Forster says that, besides its navigational use, the Pharos could be employed to signal to Fort Agame at the Chersonese, thus beginning a long system of relaying messages to other towers along the North African coast. Edward Morgan Forster was an English novelist and essayist who attended King's College at Cambridge. When World War I broke out, he became a conscientious objector and worked in Egypt as a Red Cross searcher tracing missing soldiers. Besides living in that country, he spent some time in India in the early 1920s. *A Room with a View* was his third novel, followed by *Howards End* and *A Passage to India*. He refused a knighthood in 1949. Considered by many to be one of the greatest novelists of the twentieth century, his non-fiction works *Alexandria: A History and Guide* (1922) and *Pharos and Pharillon; A Novelist's Sketchbook of Alexandria through the Ages* (1923) have been used as sources in this current volume.

Peter Fraser emphasizes in his 1972 work that the lighthouse was one of the earliest buildings in Alexandria. One drawback of a lighthouse, however, is that it is undiscriminating as a navigational aid to vessels. A lighthouse beacon could also make the city it served an easy target for attacking ships.

It will probably never be known what part Alexander had in planning the Pharos. However, the possibility that he may have done some general planning of it should not be totally excluded. Writing in the middle of the second century A.D., Arrian explicitly reports that, according to older sources, the king decided the site of the temple and of the Agora in the city. Fouad Gassir states in his *Vacation in Alexandria: Touristic Sites,* published in 1971, that Alexander designed the streets himself.

Chronicler Diodorus writes that Alexander laid out the site, traced the streets skillfully, and ordered that the city be named after him. He also laid out the walls so

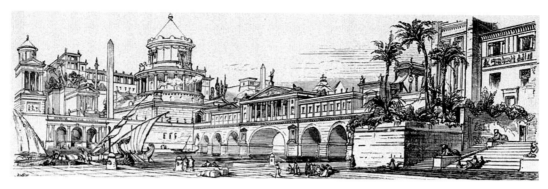
Ancient Alexandria imagined by Adolf Grauth, 1879 book by G. Ebers

that they were at once exceedingly large and marvelously strong. Alexander gave orders to build a palace notable for its size and massiveness.

Ulrich Wilcken in his 1931 book on Alexander states that during the planning phase of the city, Alexander was passionately interested in the work. He was again seized by a "longing," and decided where the gods should have their temples in the new foundations.

Charles Walker, in his *Wonders of the Ancient World*, published in 1989, fantasizes:

> As travelers are still allowed to dream, I like to think that Alexander himself arranged for the construction of this lighthouse as a sort of external symbol of Greek culture. The fire and smoke from its tall tower would guide men in the eternal, material world, while the enormous library in this same city (the finest library known to the world) would light their way in the inner spiritual world.

Walker goes on to admit, however, that "my speculation is not strictly speaking based on historic fact, for there is unfortunately no evidence that Alexander ordered the lighthouse."

One legend mentioned by Professor Angelo Solomon Rappoport says that after the death of Alexander's best friend Hephaestion, Alexander ordered Cleomenes, then ruler of Egypt, to build the lighthouse on the island of Pharos and perhaps name it after his friend. There is really no evidence for this.

Rappoport, a doctor of philosophy at Basel, published his three-volume *History of Egypt from 330 B.C. to the Present Time* in 1904. A philologist, orientalist and member of the Ecole Langues Orientales in Paris, he was quite fluent in Russian, German, and

French. Born in the Ukraine, he became a British citizen, and in 1900, was sent by the Alliance Israelite Universelle to investigate the Falasha community in Ethiopia. He then returned to London to lecture about the history of literature. Sensing trouble with Jews immigrating to Palestine, he approached Lord Cromer in 1900, suggesting that the Sudan was the best land for Jewish settlement. He wrote books on Egyptian history, Jewish folklore, the lives of Czars Paul I and Alexander I, and pioneers of the Russian Revolution. He also translated many literary works into English.

It is true that Alexander was a great believer in delegating authority to trusted individuals. However, in his 1932 study of Napoleon Bonaparte, Friedrich Max Kircheisen, writing about the Egyptian campaign, states that Bonaparte occupied himself equally with the greatest and the most trivial of matters. Nothing was unworthy of his attention. Would anyone believe that Alexander the Great was any less a man or leader than Napoleon?

Kircheisen was a German historian with a specialty in the Napoleonic Era who studied history and international law at the Universities of Leipzig and Paris. He also conducted research in geography and literature. His 1932 two-volume study of Napoleon referred to in this volume was a condensed version of his original monumental nine-volume *Napoleon I, sein Leben und seine Zeit*, considered a classic work in Napoleonic studies. He also published a classic bibliography on Napoleon in German, English, and French in 1902.

Alexandria was bounded by the sea on the north, by Lake Mareotis on the south, by the Necropolis and its many gardens on the west, and by the Eleusinian road and the Great Hippodrome on the east. A few miles to the east was Canopus, a popular pleasure resort with a very doubtful moral reputation.

Alexandria was rectangular, being built in the typical Hellenistic town planning fashion devised a century earlier by Hippodamus of Miletus. This consisted of a checkerboard layout with eight straight streets intersecting at right angles with eight more.

Two broad avenues, wide enough to accommodate both pedestrians and wheeled carriages, crossed each other at right angles, nearly bisecting the city. The longer of these, the great Canopic Street or highway, nearly five miles long and 200 feet wide, ran from the Canopic Gate in the East to the Necropolis in the West.

This broad, straight street was bordered with magnificent public buildings, temples, houses, and shady colonnades. It intersected with other spacious streets.

Canopic Street has been called by writer Michael Grant "a principal avenue wider than any in the world." Born 1914 and deceased in 2004, Grant was a highly regarded classical historian with more than fifty historical books of non-fiction and translations that appeal to both scholars and laypersons. Holding three doctorates, he was a fellow of Trinity College at Cambridge University, professor of Humanity at Edinburgh University, and president and vice-chancellor of Queen's University in Belfast. Among his more recent publications are full-length books on Constantine the Great, gladiators, classical Greece, the Hellenistic world from Alexander to Cleopatra, and the destruction of Pompeii and Herculaneum by Mount Vesuvius in 79 A.D. His autobiography was published in 1994.

Rue Rosette and its extension follow much the same line as Canopic Street today, though some place Canopic Street on modern-day Horreya Avenue. Some say the two main streets intersected near the location of the Soma of Alexander, his burial place.

When Scipio and Panaetius visited in 142 B.C., they paid no attention to the things that wealthy people thought splendid, but were most diligent studying what was

Rosetta Gate in Alexandria, May 1, 1801, R. Bowyer Historical Gallery, London

really worth seeing—the situation and the size of the city and the unique arrangements of the Pharos.

The city of Alexandria is known to have had highly impressive city gates. Some authorities believe the Rosetta Gate of Arabic times, the eastern gate leading to Rosetta and Fuwwa, also called the Canopic Gate, is the Ptolemaic Gate of the Sun. The Gate of the Moon or West Gate was at the western end of Canopic Street.

Many ancient cemeteries have been found by archaeologists in the western part of the city, since ancient Egyptians put their necropolises where the sun goes down—in the west—as representing the final phase of the soul's journey. A few authorities place the Gate of the Moon on the mainland at the end of the Heptastadium, where it abuts what is now the Grand Square.

The southern gate was called many things over its history—the Gate of Spices, the Gate of St. Mark, the Desert Gate, or the Green Gate. Caravans from the Magreb and the Egyptian hinterland traveled through this gate. The northern Sea Gate led to one of the city's three large cemeteries.

Subhi Labib, contributor to 1978's *Encyclopedia of Islam*, was an economic historian and professor of history at the University of Utah. Many of his papers from the 1960s and 1970s on Egyptian commercial policy in the Middle Ages and capitalism in medieval Islam are still discussed frequently today. Labib quotes thirteenth-century Arab observer al-Abdari as writing:

> Their uprights and lintels, despite the extraordinary size of the gates, are made of hewn stone of wonderful beauty and solidity. Every door-post is formed of a single stone as is every lintel and step. There is nothing more astonishing than the collection of these stones in view of their immense size.

Time had apparently not yet affected the gates of Alexandria. As for the gate panels themselves, they were extremely strong, covered inside and out with solid iron.

Labib emphasizes that the medieval city of Alexandria was well-fortified, since, through many periods of its history, it was considered a frontier city. Although later Arab rulers restored the city walls, they were originally built in pre-Islamic times. Newly renovated walls from 860 A.D. forward appear to have covered only half the area of those dating from the Hellenistic-Roman period. About 100 towers were built along the walls in the Middle Ages and equipped with cannon. Moats were installed in front of the walls.

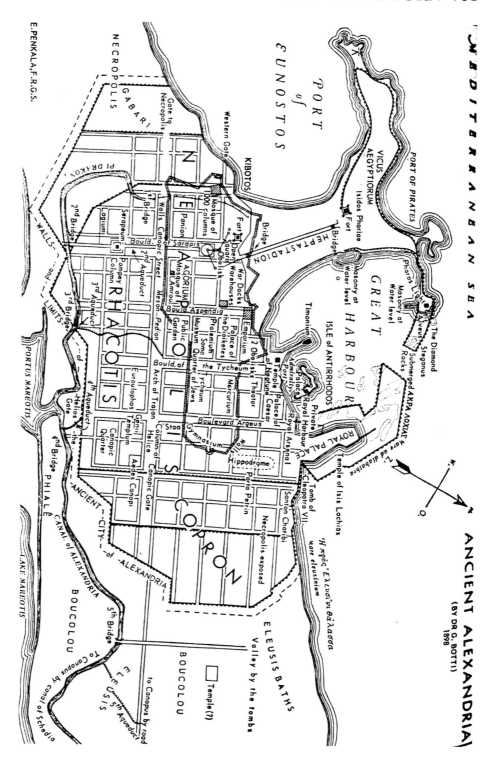

Map of ancient Alexandria by G. Botti, E. Penkala, F.R.G.S.

The city had three major regions. The Jewish Quarter or Regio Judaeorum was in the Northeast part of the city. The Greek Quarter, also called Royal Quarter, Palace Quarter, Brucheion, or Pyrucheion, was the residence of Alexandrians proper, that is, Hellenic citizens. It contained the royal residence and the most famous and magnificent of the public buildings. The Rhacotis or Egyptian Quarter was in the west. There were five smaller quarters, named after the first five letters of the Greek alphabet: alpha, beta, gamma delta, and epsilon. From the first, the population was mixed—Greeks, a large Egyptian population, Jews, and many other races.

The Alexandrian harbor-line commenced on the East with the peninsula Lochias, which had at its seaward point a fort called Acro-Lochias, the modern Pharillon. The Palace of the Ptolemies and its gardens probably occupied this peninsula. Ruins of a pier can be found on its eastern side. The Lochias formed, along with the island of Antirrhodos, the Closed or Royal Port, kept exclusively for the king's galleys that berthed at the royal dockyards. Today, the Lochias has almost completely vanished, and the island of Antirrhodos has totally disappeared. On a day with calm seas, the foundations of ancient buildings can be seen near the Pharillon.

Researcher Colin Thubron came to the conclusion that the structures of the Royal Quarter were arranged by Dinocrates so as to command a fine view of the Great Harbor and the Pharos. The Royal Quarter contained the Soma, the conical pyramid that held the tomb of Alexander the Great. It is still possible that the tomb of Alexander the Great will someday be found in the city of Alexandria, although it is not probable. It may well now lie beneath the sea, a great deal of the Alexandrian coastline having disappeared since ancient times.

If the tomb of Alexander ever were found, says Allen Drury in his 1980 book, *Egypt, the Eternal Smile*, "It would be the greatest sensation since the discovery of Tutankhamon. Like Tut, he would not be surprised by this."

Allen Drury was born in Houston, grew up in California, and graduated from Stanford University in 1939. Serving in the Army in World War II, he was later a Senate reporter for United Press International and then worked for the *New York Times* in 1954 as a reporter. He wrote the best-selling political novel *Advise and Consent*, which won a Pulitzer Prize in 1960 and was made into a movie in 1962. He later wrote both novels and nonfiction books, including works about ancient Egypt, whose political struggles he felt resembled Washington's. He completed his twentieth novel just two weeks before his death in 1998.

The royal area contained the Mouseion, or Temple of the Muses, an institution of higher learning started by Ptolemy I. The complex of buildings devoted to the study of all arts and sciences featured a library and a museum. The library contained between 400,000 and 700,000 volumes, but part of the collection was housed in the temple of Serapis in the Rhacotis quarter. The first librarian collected and edited Homer's works. The museum succeeded the once-renowned College of Heliopolis as the University of Egypt.

Euclid began a school of mathematics in the Royal Quarter. The Mouseion had a theater for lectures and public assemblies. The buildings of the Mouseion were all connected with one another and with the palaces of the Ptolemies on Lochias by long marble colonnades. The structures were adorned with many obelisks and sphinxes taken from the cities of the ancient Pharaohs.

West of the Royal Port was the Poseideion or Temple of Neptune, where mariners made their vows. The northern point of this temple, located on a promontory, was called the Timonium, built by Mark Antony after he retired there following his flight from Actium in 31 B.C. From the Poseideion to the Heptastadium, the shore was lined with dockyards, granite docks and warehouses where ships unloaded their goods.

The Rhacotis or Egyptian Quarter had as its principal buildings the granaries along the western arm of the Kibotos, a stadium, and the Temple of Serapis. The Serapeum or Serpeion is the most celebrated of all Alexandrian temples, and is near the site of so-called Pompey's Pillar. Rappoport says the Serapeum was the largest and most ornamented of all temple structures in Alexandria.

From very early times until the twelfth century A.D., waters of the Canopic Nile entered the lake through several channels. Ships sailing from Memphis came down the Nile and through one of these channels into Mareotis. Their cargoes were discharged or loaded at Portus Mareotis on the south side of Alexandria. From there, merchandise destined for export overseas was transshipped across the city to the maritime harbors on the north side. In ancient times, the Nile River had seven branches, today reduced to two at Rosetta and Damietta.

Ninth-century Arab geographer Ibn Sirapiun talks of the so-called "Alexandrian branch" of the Nile as a river running from the oasis of Faiyum to the sea at Alexandria. Some scholars believe this to have been the Asara canal that flowed parallel to the Nile and flowed into Lake Mareotis, probably the "sea" of Ibn Sirapiun. Researcher DeCosson believes that this Asara canal can be identified with the "western river" of the ancients, the Lycus River of the Romans, and, at its northern end, with the famous winding Dragon Canal on the western side of Alexandria.

Another canal seems to have run from the Canopic Nile near Naukratis and entered Lake Mareotis near Kom Turuga, once an important town and the starting-point for journeys to the desert monasteries south of Alexandria. Naukratis was at one time the most important commercial city in Egypt, and it may have been trading with Greece through this canal before Alexandria was founded.

Alexandria's Mahmudiya Canal 1900

A third canal in the area, a forerunner of the current Mahmudiya canal, was a small channel serving the village of Rhacotis before the days of Alexander, used primarily for supplying the cisterns, baths, and gardens of Alexandria, although it also served as a navigable waterway. The main stream of this canal emptied into the Kibotos ("Chest") basin in Alexandria's western harbor. It came from the Canopic Nile at Schedia (Kom el Giza), 18 miles distant from Alexandria.

Since ancient times, Alexandria had relied on the Mahmudiya Canal. In 1318, one writer called it an enchanting sight, steep-sided, covered in greenery on both banks, and surrounded by gardens. When the Canopic branch of the Nile silted up and disappeared, this canal of Alexandria was extended thirty miles eastward to the Bolbitine branch of the Nile that flowed into the ocean near Rosetta.

Neglect by the Turks allowed this extended creation to silt up, only to be reconstructed in 1820 as the Mahmudiya Canal by Mohammed Ali Pasha. A branch of this canal also probably crossed the eastern part of the city and emptied into the Great Harbor. Subhi Labib in 1978 stated that beneath each street was a subterranean channel. A remarkable feature of medieval Alexandria incorporated from ancient times, the houses were built on columns, rising above one another in as many as

Banks of the Mahmudiya Canal by Wilhelm Gentz, 1879 in book by G. Ebers

three tiers. In this manner, the city made full use of the land while securing its water supply by means of a carefully planned subterranean system of canals, cisterns and wells.

The *Romance of Alexander* written in the third century A.D. says that the future site of Alexandria was occupied by sixteen native villages, including Rhacotis, which were all watered by twelve subsidiary canals connecting with the great canal. Of these, all but two were eventually filled in; the parallel city streets of Alexandria were built over them. Anthony DeCosson states that although the *Romance* is considered poor history, it may well be accurate in geographical and topographical concerns.

Drinking water drawn from these canals was stored in underground cisterns fed by subterranean channels. Archaeologist Jean-Yves Empereur described them well in his *Alexandria Rediscovered* published in 1998. These tanks were numerous in the time of Julius Caesar and were developed even more after Augustus Caesar ordered further efforts to supply all of Alexandria with fresh water. The soil, partly sandy and partly calcareous, made for natural drainage.

Henry Blunt, who visited Alexandria in 1634, reported that fresh water was brought into Alexandria by means of a large, deep, man-made channel cut through wilderness to the Nile. Water was moved and stored in cisterns. Blunt stated that in the 1600s, only 500 of the original 2,000 cisterns remained. Napoleon's engineers, who made engravings of the arches and vaults, counted 400, but in the mid-1800s, the Egyptian astronomer Mahmud el-Falaki documented 700 of them.

An 1882 issue of *The Graphic*, in discussing the British shelling of Alexandria, portrays visitors aided by hurricane lamps exploring the cisterns. An 1872 book described Alexandria as a city "superimposed on another city of cisterns, the streets of which are subterranean canals." Water for houses was drawn from the cisterns by *saqiehs*, wheels with jars on them. Due to impurities and the threat of disease, residents would wait for one year to drink the water.

Some of Alexandria's cisterns were used as air raid shelters during World War II. Jean-Yves Empereur visited three of the shelters and began to dig into records to find others. In 1990, only one of these ancient cisterns, called el-Nabih, could be visited. However, in recent years, many more have been and continue to be rediscovered.

Old records from the Greco-Roman Museum and the Jesuit College in Cairo have documented a hundred cisterns. Recent discoveries of them have been in the area adjoining the ancient Heptastadium and beside Qaitbay Fort. Isabelle Hairy, working with Empereur's Centre d'Etudes Alexandrines, sent a monograph on cisterns to a publisher in 2008.

CHAPTER 5
PTOLEMY I, BUILDER
OF THE PHAROS

The Pharos was begun by Ptolemy I, who ruled from 323 to 283 B.C., and finished by his son, Ptolemy II Philadelphus, ruler of Egypt from 283 to 246 B.C.

Many legends concern themselves with its beginnings. Some say Alexander the Great built it; others mention Julius Caesar. A few, such as Ammianus Marcellinus, claim it was built by Cleopatra, and Arab writers many times mention her as creator of both Pharos and the dam leading to it.

However, none of these tales have any truth to them. It is clear that Ptolemy I supervised the building of the lighthouse, at a cost of 800 silver talents. Writer Peter Clayton, co-author of *The Seven Wonders of the Ancient World,* uses the very straightforward method of the weight of silver in a talent to come up with a cost figure of $8 million dollars as of 1988.

Researcher Joseph Davidovits estimates that 800 silver talents would be worth at least $50 million in today's currency. Joseph Davidovits, the author of over 130 publications and 50 patents on applied solid-state chemistry, specifically geopolymeric materials, has became famous for his revolutionary idea that Egyptians molded limestone concrete blocks in place to build the pyramids, rather than haul blocks weighing perhaps 15 tons each up ramps. His radical ideas have gradually won grudging acceptance, including current studies at M.I.T. He graduated from the Ecole Nationale Superieure de Chimie at Rennes, France in 1958 with a degree in chemical engineering, and received his doctorate from the University of Mainz. In 1970, after devastating plastics fires in France, he researched new heat-resistant materials. He has carried out decades of research on high-tech composite materials, cement technology and the containment of radioactive waste. He was presented the 1994 Gold Medal Award from the National Association for Science, Technology and Society. He published two books in 2008: *They Built the Pyramids* and *Geopolymer Chemistry and Applications*.

Ptolemy I was for a time Alexander's companion and bodyguard, and took part in the Persian campaign. After Alexander's death and various battles for succession, Ptolemy became satrap, or governor, of Egypt in 323 B.C., after deposing an incompetent predecessor.

At Alexander's death, Ptolemy, supposedly to do proper homage to Alexander, went to meet the funeral procession with an army. Kings of Macedon had been buried by ancient custom at Aegae, the ancient Macedonian hill-fort capital. There was a prophecy that when this failed the royal line would cease.

Ptolemy undoubtedly knew the prophecy well, and he may have announced that Alexander wished to return at his death to his beloved father Ammon. Ptolemy also could well have feared that had Alexander's body reached Macedon, it would have eventually been destroyed by the regent Cassander. By taking the body, Ptolemy ensured its protection, gained immense prestige for Egypt, and solidified Ptolemy's claim to divine kingship. Ptolemy, nicknamed Soter, "savior," took possession of Alexander's body and brought it to Alexandria in a gold coffin carried on a golden cart pulled by 64 mules.

In Egypt the sarcophagus rested for years in Memphis. It still sat in its beautiful car, awaiting the tomb being built in Alexandria. Eventually, the body was moved to Alexandria and placed in a mausoleum called Soma or Sema, ancient Greek for "dead body."

Mary Renault relishes the topic of Alexander's tomb, noting that the sarcophagus may well have been adorned with colored glass. The mausolea of the entire Ptolemaic dynasty were soon to be assembled around it, and priests served at Alexander's shrine.

Born Mary Challans in 1905, Renault was an English writer best known for her finely crafted historical novels set in ancient Greece. Some consider her the finest historical novelist of the twentieth century. Besides creating powerful fictional portrayals of Theseus, Socrates, Plato and Alexander the Great, she wrote a well-researched

PTOLEMY I, BUILDER OF THE PHAROS | 39

Pharos, Illustrated London News, *reprinted 1938 in book by Halliburton*

40 | A LIGHTHOUSE FOR ALEXANDRIA

Gem portraits of Ptolemy Philadelphus and Arsinoe by Ludwig Burger, 1879 book by G. Ebers

biography on Alexander from which this current volume draws—*The Nature of Alexander* (1975). In 2006, the BBC aired a one-hour documentary on her work.

Renault notes that, finally, in 89 B.C., when the Ptolemaic line had grown weak, Ptolemy IX, who needed pay for mercenaries, melted down Alexander's gold sarcophagus for coinage. The ruler was killed within a year, but the damage was done.

Caesar was to visit the tomb and gaze at the 350-year-old but apparently still remarkably preserved face. No doubt Mark Antony also came. Augustus left an imperial standard as tribute to Alexander.

Ptolemy I had ordered the assassination of Cleomenes, the unjust satrap of Egypt. Ptolemy was crowned King of Egypt in 304 B.C., founding the Lagid dynasty that lasted 274 years. Amazingly for that era, the great general and king Ptolemy I died peacefully in bed at age 84.

By about 300 B.C., Ptolemy I had witnessed the building of a series of famous architectural and sculptural works, such as the wedding tent in Susa, the Pyra of Hephaestion, the Artemision at Ephesus, the Helepolis or "City Taker" siege weapon of Demetrios Poliorketes, and the Colossus of Rhodes. Creating a lasting monument to his rule had to be constantly on his mind.

Also, with Alexander the Great's victorious campaigns, architects suddenly got to know by first-hand observation the celebrated creations of the Egyptians, Babylonians, Persians, and Medes. Babylon must have made a special impression with its temples and palaces. The king was ready and eager to attempt the construction of his own lasting monument. Ptolemy I moved his capital from Memphis to Alexandria and began the construction of royal palaces clustered around beautiful parks.

Some experts believe that construction of the Pharos began in the year 299 B.C. A long period, several decades, would have been needed for construction, due to the elements, the technology involved, and the location of the site. Also, in view of the 800-talent cost, spreading those expenditures over a long construction period would have been financially beneficial.

Hermann Thiersch wrote in 1909 that the dedication and opening of the lighthouse appear to have occurred in 279 B.C. Historical records show that, about that year, a tremendous festival took place in Alexandria in celebration of the Egyptian capital's becoming the center of world trade and Olympia for the new world. All the Greeks, especially the island Greeks, were invited by Egyptian ruler Ptolemy II Philadelphus and his wife, Arsinoe. A beautiful black granite statue of Queen Arsinoe has recently been shown in France, Germany, and Spain as an underwater exhibit from the Alexandria area traveled Europe between 2006 and 2008.

E. M. Forster in *Alexandria* writes in 1922 that the festival may also have been dedicated to the memory of Ptolemy II's parents. Posidippus of Pella, a third century B.C. poet, experienced first-hand the consecration of Pharos, and wrote an epigram in ten verses to celebrate its completion. A copy of the epigram is contained on a fragment of the Didot papyrus from the second century B.C. and is now preserved at the Louvre. The words are addressed to Proteus, sea god, guardian of seals, and master of the island of Pharos. The epigram reads:

> This safeguard of the Greeks, this watcher over Pharos, O lord Proteus, was erected by Sostratos, son of Dexiphanes, of Cnidos. In Egypt thou hast provided no high places on the islands as lookout posts; no, the bay which welcomes the ships spreads out at the level of the sea. That is why, standing erect, a tower which during the day can be seen from

an infinite distance, cleaves the skyline. During the night, soon enough in the midst of the waves the mariner will see the great lamp which blazes on its summit, and he will not fail to reach Zeus the Saviour, O Proteus, he who navigates in these parts.

Peter Fraser in his 1972 work quotes the epigram of Posidippus as: "And the sailor might run to the very Bull's Horn (a rock at the Channel entrance to the Great Harbor), yet he would not miss, in sailing hither, O Proteus, his target, Zeus Soter."

CHAPTER 6
SOSTRATUS AND THE INSCRIPTION

There is frequent mention in ancient sources of an inscription on the tower of Pharos. Strabo quotes the dedication thusly: "Sostratos the Cnidian, friend of the sovereigns, dedicated this for the sake of the safety of those who sail the seas, as the inscription says."

Lucian, born in Samosata (current-day Turkey) in the early second century A.D., gives it thusly: "Sostratos, son of Dexiphanes, the Cnidian, dedicated this to the Saviour Gods on behalf of those who sail the seas." Lucian was a professional talker, novelist, rhetorician, and biting satirist who excelled in courtroom pleadings. Over 150 of his manuscripts survive today. In his fictional *A True Story*, he parodied fantastic tales told by Homer in the *Odyssey*. He wrote of voyages to the moon and Venus and wars between planets, prompting some to call him the father of science fiction. His *Instructions for Writing History* is regarded as his best critical work. Pseudo-Lucian is the name given to many unknown writers whose works have been attributed to Lucian.

Scholars often wonder about the identity of the savior gods referred to by Lucian. E. M. Forster in *Alexandria* writes in 1922 that they could be Castor and Pollux, the Dioscuri or Heavenly Twins who became patrons of navigators and had the special talent of rescuing sailors at sea. Forster adds, however, that savior gods might also refer to Ptolemy Soter and Berenice, whose worship was a goal of their son, Ptolemy II.

Archaeological diver Honor Frost writes in 1975 that the gods in question may not be Ptolemy I and his wife, Berenice; she theorized that they would have been named in the inscription if that were so. Frost started a career in art but her love of diving rapidly took over. Her first dive was alone at night in a deep well in her London garden. In 1958, she heard of dives in Turkey off Cape Gelidonya near Bodrum, called in ancient times Halicarnassus. Frost was not only an expert diver but an archaeological illustrator as well. Her sketches helped British archaeologist Peter Throckmorton get funding from archaeological associations in the United States. The Bodrum dives are considered the birthplace of underwater archaeology, and Frost went on to do decades of underwater archaeological work. Her first book, *Under the Mediterranean* (1963) is still considered a classic. Even Noah's Ark enthusiasts cite her often, in that she is an expert on anchors.

The Isis crown that Honor Frost found under the waters of Alexandria could mean that Isis and her companion Serapis or Osiris might have been the savior gods. Ptolemy had decided that his new capital needed a god all its own, and created Serapis, who embodied aspects of the Greek god Zeus. Serapis was derived from Osor-hapi, a god already worshipped at Rhacotis. To give the God some Egyptian credibility, his consort was established as Isis. Serapis is usually represented with a modius, a small

Pharos in book by W. H. Adams, Lighthouses and Lightships, 1870

corn measure, on his head, since he was the god of the corn supply, and Egypt had become the granary of Rome. Surprisingly, Serapis was enthusiastically accepted, and soon sailors all over the Mediterranean were praying to him. The cult of Serapis was centered in Alexandria. The Serapeum there was regarded as a place of pilgrimage throughout the Greek and Roman world until its destruction on the orders of emperor Theodosius in 389 A.D.

However, according to writer Barbara Watterson, the Egyptians themselves never fully accepted this hybrid deity with his Hellenistic overtones. Watterson, who received her doctorate from the University of Liverpool, is currently a freelance lecturer in Egyptology. After publishing her well-regarded *Women in Ancient Egypt* in 1991, she wrote a second edition to her introductory work on *Egyptian Hieroglyphics* and also published *Gods of Ancient Egypt*. Her attractive *Ancient Egyptian Gods Gallery* is featured on the BBC's web site.

Most researchers believe the inscription on the Pharos was placed near the top of the first stage. There is some question as to which face of the lighthouse contained the message. Honor Frost in 1975 says the inscription was probably put on the north-northeast side, facing the harbor entrance. Peter Fraser states in 1972 that he favors the east face, where it could be seen both by those entering and leaving the harbor.

As for early Arabic authors, Mqrisi says the inscription was on the north side, while Omar Toussoun says the inscription was on the southern landward side. It is very possible the discrepancy is due to later rulers having other plaques erected in their own honor. We favor the thoughts of Honor Frost and Peter Fraser that the east face would be the most likely spot, since the inscription was probably meant to be read from shipboard.

Fraser quotes an Arab writing in the first half of the tenth century as stating, "On the Eastern side to the tower there is an inscription in Greek script, by means of inlaid lead." Frost quotes Toussoun as saying that leaden letters were let into black marble which the sea had eroded, leaving the letters to stand out in relief. Arab writer Masudi called it a tablet in lead.

As for the size of the letters, researcher Johann Adler writing in 1901 quotes Masudi as stating that they were fifteen inches high and seven inches apart. Masudi mentioned that, although the inscription was at a considerable height from the ground, the ocean often reached the inscription's base. Fraser claims that the inscription letters were twenty-one inches high and eight inches wide.

46 | A LIGHTHOUSE FOR ALEXANDRIA

Pharos close-up, from 1938 book by Halliburton

As for legends, there is mention by Syncellus of an inscription on top of the lighthouse. Fraser says this is obviously an invention. Another story presented by Hermann Thiersch mentions that the east side had an inscription to the effect that the Pharos was built by order of the daughter of Marbioush the Greek, in the year 1,200 after the deluge, to observe the stars.

As was mentioned earlier, the probable inscription begins, "Sostratos the Cnidian, friend of the sovereigns." There is great controversy over Sostratus' role concerning the Pharos. Many feel he was the architect, but other modern researchers have great difficulty believing that a mere architect would have had his name inscribed in lead for posterity.

One of these is Peter Fraser. He admits in his 1972 work *Ptolemaic Alexandria* that Pliny says Sostratus was the architect, but Fraser feels that could be an error. Posidippus says that Sostratus "set up" the lighthouse. Fraser feels this may mean that Sostratus simply paid for its construction as a gift to the city. Strabo says that Sostratus "dedicated" it. Fraser summarizes in saying that Sostratus was not the architect, but the person to whom it was dedicated, who had been carelessly referred to as the architect. Fraser believes that firm evidence for Sostratus as a practicing architect is very slight, since only Pliny refers to him as such. Fraser feels that the architect will probably remain unknown.

Others have attempted to clear up an apparent misunderstanding between Sostratus of Cnidus, who did engineering work in the 330 B.C. period, and Sostratus the diplomat, who is recorded as an envoy of Ptolemy II Philadelphus at Delos in the 270 B.C. period. These writers have assumed that the diplomat is not the same man as the earlier engineer, but, rather, the engineer's grandson living in Egypt in the third century B.C.

Hermann Thiersch, on the other hand, writes in 1909 favoring the idea that Sostratus embodied both qualities, architect and diplomat, combined in one person. Thiersch feels that others have been unduly swayed by many records of edicts honoring Sostratus for diplomatic service. Sostratus was considered a great diplomat. Thiersch says that on Delos, the Nesiots immortalized him as their negotiator and spokesperson in Egypt. Many of the other islands revered him as well. He was most probably a hero and representative for all the Greek island dignitaries who came to the dedication ceremonies for the Pharos. He was undoubtedly a member of the State Council.

Thiersch, in studying Sostratus, feels that the character of his various building efforts, in their uniformly constant technical interest and omission of glitter, shows a pronounced talent. In his work of diverting the Nile, Sostratus delivered the city of Memphis to Ptolemy I without a siege, according to mid-second century A.D. writer Lucian. Also, Sostratus was the first to erect a suspended corridor in Knidos around 310 B.C. The suspended corridor was one of the most significant accomplishments of Greek architecture at that time, building structures not next to one another but over one another. These projects required a man with great technical knowledge. A simple diplomat would not have been able to engineer them. Thiersch feels that Sostratus stands among the ancients as one of its few architects and one of its greatest engineers.

Sostratus was born on Knidos. His father, Dexiphanes, was chief aide to Dinocrates, who Alexander the Great used in his design work. Dinocrates accompanied Alexander on all his campaigns. The last time we find Dinocrates' name mentioned in sources is 323 B.C., when he built Hephaestion's tomb in Babylon. His chief helper, Dexiphanes, did the most technically difficult work on Alexandria's Heptastadium and its pipes and ducts. Thus, Sostratus' father, Dexiphanes, was obviously more a building engineer than an architect. His son probably helped him, gaining experience.

This background may have motivated Ptolemy I Soter to hire Sostratus, then let him acquire experience and skills to the point that the ruler had enough confidence to have Sostratus build the Pharos. E. M. Forster in his *Pharos and Pharillon* written in 1923 notes that during this period, the architect could also have consulted such experts as Aristarchus, Eratosthenes, Apollonius of Perga, and Euclid.

Johann Adler writing in 1901 also is not surprised that multi-talented Sostratus' name is inscribed as its consecrator, since this project was amazing due to its height, and must have made a great impression. Adler agrees with Hermann Thiersch in saying that a special place of honor shall someday be clearly made for Sostratus among the masters of his specialty.

Thiersch theorizes that Sostratus made a gigantic gift, perhaps unlike any other ever made. Still, it does seem highly irregular that the dedication be to anyone other than the ruler. According to Patrick Beaver writing in 1973, Pliny the Younger states: "I cannot but note the singular magnanimity of kind Ptolemy, who permitted Sostratus of Cnidus to grave his own name in this building." Writing in modern times, Beaver has been the author of a series of general books, including *History of Lighthouses*,

History of Tunnels, a work on Brunel's huge *Great Eastern* ship, and *Crystal Palace* (on Victorian enterprise).

Mid-second-century A.D. writer Lucian, who always enjoyed fantasy and deceit concerning famous places, created a sinister legend about the inscription:

> Do you know what the Cnidian architect did? He built the tower on Pharos, the mightiest and most beautiful work of all, that a beacon-light might shine from it for sailors far over the sea and that they might not be driven on to Paraetonia, said to be a very difficult coast with no escape if you hit the reefs. After he had built the work he wrote his name on the masonry inside, covered it with gypsum, and having hidden it inscribed the name of the reigning king. He knew, as actually happened, that in a very short time the letters would fall away with the plaster and there would be revealed: 'Sostratus of Cnidos, the son of Dexiphanes, to the Divine Saviours, for the sake of them that sail at sea.' Thus, not even he had regard for the immediate moment or his own brief life-time: he looked to our day and eternity, as long as the tower shall stand and his skill abide.

The legend has not been taken seriously by most researchers. Adler calls it a ridiculous fairy tale not even worth refuting. Lucian was known to tell wild tales, especially cynically humorous ones.

Speaking of legends, the wildest one concerning Sostratus is related by David Carroll in his book, *Wonders of the World*. Carroll graduated from Harvard and then spent two years in the Peace Corps in Nepal as curator of the Royal Nepal Museum. He catalogued the Henry Welcome Collection of Tibetan Art at the University of Southern California and has run several art galleries and a research organization. He has written thirteen books, including one on the Taj Mahal.

Carroll tells of the architect's being betrothed to a girl from a distant land. On the night of her arrival, a great windstorm blew her ship off course, and, because the Alexandrian coast had no beacon, the vessel was lost at sea. Vowing to construct a tower that would spare others from such tragedy, Sostratus chose the small island of Pharos and began work on his lighthouse.

Pharos, 1630 atlas of Jansson Jansonius

CHAPTER 7
HIGH ENOUGH
TO TOUCH THE STARS?

All writers agree that the Pharos was very tall. Because it stood on a low reef, hardly rising above the waves, it needed to be an unusually high structure if it were to have any effect at great distances. However, as to the exact height and structure of the Pharos, we encounter great difficulty. Literary information on the Pharos is surprisingly scant. It has been named in all centuries as one of the wonders of the world, yet it was never really described in antiquity. What Greco-Roman information exists is full of gaps. The frequent Arab descriptions of later time are much more detailed but may have some exaggeration. Also, the Arab figures are of a structure left 1,000 years after the original construction. Who knows how many height changes occurred over this lengthy period?

In an episode of *Deep Sea Detectives* aired on television's History Channel in 2006, commentators stated that legends told of the lighthouse's being 1,500 feet tall. What a comment to make to entice viewers to watch the entire show! Most writers throughout the ages have estimated its height at between 350 and 600 feet; a recent figure of 440 feet is frequently used. One travel book goes in the opposite direction, saying it was only 220 feet high. To quote a more modern source, the Empire State Building's Internet site says, in writing about its large lobby depiction of the Pharos, that the original was 600 feet high.

Direct statements concerning the size of the lighthouse in classical literature are exceedingly rare. The earliest one is by Epiphanius, writing about the year 400 A.D.

52 | A LIGHTHOUSE FOR ALEXANDRIA

When he went through Egypt, it was under Moslem rule. He was searching out every place of miracles in Palestine and the holy graves in Alexandria, and was only interested in the miraculous side of the Pharos. The legends, he was told, were that the tower was built of glass and lead, and that it was astonishingly high.

Epiphanius gives the figure of 306 *orgyien*. Thiersch uses an involved method to calculate this to be the equivalent of 373 feet. Adler accepts this same figure of 306 *orgyien* which he calculates to be 356 feet measuring from the fire on top to the ground. This is the same measure that Mohammed Pasha, court astronomer of the vice king Ismail Pasha and scholar of merit on antique Alexandria, came up with in 1872. The figure from Epiphanius dates to almost 700 years after the Pharos' creation; there may very well have been changes to the lighthouse over such a period.

As for other Arab writers, one would do well to keep in mind what Thiersch says. Many estimate the tower's height with obvious precision,

Tall, twisting Pharos fantasy, 1879 book by G. Ebers

yet to be sure, no one is right about it. Adler says that Ibn Ali Jaqubi wrote in 891 A.D. that the tower was sturdy and strong with a height of 175 *elles*, which Adler calculates after involved figuring to be 283 feet.

Adler reminds us that this Arab measurement would have been based on a substantially reduced structure, the reconstruction by Ammonios in 500 A.D. Thiersch, on the other hand, argues throughout his book, *Pharos; Antike Islam und Occident*, that, until 785 A.D., there was no substantial change in the tower of antiquity.

Idrisi's eleventh-century A. D. description says that from the ground to the middle gallery or stage, the measurement was exactly seventy fathoms, and from this gallery to the summit, twenty-six. This would amount to 576 feet.

Trading card depiction of Pharos 1880

To throw in another figure, we might mention that Adler calculates the entire height above water at 128 meters, or 422 feet, including the statue on top.

Perhaps the most interesting calculations are those determined indirectly, using ancient statements about how far out to sea the tower light could be seen. Johann Adler says that direct statements about the height of the flame above the ocean during the antique period unfortunately are lacking.

Only first-century A.D. Jewish historian Josephus affords a bit of help, stating that the left side of the military harbor ended in a high city wall; the right side, he tells us, was protected with a very high tower. The tower aided sailors up to a distance of 300 stadia, so that mariners, because of the difficulty of entry at night, could anchor at a suitable distance. Calculating each stadium at 164 meters, 300 stadia equal approximately 48 kilometers, that is, 28.8 miles. Assuming that the horizon of the seafarer is 5 meters, or 16.5 feet, above water-level, a height of 125 meters, or 412 feet, can be calculated.

Born in Jerusalem 37 A. D. to a distinguished priestly family, Josephus became known as a Roman citizen named Titus Flavius Josephus. He recorded the destruction of Jerusalem in 70 A.D. and wrote two important books, *The Jewish War,* documenting the Jewish revolt against Rome, and *Antiquities of the Jews,* relating the history of the world from a Jewish perspective. He and 40 remaining fighters hid in a cave to draw lots and carry out a suicide pact. Joseph was the only survivor. He provided intelligence to the Romans, gained patrons in Rome, and wrote all his works there. He always remained in his mind a loyal Jew, emphasizing the compatibility of his beliefs with cultured Greco-Roman thought.

D. Alan Stevenson writes in his classic 1959 book on lighthouse history that to a seaman's eye some fifteen feet above sea level, a height of 450 feet would yield a range of 29 miles, and fifty feet more or less would alter the range by 1.5 miles. Therefore, a height of 450 feet would closely match Josephus' 28.8-mile visibility range.

Stevenson was born 1891 into a long line of Scottish engineers. The Lighthouse Stevensons included author Robert Louis Stevenson as one of its members. The family

Pharos depiction by Fischer von Ehrlach, 18th century

built 97 manned lighthouses around the coast of Scotland. D. Alan was the eighth and last of the family line. During World War I, he was quickly commissioned into the Royal Marines to work on a secret mission to erect lights in the Dardanelles. He soon became a partner of the family firm, which built lighthouses, harbors, bridges, canals, roads and railways, both in Scotland and around the world. In 1959, he published *World's Lighthouses before 1820*, considered the most authoritative lighthouse book on early structures. That work is referred to in this current volume.

The History Channel's *Deep Sea Detectives* episode televised in 2006 mentioned legends saying that the beacon of the Pharos could be seen 300 miles out to sea. This claim makes no sense in light of Stevenson's calculations, or mid-second-century A.D. writer Lucian's statement that the light was visible 100 miles away. In modern times, the U.S. government's National Park Service gives the range of the Cape Hatteras Lighthouse at 24 nautical miles, adding that the range of a lighthouse depends more on height and air clarity than on the power of its beacon. In dense fog at a visibility of 100 yards, a 10-billion candlepower beam would be visible for only half a mile.

One has to be careful what the word "visible" means. The National Lighthouse Museum states that the Navesink Twin Light of New York Harbor, visible for 22 miles, casts a glow on the horizon that can be seen for over 70 miles. Larry Radka, writing in his often fanciful but always interesting book, *The Electric Mirror on the Pharos Lighthouse*, discusses the 1881 Australian lighthouse on South Head near Sydney. One of his sources maintains that the glare of the light in the sky could be seen at a distance of over 60 miles, far beyond the distance at which it would cease to be directly visible.

As a curiosity, one could look at the 30-story glass pyramid of The Luxor, a unique resort hotel and casino built in Las Vegas in 1993 to pay homage to ancient Egyptian art and architecture. It claims to have the brightest, most powerful beam of light in the world. At its top is a 315,000-watt, 40-billion-candlepower beacon that sends a shaft of blue light 10 miles into space. Claims are that airline passengers can see the beam 250 miles away. One reason it was included in the resort's building plans was because ancient Egyptians believed their souls would travel up to heaven on a beam of light.

For decades, modern lights with the greatest visible range, at 1,092 feet above the ground, were the Freedom Lights on the Empire State Building. Installed and switched on in 1956, each of the four arc mercury bulbs was 450 million candlepower. They were visible 80 miles away on the ground and 300 miles away by aircraft. The *New York Times* wrote of them on March 4, 1956, that the installation of the lights created the brightest continuous source of man-made light in the world. In 1964, the building went with a different, less intense form of lighting that could be colored and changed for various holidays and events.

The world's tallest lighthouse today, the steel tower near Yamashita Park in Yokohama, Japan, is 348 feet tall, has a power of 600,000 candles, and has a visibility range of 20 miles. It seems strange that discussions of both the Empire State Building's famous floodlights and the Yokohama lighthouse, which appeared in the *1991 Guinness Book of World Records*, have been dropped from newer versions of that publication, probably due to lack of space. In the arena of lighthouses and brilliant lights, fame is fleeting and may soon vanish from view. It is therefore always comforting to contemplate the Pharos of Alexandria's permanence of image and steadfast fame.

Reflecting on all calculations based on the distance the Pharos was visible at sea, it is safe to agree with Stevenson that the lighthouse was 450 feet high and visible 29 miles out to sea.

CHAPTER 8
SQUARE, OCTAGON, AND GLOBE

There are just as many problems in determining the shape and structure of the Pharos as in establishing height. To the questions, "What did it look like?" and "What was it made of?" one must reply that it all depends on which period of its 1,600-year history one is considering. It had different heights, building materials, and shapes over its long life.

All researchers accept the basic form of the Pharos as being a square, an octagon, and a globe, sphere or cylinder in ascending order. Most researchers believe this form remained the same from the tower's creation until the late Arab period, perhaps about 1100 A.D., after repeated earthquakes had destroyed the globe and octagon sections.

Johann Adler, in his theory of a substantial renovation of the lighthouse about 500 A.D. discussed in his 1901 work, not only questions whether or not the height was reduced and the lantern apparatus altered. He also feels the three-part shape originated with the 500 A.D. renovation. Most reject this theory and assume that the square, octagon, and globe form was present from the creation of the Pharos.

Hermann Thiersch summarizes in his 1909 book that the bottom, square stage was at least 200 feet high; the second, octagonal stage was 150 feet high; and the third, sphere-shaped stage was 80 feet in height, with a 20- to 30-foot-high statue topping off the structure. This would total 460 feet including the statue. The three parts were in a 2 to 1-1/2 to 1 proportion, similar to what can be seen on coins from ancient Alexandria.

58 | A LIGHTHOUSE FOR ALEXANDRIA

Thiersch version from his frontispiece 1909

SQUARE, OCTAGON, AND GLOBE | 59

The tower proper was built of local nummulite limestone, quality stone called *kedan*. Nummulite limestone is of medium hardness. Patrick Beaver writing in 1973 says that these blocks were fused together with melted lead, which hermetically sealed the joints. D. Alan Stevenson writes in 1952 that the melted lead method was used 2,000 years later when John Rudyerd built the second Eddystone Lighthouse, off Plymouth, England in 1709. Geographer Idrisi says that the stones were strapped together by metal ties, probably iron clamps.

The use of limestone was not new. When the royal bark of Khufu was unearthed from a pit near the base of the Great Pyramid in 1954, the pit had been very effectively sealed by being overlaid with huge limestone blocks joined by thick mortar. The mortar was made of limestone powder, crushed gypsum, and specks of ground potsherds.

Writing in *National Geographic*, Farouk El-Baz stated that when the second pit at the base of the pyramid was uncovered in 1985, it revealed the same huge blocks of limestone laid on edge, each weighing 15 tons and measuring five to six feet thick. Joseph Davidovits in his groundbreaking 1988 book, *The Pyramids: An Enigma Solved*, notes, however, that limestone used in the Old Kingdom by the pyramid-builders was of a very hard type of limestone not found during the Pharos lighthouse construction period of the New Kingdom.

Some say that the limestone of the Pharos was faced with marble. Strabo stated concerning the lighthouse of Alexandria that on the extremity of the island was a rock washed all around by the sea that had upon it a tower admirably constructed of white marble. White marble is a translation of *leucos lithos*, meaning literally, brilliant or white stone. However, the larger pieces that

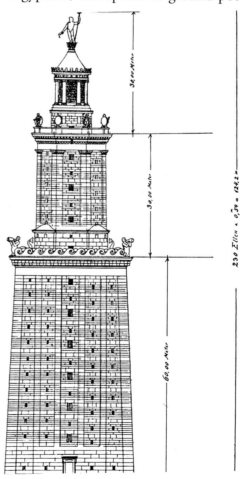

Detailed version of Pharos by Thiersch 1909

diver Honor Frost found decades ago in the Alexandrian harbor were only Aswan granite. In Ptolemaic architecture, stone was covered with plaster before being painted. Mid-second-century A.D. writer Lucian states that Sostratus covered the dedication in his name with plaster. This could not have worked if it were the only plaster area.

In recent archaeological work at the great Maya city, El Mirador, located in northern Guatemala 225 miles north of Guatemala City and built more than 2,000 years ago, experts have found that the chief building method was to fit and mortar limestone blocks and finish them with stucco and red paint. Writing in *National Geographic*, Ray Matheny reported that the city overlies an outcrop of limestone; wood burned to process lime mortar and stucco was also abundant. Ferric oxide, a red pigment possibly from a mixture of crushed hematite and a medium such as water, was painted onto the stucco, perhaps to deter erosion, but also to convey religious import and to signify blood as the power of kings. Matheny says that cut limestone blocks were uniformly shaped with stone instruments, carefully fitted, set with lime mortar, and then plastered with a lime stucco skillfully finished for durability.

Writing in 1988, Joseph Davidovits says that in the Egyptian New Kingdom building period at the time of the Pharos, stucco and polychrome paint coatings were used to hide imperfections from poorly-masoned or poorly-worked stone. In view of these common building methods 2,000 years ago, it is probable that the Pharos was built of local limestone blocks faced with a stucco or plaster painted white to achieve overpowering brilliance.

The lighthouse stood in a colonnaded court. The columns were of reddish-purple Aswan granite; fragments of them lying beneath the sea are visible today. Davidovits in his 1988 book adds that most of the large statues built during the New Kingdom and later were cut from this type of oriental red granite or pink syenite, a soft granite from the Syene/Aswan area that was relatively easy to carve, but still hard enough that it could not be scratched by a fingernail.

Most syenite monuments have been found in northern Egypt, mostly in the Delta, and were erected during the Late and Ptolemaic periods. Davidovits emphasizes that the greatest accumulation of these is found in the Ptolemaic capital of Alexandria, where the entire land is scattered with the ruins of syenite statues, walls, and obelisks.

It is interesting to note that, in Egyptian mythology, red stones represented the blood of Isis, a goddess of fertility. Also, in the ancient mythology of Thebes, sandstone and pink granite represented the body of Ammon.

John Marlowe, in his 1971 *Golden Age of Alexandria*, says that sculptures on the outside of the Pharos were decorated with marble and bronze. Thiersch notes that from Roman coins, it appears the entrance doorway had an architrave and entablature. It was a high-beamed entrance with a ramp leading to it. Johann Adler puts the height of the gate threshold at 25 feet above the rock.

British archaeologist Richard George Goodchild reported in a 1961 *Antiquaries Journal* article that a mosaic discovered decades ago shows in the center of the lower story a large black-filled doorway with a flight of steps approaching it. Goodchild, who died in 1968, was for years the leading authority on the ancient Roman areas of Tripolitania and Cyrenaica in modern-day Libya, holding the post of Controller of Antiquities, Government of Cyrenaica. After early works in 1939 on archaeological sites in Britain, he wrote many interesting papers, including "The Coast Road of Phoenicia and Its Roman Milestones," "Libyan Forts in South-west Cyrenaica," "Euesperides: a Devastated City Site," "Mapping Roman Libya," an essay on harbors, docks, and lighthouses, "Benghazi, the Story of a City," and *Christian Monuments of Cyrenaica*, a major work published in his name posthumously in 2003 by the Society of Libyan Studies in London.

Edgar James Banks writes that a shaft went from the base to the very top. Fuel and other items were raised by a windlass, or endless rope. Born in 1866, many today feel this entrepreneurial archaeologist was the basis for the character Indiana Jones in the movie *Raiders of the Lost Ark*. He obtained from President McKinley the appointment of American consul to Bagdad in 1898, allowing him to buy hundreds of cuneiform tablets and resell them to dozens of museums and universities in Utah and other Southwest American states. After failing to get permission to lead an expedition to the ancient site of Ur, he was sent by the University of Chicago as field director on an expedition to Babylonia during 1903-4. Money for the trip came from the Oriental Exploration Fund, largely funded by John D. Rockefeller. Work by Banks was done on the mound of Bismya in modern Iraq, eventually found to be the site of the ancient city of Adab. He lectured at the University of Notre Dame each year from 1907 to 1919. Banks was also movie consultant to Cecil B. DeMille on bible epics and climbed Mount Ararat in 1912 in search of Noah's Ark.

The Arabs tell us that in the Pharos, an inclined plane led up the first two stages. The slope was so gradual that a loaded horse could be driven to the top. Other writers mention a spiral stairway encased in marble circling the central shaft. Writer Fouad

Gassir says that workmen climbed to the top of the lighthouse through an ascending street similar to the Ahmed Ben Toulon minaret now in Cairo.

Two currently-standing structures in Copenhagen might give us an idea of what the ascent through the Pharos tower might have felt like. Climbing the steeple of Our Saviour Church in Copenhagen was described in a March 13, 1983, letter to the *New York Times* by George Faleck, who found it both breathtaking and hair-raising to walk up the copper-clad steps holding on to a waist-high railing that wound around and up the outside of the steeple. Faleck also discussed the Rund Taarn tower, a circular structure 30 feet in diameter with an inside spiral stone ramp 10 feet wide which led to a wide exterior platform on top that contained an astronomical observatory.

The square interior shaft-like space of the Pharos was said by Adler to be the most unique feature of the entire building plan, giving rise to mysterious legends of a fountain or light area. Anyone throwing something into it would never know where it came to rest. This shaft was certainly in the Sostratus structure; to build it later would have been technologically impossible. It served as a work shaft for the day's activity, sending up fuel to the story just under the last one. Material was then moved up to the fire basin. Due to the close proximity of the shaft to all places within the structure, it became possible to continuously use the greatest part of the tower as a warehouse, so that during the summer the fuel for winter could be stored.

Hermann Thiersch's description in his 1909 volume has an inclined ramp or spiral staircase forming an outer frame, around which were small rooms with little windows, obvious storage space for fuel to some researchers. Adler says that the practical design of this shaft was not invented in Alexandria but in Babylonia with the construction of the hanging gardens of Semiramis, one of Nebuchadnezzar's splendid creations.

As for the number of rooms, Don Miguel Asin y Palacios and Don Modesto Lopez Otero, with the help of the Duke of Alba, presented in the 1933 *Proceedings of the British Academy* a detailed description of the Pharos written 1165-66 A.D. by Yusuf Ibn-al-Shaikh, who had visited Alexandria for a few months. Born 1871, Don Miguel Asin y Palacios was a Spanish scholar and Roman Catholic priest with a love of ancient Arab sources. He became professor at the University of Madrid in 1903, specializing in medieval Spain, and founded the journal *Cultura Espanola*. He dropped a bombshell on the literary world in 1919 with his book proclaiming that Dante's *Divine*

Comedy likely had Islamic sources for ideas and motifs. He survived the 1936 Spanish Civil War even though thousands of priests were assassinated. Asin's works on Islamic mysticism, Teresa of Avila and John of the Cross are widely admired.

The Asin article based on Ibn-al-Shaikh's observations mentioned a total of 50 rooms. However, some sources have reported over 300 rooms, so intricately arranged that no stranger could find his or her way among them without a guide. Legend had it that, during the reign of d'el Moktadir, when the army of Mauritanians entered into Alexandria under the leadership of Sahib el-Magreb, horsemen entering the Pharos got lost in a labyrinth of passageways, went into the glass crab opening, and fell into the sea, drowning.

A closed room led to the basement of the tower, which went clear down to the rocks on which the Pharos rested. According to Thiersch's details, deep below in the foundation was a cistern fed by a drinking water pipe running from the dam of Heptastadium. Supporting this cistern were four giant crabs, made from bronze or glass. Many stories were fabricated by the Arabs about them. However, they may well have existed.

Gregory of Tours mentions the glass crabs. Born 538 A.D. in France, he became bishop of Tours and a Roman citizen, and is the main source for Merovingian history, a transition period between Roman and Medieval history. The city of Tours sat on the Loire River at the intersection of five Roman roads and was a pilgrimage site for the cult of Saint Martin of Tours. Gregory's chief work was *Historia Francorum* or *Ten Books of Histories*, but he was also known for his believable accounts of the miracles of the saints, especially four books on the miracles of Martin of Tours. With the coming of Christianity, efforts were made to remove some obviously pagan structures from the wonders of the world list, including Gregory's removing the walls of Babylon, replacing them with the Pharos.

Veda Vererabilis and Gregorius Cedrenus also mention crabs of glass, so they may well not be just an Arab fantasy. Crabs were used in the Baptismal Church in Jordan and the church at Nazareth, and perhaps also under the theater of Heracles in Bithynia.

Gregory of Tours says in quoting the text of a late Latin manuscript that the glass crabs of the Pharos were so huge that a man stretched out lengthwise could be placed between their claws. Hermann Thiersch says that these crabs seem more and more to have become the reason why the structure was named among the Seven Wonders, whereas, in earlier times, it was believed that the sheer size of the building and its luminous apparatus had earned the Pharos its wonder status.

A LIGHTHOUSE FOR ALEXANDRIA

E. M. Forster, writing in *Pharos and Pharillon* published 1923, discounts the lighthouse crabs, saying that there were crabs at Alexandria, but these were copper crabs, quite small, under Cleopatra's Needle. We respect the judgment of ancient writers and Thiersch that the Pharos crabs were indeed real and immense.

A book by the Metropolitan Museum of Art on Cleopatra's Needle in New York discusses the use of crabs as structural supports. It states that, in 1877, English engineers at Alexandria filled in spaces around the base of the obelisk with masonry after discovering that two of the bronze sea crabs on which Roman engineers had rested the shaft had been lost. Apparently, ancient robbers had taken the crabs and replaced them with boulders. American engineer Henry Gorringe, who moved the obelisk to New York City in 1880, donated the two remaining crabs from under the structure to the Metropolitan Museum. He had four newly-cast bronze crabs made by metalworkers at the Brooklyn Naval Yard to help properly support the obelisk after it was moved to New York's Central Park. Each crab weighed 922 pounds.

Pharos version by Dutch artist Heemskerck 1550

Johann Adler wrote in 1901 that he believed the entire structure of the Pharos, its fort, gates, defense routes, staircases, and barracks, was a square 541 feet on each side. The tower itself was in the middle of the fort's northwest wall. Each side of the lighthouse base measured 100 feet. Outside the large courtyard surrounding the tower was a sidewalk going around the quadrangle. Beyond that was a wide platform and sea wall which sloped down to the water and was attached to the rocks.

Resting on the tower base, Alder tells us, was the 200-foot-high first stage. The second stage of the lighthouse was a pyramidal octagon that may have been almost prismatic. Many estimate the height of this stage at about 100 feet, but one could assume that the Arab restoration was smaller than the original, which would have measured about 150 feet. This second stage was filled with the interior spiral ascent. At the top was a large terrace about 180 feet in circumference.

The third stage, variously referred to as a sphere, globe, or cylinder, was about 90 feet around. This level held the lighthouse's lantern. It was a very narrow stage, with the stairways and shaft taking up the entire area. The height of this third stage was about 80 feet. Some believe there was a terrace on top of this section, as well as on the other two stages. Richard Goodchild wrote in 1961 that the so-called third story on the Pharos was really only a circular base supporting the top statue.

At the top of the square first section was a broad terrace, decorated with columns, balustrades, and ornamentation of marble. On its balustrades, according to coins of the era, sat tritons blowing their conch-shells. Masudi, the "Arabic Herodotus" who wrote around 930 A.D., mentions figure-like bronze embellishments on the upper part of the tower. Three of the original four tritons are mentioned. Seemingly one had lost its shell horn, for it now pointed empty-handed toward the sun.

Of the other two bronze figures, acoustic signals are mentioned. Hermann Thiersch states in his 1909 work that one turned towards the ocean, letting out a terrifying sound if an enemy were coming from the sea. One could hear the sound of the statue's warning two or three miles away. The other figure sounded a melodious tone, with each hour having a different sound. Thiersch makes an amusing point that one sees at the top of the Pharos tritons with shell horns as acoustic signals, and at the bottom, crabs, thereby creating an ocean structure that cleverly uses motifs from the floor of the ocean for decoration.

Concerning the automation of these tritons, Peter Fraser writing in 1972 says that mechanizing them was by no means impossible. The regularity with which the tritons appear on coins, vases, and the Begram vase suggests that they perhaps had a special function. Researcher Charles Picard has the simpler explanation of "Alexandrian illusionism." This was a new art of the period used in such buildings as the funeral monument of Hephaestion. In the funeral structure, large statues of sirens on top seemed to sing memorial songs, while actually choirs inside the sirens did the real work. Picard suspects a similar illusion with the tritons of the Pharos.

Adler wrote in 1901 that machines such as bellows and wind sounding boards invented by Heron could have been set up in the uppermost cupola-arched workroom without difficulty to provide acoustic signals through the tritons. One should recall that, about 300 B.C., the Aristotelian heritage of science and mathematics was centered in Alexandria; the city attracted nearly all the major scientists of the period, Euclid among them.

As for the various moving devices of the Pharos, Ctesibius (c. 310-240 B.C.) was a contemporary of pneumatic compressed air inventor Archimedes and was also founder of the Alexandrian school of mechanics. In his *De Re Aedificatoria*, Vitruvius credits Ctesibius with inventing the first hydraulic and pneumatic machines, as well as the water clock to tell time after sunset. The concept of a hydraulic organ could also be attributed to Ctesibius, in which air compressed by water would make reeds of various heights vibrate.

Philo of Byzantium, a disciple of Ctesibius, lived in Alexandria. He wrote a treatise on mechanics around 250 B.C. titled *Pneumatics*. Most of the work's contents still exist today. The first three books discuss applications of levers, harbor engineering, and the technicalities of hurling-type war machines. Other books discuss compressed air machines and automatons.

Scientists of the time knew how to utilize atmospheric and steam pressure and were familiar with laws of siphoning. In fact, under Alexandrian medical scientist Erasistratos, a mechanical model of human anatomy was created, a pneumatic machine made up of three systems of tubes representing the living human being.

CHAPTER 9
A MIRROR OF LIGHT

Most narratives on the Pharos describe the third, lantern-level stage as containing a fire basin, with a square lantern resting on four corner pillars. Adler believes that both fire basin and pillars were made out of fireproof stone such as basalt or basalt lava, a necessity due to the strong heat generated. The lower outer walls and pillars were made out of *turra* stone.

The fire basin was twenty feet in diameter with a depth of ten feet. The burner was supported by stone arches and an appropriate cover with tile-like plates made out of basalt lava. With such a set-up, it would be easy to control the quantity of luminous matter. The lantern portrayed on coins clearly supports the premise of an open fire, be it of wood, pitch, or an asphalt mixture. A wood and pitch fire was favored by German lighthouse experts Hermann Thiersch and L. A. Veitmeyer. A resinous wood fire is mentioned by others. The fire was kept going continuously.

Johann Adler states that he favors petroleum for the lantern's fuel. There would be no storage problem as with wood. Also, timber was very scarce in ancient Egypt, with acacia and tamarisk being the only native trees. Petroleum burns without creating ash, and gives more light than an equivalent weight and volume of wood. Also, an oil flame is reddish, and its long light waves are least absorbed by mist, haze and fog among all means of fueling. Probably many years of experiments took place by physicists and mathematicians before the best material was found. A square, open lantern would allow for steady burning by occasionally closing the opening according to the wind's direction.

68 | A LIGHTHOUSE FOR ALEXANDRIA

Adler states that it is not impossible, indeed, it is very probable, that the lantern was an addition from a later date, resulting from progress in the area of mathematics that Ctesibius and Heron had achieved. It is also quite probable that through Heron, because of his work in the area of catoptrics, the study of mirrors, reflection and the strengthening of light effect in the last century before Christ, ultimately a large metal mirror was set up in the south wall of the lantern and used for many years.

As for the distance the light could be seen out to sea, we favor Josephus' figure of 28.8 miles. As mentioned earlier, lighthouse expert Stevenson says that a tower 450 feet

Pharos magazine ad 1938 Climax Molybdenum Co.

high would have a

light range of about 29 miles. Some claim mirrors could have greatly increased this range. However, Stevenson emphasizes:

> But though mirrors could increase the candle power of oil lamps, if such were used, and extend their effective range to a degree that would appear astounding to the ancients, they could not extend the direct visibility of either a wood fire or an oil lamp beyond the geographical range limited by the height of the tower.

Such claims as Lucian's, writing in the mid-second-century A.D., that the light was visible 100 miles at sea, or a day's sail, would then seem completely false. However, fantastic claims have persisted. Writing in 1971, Fouad Gassir discussed some sources as saying the lights of the Pharos could be seen in Istanbul 600 miles away.

Ancient geographer Idrisi says the light seemed so like a star that mariners often aimed for the other shore, only to be wrecked on the Marmorica coast. This phenomenon is not unknown to lighthouses of modern times. Some now have two lights, one at the summit and one below, to avoid the star error.

Writer L. Sprague de Camp in a 1965 article called the Pharos "The Darkhouse of Alexandria." He theorized that the structure was originally just a simple tower serving as a landmark by day without illumination, a beacon not being installed until the middle of the first century A.D. He sees the first evidence of a light in the form of a verse by Lucian in the mid-second-century A.D. and a coin of Domitian, who reigned from 81 to 96 A.D. De Camp admits that Richard Goodchild and Strabo assumed in their descriptions that the Pharos was a lighthouse from the beginning. He agrees that there is no strong evidence either way. Born in 1907 and trained as an aeronautical engineer, de Camp was a science fiction writer who also enjoyed debunking doubtful history and false claims of the supernatural.

Since many say the Pharos could be mistaken for a star, including ancients such as Statius and Pliny, William Henry Davenport Adams concludes it could not have been the wavering light of an ordinary fire. He concludes that its lighting apparatus may have been more complete than previously supposed. An author and journalist born in London in 1828, his 140 books included volumes on the British military, Farragut, the Arctic, Venice, Pompeii, the Incas, famous caves, Hindu mythology, Charles I and II, chivalry, Egypt, celebrated women travelers of the nineteenth century and his book on lighthouses to which this current volume refers. He also published translations of French authors, including famous historian Jules Michelet.

Writer Edgar Banks says that, in spite of the Arab conquest, it seems that the fire on the Pharos was kept going. Adamnanus' pilgrim report of about 660 A.D. says the illumination of the light was still continuous and well-regulated, with ignition material being wood and bundles of sticks drenched with pitch. Adler says that the original excellent but costly way of lighting the tower with petroleum delivered inside an open lantern had given way to wood-burning. Thus, he assumes that Ammonios' construction about 500 A.D. changed the upper part quite a bit and diminished it.

Some claim that there were several mirrors in the tower. If that is true, one can assume that there was one huge mirror that most writers emphasize. Thiersch discusses ancient writer Abd-Allah ben Amr's statements that there were in the world four marvels, one of them being the mirror suspended at the summit of the Pharos of Alexandria. Using it, one could see travelers from Constantinople. Thiersch theorizes that the mirror was made of iron from China. E. M. Forster in *Alexandria* writes in 1923 that its reflective surface could have been finely ground glass, transparent stone, or highly polished steel. One Arab writer says it had the appearance of transparent slabs of stone.

Hermann Thiersch noted in 1909 that some legends claimed that, with the mirror, one could see ships arriving from Rome, and view boats sitting in the harbor of Cyprus. D. Alan Stevenson in his 1959 book considers stories of seeing enemy vessels 100 to 200 miles away absurd. He believes, instead, that perhaps the reflection in the sky of the lighthouse fire during some uncommon atmospheric condition accounted for the phenomenon.

However, Thiersch says that the legends of the mirror showing distant ships may have had some truth. Small openings in the wall of the lantern-like foundation would throw inverted images of the ocean onto the opposite wall of the dark inner area, serving as a *camera obscura*. The telescope apparatus probably consisted of several mirrors. The main mirror, which everyone always referred to, was a large, concave mirror, so positioned in the dark inner area of the shaft midway down that pictures of ships appearing on the horizon could be seen greatly enlarged. Thiersch thought that it might possibly be a mirror in the form of an eight-sided pyramid hung with its top directed downward. Small openings in the cylinder wall lining of the uppermost story let in light. The pyramid would direct the rays downward, where they would be caught by the concave mirror placed horizontally on the first terrace.

Thiersch states that the dark, enclosed middle shaft area of the octagon level provided in effect the service of a giant telescope. It was perhaps the antique forerunner of the great Herschel telescope that in the 1780s was able to give viewers a thousand-fold enlargement of images (Herschel's device was at the time considered a wonder of the world comparable to the Colossus of Rhodes). These instruments were not exceeded in optical power by any other, but eventually proved too troublesome to operate. The metal concave mirror at the base could also have been used for stargazing.

D. Alan Stevenson admits that it was certainly not impossible that a kind of *camera obscura* could have been constructed with mirrors to show ships at a distance. However, legends of images from farther than 25 miles away are ignored by Stevenson.

It is known that Alexandrian scientists were familiar with studies in optics. A study by Euclid in two parts, *Optics* and *Catoptrics*, provides explanations of shadows, images produced through cracks, the apparent sizes of objects and their relationship to distance from the eye, and phenomena produced by flat and spherical mirrors. There is also an interesting theory on reflection, with one proposal stating that fires could be lit using concave mirrors directed at the sun.

Hermann Thiersch in 1909 discussed legends that the mirror was used as a burning glass that could destroy enemy ships. Mirror operators would supposedly let enemy ships approach the city. When the sun passed the meridian, and was on the wane, they positioned the mirror to pick up the sunlight and direct it at enemy ships to burn them. Legends say that Romans paid tribute to be exempted from having their boats burned. Archimedes of Syracuse, who was closely linked to Alexandrian scientists, allegedly invented the famous burning mirrors that were used to defend Syracuse.

The great mirror atop the Pharos was eventually destroyed. One legend relates that Byzantine Greek Emperor Masoudi, in the beginning of the eighth century, could not attack Egypt because the mirror detected or destroyed his ships coming from Constantinople. Masoudi concocted a ruse, under the pretense of embracing the Moslem faith. He sent a dignitary and an ambassador before Calif Walid ben Abd el-Melik. They presented the Egyptian ruler with rich gifts. These schemers also told him that Alexander the Great's treasure was buried under the Pharos. Calif Walid had the mirror removed and almost the entire upper half of the tower dismantled, ruining the top two stories. Alexandria's citizens finally intervened to stop the destruction. After the trick was discovered, the mirror was so heavy that workers could not get it back up. Some say it fell and broke while being moved.

A different version of the legend says that a Greek boat commanded by a captain named Sodoros came to Alexandria bearing rich gifts of gold and beautiful clothes. He cast anchor under the mirror, as was the custom for all merchant ships. The officer who guarded the tower came with his men to eat his meals every day on board. The captain thereby gained the good graces of the tower commandant, allowing him to come and go from the tower at will. One day the captain and his men prepared a great feast for the commandant and his men, who all became so tired that they fell asleep. The captain and his men arose at night, destroyed the mirror, and left harbor the same night.

Allegedly, when Hakim bi Amrillah ruled in Egypt (996-1020 A.D.), a man came before him and offered to restore the mirror. Hakim replied that he did not see the need, since, at this time, the Greeks paid regular tribute, and the two countries enjoyed a lasting peace.

Richard Goodchild reports that in the Cyrenaica mosaic found a few years ago, a round object with a black circumference and center is found below the point of the top statue's sword. It is seen behind the left-hand crenellations of the lighthouse platform, and seems to be a free-standing object, perhaps completely circular. Goodchild says that this disc brings to mind Arab stories of a large mirror still on the Pharos after the Arab invasions that was later destroyed.

CHAPTER 10
TOP STATUE RULING ALEXANDRIA

We have earlier mentioned that a statue twenty or thirty feet high topped the Pharos. There is great uncertainty and controversy over who the figure was. Hermann Thiersch leans toward a Poseidon or a heroized Ptolemy. Other modern-day writers also favor Poseidon's being the logical choice, though Peter Fraser states that it was Zeus Soter, while Richard Goodchild believes the statue to be Helios, the Greek personification of the sun. One might even wonder if it might not have been a statue of Alexander the Great, based on the Helios image, especially in view of the rumors of Alexander's treasure's being buried there. We note that one of the twin sons of Marc Antony and Cleopatra was named Alexander Helios.

Johann Adler wrote in 1901 that he favored the theory that the top figure was a bronze statue of Isis Pharia. The cult of Isis was probably associated with the Pharos. Isis is often shown beside the Pharos on Alexandrian imperial coins, her robe outspread and holding a sail. Also, divers working an area north of Qaitbay years ago found a thirty-foot statue of Isis. Some also say they have seen a rock-cut temple underwater, undoubtedly dedicated to the Egyptian goddess.

An ancient glass cup found at Begram, Afghanistan, shows the figure atop the Pharos to be a beardless male figure holding an oar or rudder. Researcher Charles Picard says it may be a Ptolemaic ruler in heroic guise. Goodchild concedes that the beardless male figure is not a Poseidon or a Helios. It could have originally been a heroized Ptolemaic ruler, and then changed during the many centuries of Roman rule.

74 | A LIGHTHOUSE FOR ALEXANDRIA

Begram vase first-century B.C.- third century A.D., Kabul Museum

To be added to the argument is a mosaic panel in the pavement of a Byzantine church excavated at Gasr el-Lebia (Cyrenaica) in 1957. It is assumed the mosaic dates to 539 A.D. One can see in the mosaic a three-arched structure with a statue on top across the water from the Pharos. Its green color indicates bronze. The statue is naked, male, beardless, with the right forearm extended horizontally. The face is looking to the right, away from the Pharos.

In this mosaic, the Pharos masonry is outlined in black, with yellow filling and white highlights. Two stories are shown, each story capped with crenellations. A statue stands centrally on the upper level. Like the one across the water, it is bronze, naked, male and beardless. It has the rays of Helios on its head, and in its outstretched right hand is a downward-pointing sword. The left arm, flexed a bit at the elbow, is held close to the body. It is often difficult to identify items in art. However, Goodchild feels that in the case of the mosaic, the exaggerated emphasis on the two statues seems to be passing down a truth about the top statue's being Helios.

In the collections of the British Museum is a hematite gem. On its reverse, seal side is what may be the Alexandrian lighthouse. The statue on top is a Helios. It differs from the

Pharos mosaic sixth century A.D. from church floor in Libya

mosaic one, with the left hand upraised, and the extended right hand holding a globe. Goodchild believes that the testimony of the Gasr el-Lebia mosaic coupled with that of the British Museum gem would seem to suggest that a bronze Helios statue of colossal proportions stood atop the Pharos during at least one phase of its existence. Goodchild emphasizes that Helios would not have been any more out of place atop the Alexandrian lighthouse than he was in his role as the Colossus of Rhodes.

Peter Fraser writes in 1972 that coins of the period are too small to identify the statue on top. On some, the figure seems to be carrying a cornucopia and scale, and, on other coins, a lance or scepter as well.

Poseidon at Virginia Beach by Katie Kellert
flickr.com

Another version has the bronze figure holding a disc in its right hand and its left raised as if holding a trident. Fraser accepts none of the versions, since coins and art work often change to honor the current ruler. He feels the epigram of Posidippus shows the statue to be that of Zeus Soter, and some modern-day writers agree with him.

Hermann Thiersch writes in 1909 that the figure on top, which he believes to be Poseidon, looks like it could be a weather vane at first glance. However, no part of it offers the wind a catching surface. Instead, he suggests that this was a statue that could turn and point, with its outstretched right hand serving as the pointer of a clock which designated the hour at its base. The shell in its hand was necessary for accuracy.

Thiersch conjectures that the axle of the figure was set on an asbestos pipe which went down through the fire basin past the octagon into a cistern, where it rested on the surface of a float. The flowing of water into this container was regulated by a small opening in a vessel above the water container. When the lower container was filled and the float rose, the pole was raised and turned itself at the same time, as it was guided in winding fashion by a nut.

The great weight of the axle pole was counterbalanced by large weights over rollers. The weights had to exceed the weight of the axle in order to overcome the rubbing of the screw and the pole. The staircase of the Pharos, with its railing, threw dense shadows over the south tower walls parallel to the equator. One could read the hour on the wall.

Many researchers agree that the figure held something that pointed, perhaps a lance. The lance was possibly heavily gilded to produce a heliostatic effect, catching and reflecting the sun's rays. Approaching skippers could thereby gain course direction by day at least 29 miles out from Alexandria. Johann Adler in 1901 emphasized that the statue thus served as a day-sign, simultaneously conveying the impression of ruling over the entire area.

CHAPTER 11
THE ALEXANDRIA OF ANCIENT ROME

In the Alexandrian War of 47 B.C., the Pharos endured its first test, a serious test not without damages. At Alexandria, Caesar received news of Pompey's death. There were riots and mass demonstrations, and many of his soldiers were killed. He ordered legions from Asia that had been formed from Pompey's army. Caesar himself was unable to get out of Alexandria, due to the prevailing northwest winds. He tried to get King Ptolemy and his sister Cleopatra to disband their armies and appear before him.

He then got word that Ptolemy's army was marching on Alexandria. Caesar's forces were very small, just 3,000 men. The king's army, under Achillas, took over nearly the entire city of Alexandria with 25,000 troops, all except the part of the city that Caesar held. The king's forces then attacked the palace and tried to take over 72 warships of Rome in the harbor. Caesar burned all the ships, since he could not guard the area with his small force.

In Caesar's time, the entrance to the harbor was so narrow that anyone who controlled the Pharos lighthouse could stop any ship from entering. This fact greatly disturbed Caesar. Therefore, while the enemy was busy fighting, he landed troops on the island of Pharos, seized it, and installed a garrison there. This guaranteed his being able to receive supplies and reinforcements by sea. He had already sent out to all neighboring provinces asking for reinforcements.

78 | A LIGHTHOUSE FOR ALEXANDRIA

Caesar wrote that the lighthouse was an extremely high tower and that he considered it a wonderful piece of engineering. He also noted that there were houses on the island where Egyptians lived, in a fairly large village. Any ship that strayed just a bit off course because of bad weather or poor navigation was likely to be plundered by the inhabitants, whom Caesar said behaved exactly like pirates.

The Alexandrians retook Pharos and forced Caesar's ships to lie outside the harbor, in danger from both the weather and from any attack coming from the western harbor. However, the forces of Alexandria were unable to prevent Domitian from entering the royal harbor. He arrived with the 37th legion and supplies in a large convoy of ships.

Cleopatra carried into palace, illustrated by Ferdinand Keller, 1879 book by G. Ebers

Roman ships defeated the Alexandrian vessels and Caesar managed to retake the lighthouse, fort and island of Pharos. He now advanced to attack the enemy along the causeway leading to the city, which had two bridges to allow the passage of water between the harbors. Caesar was surprised by a sudden charge of boats from the rear. More than 100 of his men, including Caesar himself, were driven into the water and had to swim to safety.

According to Johann Adler, both bridges to the Heptastadium, together with the Pharos, were damaged considerably in the Alexandrian War. Some say that Cleopatra undertook the necessary restorations, thereby incorrectly preserving her name in some sources as the builder of the tower and dam. Thiersch disputes Adler's claim that the lighthouse was damaged. Thiersch says that the damage caused by the war seems more to concern the dam leading to the lighthouse, with its moles, or breakwaters, than the lighthouse itself. Thiersch feels this is important, since it then follows that the tower was still intact when it started to appear on coins during Domitian's reign.

Cleopatra lived with Julius Caesar up to the year 44 B.C., when he was assassinated. After the Alexandrian War and the death of Caesar, when Octavian became master of the Mediterranean, Mark Antony came to Egypt. Strabo's ancient account reports that Antony built himself a dwelling place on the water, near the Pharos, upon a little mole which he cast up in the sea, and there secluded himself from the company of mankind. On the very tip of this mole projecting into the middle of the harbor, he built a royal lodge he called Timonium, since he was choosing to live the life of a Timon, in solitude from his friends.

At age 25, Cleopatra began her love affair with Mark Antony. After Mark Antony's defeat in the naval battle of Actium in 30 B.C., he committed suicide by stabbing himself with his sword. This marked the end of Greek rule in Egypt. The period of Roman rule in the region lasted 600 years, starting from 30 B.C. Cleopatra tried to seduce Octavian but failed. It is believed that Mark Antony and Octavian were buried in the royal cemetery of Soma, where the Canopic road met the sea. After Cleopatra's death, she was buried near Mark Antony.

Researcher Fouad Gassir relates how Augustus visited the royal burial-place to see Alexander's body, adding a golden crown and a garland of flowers to the other ornaments on his sarcophagus. Augustus planned to build a new capital only four miles from the Canopic or eastern gate of Alexandria to punish the Alexandrians severely. This new city of Nicopolis would occupy the very spot where he had routed Mark Antony's forces. Several temples were begun but never completed and the place was soon abandoned.

On his return to Rome, Augustus carried with him the entire royal treasure of Egypt, including jewels, ornaments, and furniture, as well as the crown of Upper and Lower Egypt. These were paraded on wagons through Rome's streets. Shown in chains were Alexander Helios and Cleopatra Selene, the children of Antony and Cleopatra. Vespasian had himself proclaimed emperor in Alexandria in 69 A.D.

Of the prosperous Roman period, Angelo Solomon Rappoport wrote in 1904 that the Alexandrian harbor was crowded with masts, strange prows and uncouth sails. Quays were always busy with loading and unloading. In the streets appeared men of all languages and dresses, copper-colored Egyptians, Jews, Greeks, Italians, and Asiatics from the neighboring coasts of Syria and Cilicia. There were also dark Ethiopians, painted Arabs, Bactrians, Scythians, Persians, and Indians, all in their national costumes. Rappoport wrote, "Alexandria was a spot in which Europe met Asia and each wondered at the strangeness of the other."

The Caesarium, temple of the Caesars, was added as a place where divine honors were paid to the emperor. It was still later called the Sebasteum or Augusteum and marked by two obelisks, Cleopatra's Needles, which were removed in the nineteenth century to London and New York. Another striking building was the Dicasterium or court of justice. Rappoport reported that temples and palaces covered more than one-fourth of the city.

John Pentland Mahaffy, writing in 1895, said of the city, "Its dilapidation was the effect not of time but of the hand of man. Its dry atmosphere preserved for centuries after their erection the sharp outline and gay colors of its buildings." Mahaffy was educated at Trinity College in Dublin, where he later became professor of ancient history. He was an Irish classicist, Egyptologist, papyri expert, and Doctor of Music. Besides writing numerous scholarly works, he played cricket for Ireland, was a very able fly fisherman, claimed to know the pedigree of every racehorse in Ulster, and was known for his biting wit. Oscar Wilde accompanied him to Greece in 1877. Mahaffy's works included *The Silver Age of the Greek World* and the classic 1895 book *Empire of the Ptolemies* to which we refer in this volume.

In A.D. 120, when Emperor Hadrian came to Alexandria, he found almost intact the original city of the Ptolemies. In the Roman period, Egypt became known as the granary for Rome and Alexandria became famous as a grain exporting center. Rappoport, however, wrote in 1904 of one year when the Nile did not rise to its normal height, and much of the grain-producing land of the Delta dried to sand. Granaries in Rome were unlocked that year to feed the Alexandrians, who witnessed the odd view of ships unloading wheat for them instead of taking it away.

Researcher Anthony DeCosson writing in 1935 stated that, besides the grain crop, in the prosperous period of Greco-Roman rule, the regions of Maryut, Lake Mareotis, and Alexandria saw the cultivation of grape vines, olives, figs, dates, almonds, and other fruit trees. Food from the Thebes area came in, along with gold, porphyry (rock with fairly large crystals), and other minerals of Egypt's eastern desert.

THE ALEXANDRIA OF ANCIENT ROME | 81

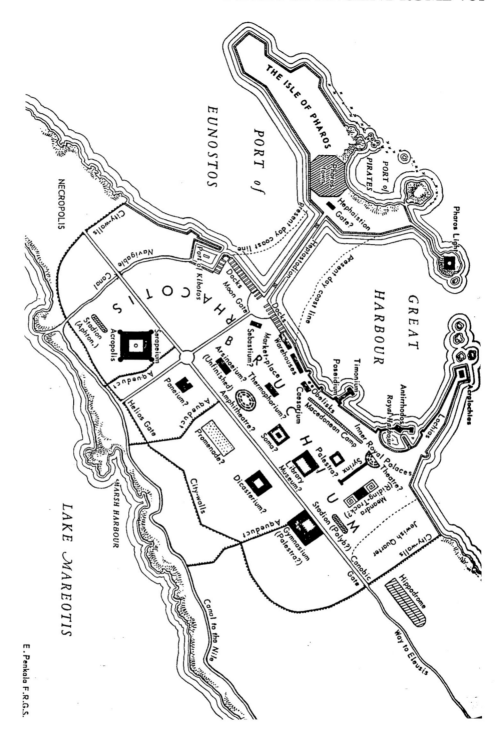

Alexandria in the time it became a Roman provincial town, G. Parthey 1838, E. Penkala, F.R.G.S.

Wine, oil, and cattle of the Maryut region west of Alexandria were carried in boats to Portus Mareotis, the lake port of Alexandria.

Papyrus of fine quality grew near the perimeters of the lake and its eight islands, and enormous quantities of it were shipped out of Alexandria. Glass-making arose in the region in early times, with materials for the manufacture of glass being exported from the Nitrian desert as late as the eighteenth century. There are still traces of glassworks at Marea and Taposiris. Quarrying was in constant demand. Today one can see numerous quarries with their saw-marks all along the limestone ridges of Abusir.

Plaster-making, pottery, and masonry were important trades in view of the numerous buildings, wells, and catacombs of the area. The region of Mareotis just west of Alexandria was famous for its wines; Horace described Cleopatra's mental condition with Antony as "disordered by Mareotic wine." The neighboring region of Taenia was also noted for its sweet wine.

Writing in the July 1988 issue of *National Geographic*, David Soren reported that, in 365 A.D., a powerful earthquake with an epicenter apparently 30 miles southwest of the port of Kourion on Cyprus struck with devastating force. Accompanying the quake was a tsunami whose huge wave hit the coast of Greece to the west and Alexandria Egypt, 250 miles to the southwest. The earthquake came in three waves, the second with tremendous power seldom seen outside of an atomic explosion.

Fourth-century historian Ammianus Marcellinus wrote that a little after daybreak, following heavy and repeated thunder and lightning, all the earth trembled and shook. The sea was pushed back so that it withdrew from the land to reveal an abyss of hills and valleys, with fish and ocean creatures stuck fast in the slime. Many ships were stranded as if on dry land.

The roaring sea then rushed back, dashing itself upon islands and broad stretches of the mainland and leveling many city buildings. The great mass of onrushing water killed thousands of people, and many ships were destroyed. Other ships, driven by the mad blasts of sea, landed on the tops of buildings. Some were driven almost two miles inland.

Although we have no proof that the tidal wave damaged the lighthouse of Alexandria, we may assume from the description of Marcellinus that the base of the Pharos underwent some damage. Bishop Epiphanius at the beginning of the fifth century wrote that he saw and admired the Pharos. From then on, however, the condition of the Pharos seems to start to decline.

Under the reign of Emperor Anastasius I from 491-518 A.D., an extensive renovation seems to have been undertaken. Johann Adler considers this to be a second and extensive renovation, believing that the Alexandrian War caused the first great damage to the tower which Cleopatra undertook to have repaired.

The Sophist Procopius of Gaza gives the best report, stating that the surf breakers set up to protect the foundation and walls of the Pharos on its north side were neglected for decades, to the extent that the collapse of the tower was feared. Emperor Anastasius averted this danger by ordering the repair of the lighthouse. The architect was supposedly the patrician Ammonios (not a technician of the same name who built a water line on Samos). Procopius mentions the renovation of several surf breakers in the form of a curve on the north side, and the fixing of the underpinnings of the tower. Adler says that Ammonios demolished the upper part of the tower, but let the lower stand. However, Adler admits that Procopius makes no mention of the new structure of the upper story.

At the lighthouse site, there are strong breakers and north winds. All of this, combined with numerous earthquakes that wracked the area from 800 A.D. on, certainly left the lighthouse exposed to very harsh elements. A 2003 report studied records from 320 A.D. to 1900 A.D., combined with earthquakes recorded by instruments from 1900 through 1998. Within 120 miles of the site, earthquakes ranging from 6.3 to 6.7 magnitude occurred eight times in 900 years. The site was indeed a challenging one for a tall, vulnerable lighthouse to occupy for so long.

St. Menas marble relief, fifth century A.D.

CHAPTER 12
RELIGIOUS FEVER HITS THE CITY

There is very little mention of the lighthouse in the years after the dedication in 279 B.C. One of the few traditions near the 279 B.C. date is that of the composition of the Septuagint, the oldest Greek version of the Old Testament, within the lighthouse or on the island surrounding it. In using the phrase the Septuagint, what most refer to in discussing Alexandria was the Greek version of the Torah, which had been published in five volumes or rolls, and hence the name Pentateuch, meaning five scrolls. The entire Greek Bible that became known as the Septuagint referred to the entire body of seventy Holy Books, which most scholars believe was also translated into Greek at Alexandria over a period of years starting about 270 B.C.

The tradition of the Alexandrian translation of the Torah is based on a work by a man named Aristeas written to a friend named Philocrates. The work supposedly gives an eyewitness account written by a highly placed courtier in the court of Ptolemy II Philadelphus concerning the translation of the Jewish Old Testament by 72 scholars, six from each of the Hebrew tribes, in the third century B.C. It states that Demetrius of Phalerum, director of the library at Alexandria, told the emperor that 200,000 books had been collected, but that the library lacked a translation of the Jewish Laws. This was considered an important gap, since there was a large Jewish population in Egypt centered in Alexandria.

Aristeas and Andreas were sent by the king to deliver a letter to Eleazar the high priest asking that 72 qualified translators be sent to his court to produce the work for his library. Many gifts were sent to Eleazar for the temple. Supposedly, the 72 elders returned to court with Aristeas and Andreas. They showed the king Hebrew parchments written in letters of gold. After seeing them, the king bowed down seven times, and assigned elegant rooms for them. Then followed seven days of banqueting for the guests, during which time the king asked each of them various ethical questions. The elders answered calmly and with great wisdom. Three days later, royal librarian Demetrius took the 72 scholars to the island of Pharos. There in secluded but luxurious houses, or in the lighthouse itself, they went to work. The translating of the Old Testament into Greek was finished in 72 days. Demetrius then called the Jewish community together and had it read aloud. The reading was followed by a tremendous ovation.

Since the translation was done so accurately and read so richly, no revision was to ever be permitted. A curse was placed on anyone who revised, added, or deleted anything. Later writers added to the legend; Philo and latter-day authors such as Pseudo-Justin, Irenaeus, and Clement of Alexandria all claimed that the translators worked independently. When each had completed the entire translation and their works were compared, they were found to be completely identical.

Researchers generally feel that the Aristeas story is a historical romance written by an Alexandrian Jew in the latter half of the second century B.C. or the first years of the first century B.C. Therefore, they call the writer pseudo-Aristeas.

Hellenistic scholar Elias Bickerman claimed in 1988 that he found numerous errors in the work. One is the fact that Demetrius was never chief librarian, but, rather, a famous lawgiver and adviser of Ptolemy I. Born in 1897, Bickerman is considered a

St. Mark sermon in Alexandria by Bellini 1504-7

leading scholar of Greco-Roman history, ancient Judaism, Iranian history, and Russian literature. He studied at the University of Petrograd from 1915 to 1921, then continued his studies at the University of Berlin. Escaping to France in 1933, he left for New York in 1942, and became professor of ancient history at Columbia University until he retired in 1967. He also taught at the New School for Social Research and was research fellow at the Jewish Theological Seminary of America, continuing his research until he died in 1981. He was noted for providing original solutions to many neglected problems of ancient history.

Bible scholar Suzanne Daniel, writing in *The Encyclopedia Judaica*, says that what the letter of Aristeas relates about an official translation of the Pentateuch made in Alexandria at the beginning of the third century B.C. may be taken as valid. Daniel was at one time associate professor of Judeo-Hellenistic studies at Hebrew University in Jerusalem, and her 1966 monograph on word choice in the Alexandria Septuagint translation is referred to often. Daniel says that the translation is strikingly faithful to the Jewish Old Testament and yet not servile to the original. The syntax of the Greek is respected and even judiciously exploited.

In his 1988 book, *The Jews in the Greek Age*, Elias Bickerman calls the Septuagint the most important translation ever made, saying that it opened the Bible to the world and the world to the Word of God. Says Bickerman, "Without this translation London and Rome would still be heathen and the Scriptures would be no better known than the Egyptian Book of the Dead." In Philo's time (Philo lived from 20 B.C. to 50 A.D.), the Jews of Alexandria celebrated each anniversary of the translation with a festival on the shore of the island of Pharos, where they believed the translators lived during their work.

St. Mark the Evangelist had a large role to play in Alexandria's religious history. Tradition says that he came to Alexandria in person and converted the city's residents to Christianity in 43 A.D. While there, according to legend, he miraculously healed a cobbler named Anianus, who had hurt his hand with an awl. The cobbler became a Christian and eventually the bishop of Alexandria. St. Mark was arrested in Alexandria on Easter, 68 A.D., while celebrating Mass, and was killed when followers of Serapis dragged him through the streets with a rope around his neck. Legend has it that a hailstorm forced his killers to flee.

His body was dumped near the seashore. Christians recovered it and buried it at the site of the present El Morkossia. In 828, two Venetian merchants stole St. Mark's body and carried it off to Venice, placing it in the Basilica bearing his name, where it

88 | A LIGHTHOUSE FOR ALEXANDRIA

lay beneath the High Altar of St. Mark's Church for centuries. Only after negotiations between Vatican and Egyptian authorities was part of the body restored to the head in a Cairo cathedral in June 1968, the nineteen-hundredth anniversary of St. Mark's death.

Georg Moritz Ebers wrote in 1879 of religion in Egypt, "Christianity was born in Palestine, but it was educated in Alexandria." Ebers was a German Egyptologist and novelist of the mid-nineteenth century. After studying oriental languages and archaeology in Berlin, he taught in Leipzig. He discovered a famous medical document in Thebes during the winter of 1873-4 that became known as Papyrus Ebers. He later wrote historical novels on Egypt, including *Serapis* and *Cleopatra*. In his classic 1879 work, *Aegypten in Wort und Bild* or *Egypt: Descriptive, Historical, and Picturesque*, Ebers took singular pride in the volume's artwork, calling the prints unsurpassed and portraying not just the area as it was but also as it was mirrored in the mind of the artist. Some of those drawings are reproduced in this current volume.

The native Christians of Egypt came to be called Copts. One of the chief teachers of Christianity after the apostles was Apollonius of Tyana, a wandering prophet-healer likened by some to Christ. In his life of Apollonius, Philostratus stated that Alexandria was passionately fond of Apollonius before he had ever been seen there.

As he walked from the ship to the town, they gazed upon him as though he were a god. Apollonius encouraged this devotion by claiming that, in a previous incarnation, he had been the humble steersman of an Egyptian vessel. He claimed that his home in the former life had been a miserable hovel on the island of Pharos, where Proteus lived in olden days.

Arab cemetery by F. C. Welsch in 1879 Egypt book by Ebers

In the third century A.D., the Alexandrian School of Christian Learning produced noted scholars Clement and Origen. Also at Alexandria, the heresy of Arianism was formulated. Alexandria was rocked with religious strife for many years, starting 281, in the Epoch of Martyrs, when many Christian leaders were executed. In 415, the intellectual leader Hypatia, teacher of pagan Neo-Platonist philosophy, was lynched by a crowd of angry Christians.

The entire area around Alexandria was a religiously exciting one for hundreds of years. The remains of St. Menas, an Egyptian soldier and martyr tortured and beheaded while on service in Asia Minor in 296, were buried a few miles southeast of Alexandria. Tradition said that when friends were bringing his body home, camels carrying St. Menas stopped on the edge of the Libyan Desert and would not move. Soldiers buried him on the spot, where it was said 90 springs of water burst from the ground. The water was said to have great healing powers.

A magnificent shrine was built over the grave in his honor about 350 A.D. When the number of pilgrims became too great, Emperor Arcadius (395-408) added a splendid basilica to the original building. In the fifth and sixth centuries, according to Anthony DeCosson, pilgrims came from all over the Mediterranean to visit it and be cured of their diseases by the beautiful water of St. Menas that supposedly carried away all pain. A town grew up around the church.

Although the area was plundered by Bedouins and finally destroyed by the Abbasids in 900, an Arab traveler of 1086 reported that the church still contained statues and sculptures of the greatest beauty. The last residents of the city of St. Menaswas left in the thirteenth century and the remains of buildings were buried under the sand. The site, known to the Bedouins as Karm Abu Mina or Vineyard of St. Menas, was rediscovered in 1905 by German archaeologist Carl Maria Kaufmann.

An ancient Christian pilgrim route grew up, running south outside of Alexandria through St. Menas and then southeast. It was a pleasant trip, 40 miles south by sailboat, a day and a half's sail on Lake Mareotis and the Naukratis canal. Christian monastic communities grew up in the Mount Nitria and Wadi el Natrun desert areas. The Wadi el Natrun monasteries were also known in ancient times as Scetis.

Interestingly enough, this route also made up a small part of the ancient caravan route of Darb el Haj, which ran about 1,600 miles between Algeria and Mecca. Muslim pilgrims walked over the wavy camel track routes in the areas south of Alexandria through Abu Menas and Wadi el Natrun to eventually reach Cairo.

Surrounded by natron (salt) lakes, Mount Nitria, by the end of the fourth century, was the most famous monastic center in Egypt. It was far enough from Alexandria to be in deep desert, but close enough across the lake to be very convenient for city residents needing purification and meditation. Anthony DeCosson wrote in 1935 that less hardy and more worldly city-dwellers settled in numerous monasteries near the city on the road leading west from Alexandria to Cyrene. These sanctuaries were at Pempton five miles out, Enaton nine miles out, and Oktokaidekaton eighteen miles out. By the beginning of the eighth century, Nitria was probably in ruin.

It is most interesting to note that, while during the years of Greek rule, pilgrims traveled to festivals at the great Temple of Osiris westward from Alexandria on the long arm of Lake Mareotis, later pilgrims after 325 traveled southward across the lake to the Christian shrines at Mount Nitria, Scetis, and St. Menas.

The St. Menas Monastery in the Maryut Desert south of Alexandria was registered as a World Historic Site by UNESCO in 1979. It was finally placed on UNESCO's List of World Heritage in Danger in 2001. Authorities at the time were filling the crypt containing the tomb of St. Menas with sand to help prevent the collapse of the monastery. Also, the site was being threatened by a regional land reclamation project that had caused a dramatic rise in the area's water table. The clay-type soil supports buildings when dry but becomes semi-liquid with too much water. As with everything in and around Alexandria, preserving ancient artifacts is a constant dilemma and struggle.

Maiden of Coptic faith by Gustav Richter, 1879 book by G. Ebers

CHAPTER 13
THE LIGHTHOUSE DURING ISLAMIC TIMES

In 616 A.D., Alexandria was taken by Chosroes, king of Persia. In 640, Alexandria was besieged by Arab General Amr Ibn al-'As, one of the most famous of Sarasin leaders. Fourteen months later it was finally taken, in 641. During that time, Heraclius, the emperor of Constantinople, did not send even one ship to help Alexandria.

A contemporary of Mohammed, Amr was the Arab military commander who first suggested and then led the Islamic invasion of Egypt in 640. He founded the Egyptian capital of Fustat and built in its center the first mosque on the continent of Africa, the Mosque of Amr Ibn al-'As. Some old stories claim that Amr, acting on Caliph Omar's orders, burned down the ancient Library of Alexandria, but this legend is most certainly false. Sunnis honor Amr as the close companion of Islamic prophet Mohammed.

Historian Subhi Labib wrote in 1978 that when the city fell into Arab hands it was still a great and splendid city, though its glory had diminished. Arab newcomers were overwhelmed by the city of Alexandria, whose buildings and monuments must have seemed to them the work of a divinity. Anthony DeCosson in 1935 stated that conquering Islamic General Amr reported to his master, Caliph Omar, "I have taken a city of which I can but say that it contains 4,000 palaces, 4,000 baths, 400 cellars, 12,000 sellers of green vegetables, and 40,000 tributary Jews." The entire area from Alexandria to Cyrene was at that time one continuous chain of towns and a nearly unbroken tract of cultivated land.

Stephan Schwartz in his 1983 book, *Alexandria Project*, presented the words of a lowly soldier describing Alexandria at the time of the Islamic conquest: "The moonlight reflected from the white marble made the city so bright that a tailor could see to thread his needle without a lamp. No one entered the city without covering over his eyes to veil him from the glare of the plaster and marble."

Schwartz was research director of the Mobius Group that used "remote viewing," whereby sensitive people with some psychic ability find people or buried objects from a distance of thousands of miles. He was at one time an editorial staff member of *National Geographic*, associate editor of *Seapower* magazine, and special assistant for research and analysis to the Chief of Naval Operations. His remote viewing tests at the harbor near the Pharos, conducted from 1979 to 1980, were described in his 1983 work, *Alexandria Project*, which is referred to in this current volume. He is a board member of various forward-thinking foundations and writes the daily *Schwartz Report*, sending subscribers information on trends affecting the future of human life and emphasizing the interconnectedness of all being.

Historian Subhi Labib wrote in 1978 that the famous twelfth-century Arab geographer, Yaqut (also spelled Yakut), writing much later, seemed to tone down Alexandria's brilliance when he declared that the town during the night was as dark as any other. Former slave Yaqut ibn 'Abdullah al-Rumi al Hamawi was an early thirteenth-century Syrian geographer and biographer who also earned a living copying and selling manuscripts. His *Mu'jam al-Bultan*, or *Dictionary of Countries*, was a geographical encyclopedia of all medieval knowledge of the known world, written after travels to Egypt and other countries. His other major work, *Mu'jam al-Udaba* or *Dictionary of Learned Men*, was a collection of biographical sketches on men of the era. His work was important for combining Greek and Arab views on science and cosmology. He was one of the last scholars to gain access to libraries east of the Caspian Sea before the Mongols devastated the area.

From 670 A.D. on, we are left with Arabic sources, which are indeed plentiful but have to be used with some caution. Johann Adler states that they are indispensable, nevertheless, because of some important statements on renovations. Thiersch agrees, adding that the writings of the Arabs are important, and not just for the later period. Within their writings is concealed valuable information about antiquity. These sources are equal in importance to antiquity; to dismiss them is wrong. Thiersch states that there is in some of their fantastic exaggerations more reality than is generally accepted.

Hermann Thiersch wrote in 1909 that, for the Arabs, the Pharos was in no way the self-evident structure taken for granted by the Egyptians and Greeks. Nearly every Arab geographer of significance had something to say about it. In fact, they say more about it than do the ancients themselves.

Under the Mamelukes, the city became an important center of trade handling all goods coming from the Orient. Alexandria was also well-known for many years as a center for the textile industry. Its mats were famous around the world and its textiles were exported as far as India. It also served as an exchange center for the silk trade, and there were workshops for raw silk and brocade.

It is believed that much of the fabric donated by the popes to Italian churches in the eighth and ninth centuries was produced by workers in Alexandria. Subhi Labib, an expert on commerce in medieval Egypt, wrote in 1978 that there were 14,000 looms in Alexandria at the beginning of the fifteenth century and adds that, even as late as the twelfth century, Alexandria was said to enjoy a special place in international trade.

Benjamin of Tudela named 28 Christian cities or countries alleged to have commercial representation in Alexandria, and William of Tyre

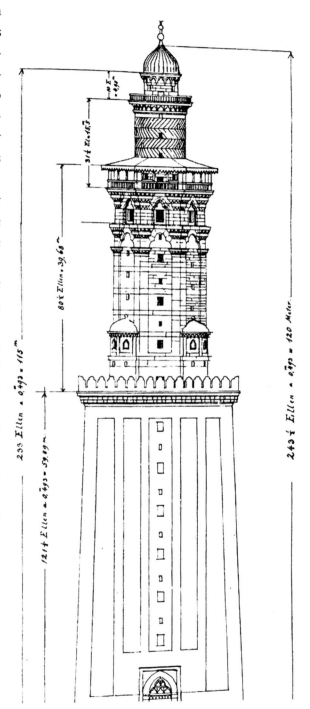

Pharos Arab period by Thiersch 1909

said that the city had in this period become the emporium of East and West. Economic historian Subhi Labib stated in 1978 that neither the establishment of the Crusader states nor that of the Mongol empire affected its position in world trade or detracted from it. Besides Christians from the West, the Byzantine Empire and Ethiopia, Muslims came to the city from Spain, North Africa, Mesopotamia, Syria and India.

Johann Adler discussed in his 1901 book a hearsay report of Ibn Hordadbeh of Tunis in 849 that the Pharos had 366 rooms and a chapel on its top, that its base was washed by the ocean, and that one entered it on a ramp. According to Hermann Thiersch, the building apparently then underwent a major renovation of the upper two stories, done in the style of the Arab early period, with an air-dried brick core faced with stucco. This repair was done by Ibn Tulun about 875. A short time later, between 883-895, the west corner of the structure was repaired by Chamarya, Ibn Tulun's son. Some of its supporting pillars had been battered and had fallen towards the sea.

Geographer Masudi, who died in 956, was one of the best authors of the age. Adler quotes him as saying the Ibn Tulun-renovated tower was in three sections. The lowest part was a square and very high, consisting of white square stones poured from lead. The second was eight-sided, about half as high as the first one, and made of bricks with stucco over them. A wide platform on which one could walk surrounded the octagon. The uppermost part, on top of which Ahmed Ibn Tulun had a wooden cupola mosque and prayer room built, was round and accessible by a ramp.

In 1909, Hermann Thiersch corrected Masudi's figures, coming up with heights of 196 feet for the first floor and 107 feet for both the second and third floors, including the chapel on top. The entire height of the Tulun renovation totals 410 feet. Although the date of this renovation is controversial, it seems very probable it was in Tulun's period. It was also at this time that the first new tower construction in Egypt took place, a minaret mosque built in Cairo by the same Ibn Tulun.

Therefore, if, from 875 on, the Pharos is still being described as a three-part structure, Thiersch says it is a reconstructed version by Arab master craftsmen, and probably a good imitation. Repeated earthquakes and windstorms damaged and continuously changed this Arab reconstruction of the tower's upper part. One such quake, which was felt in Egypt, Syria and surrounding areas, destroyed the top part of the tower in 956.

Alexandria rapidly declined in importance between 800 and 1000 A.D. The final invasion of Egypt occurred in the mid-tenth century under Khalif al-Mu-izz, culminating in a five-month march by General Gohar from Tunis. Covering over 1,500 miles, it ended at Giza on July 6, 969. Cairo was founded on the same day.

The building of Cairo severely reduced the importance of Alexandria. With the construction of Cairo, port city Alexandria fell into neglect. Johann Adler emphasized in 1901 that we know nothing about any lighthouse restoration that followed, because of an almost 200-year pause in the literature.

Besides the important description of Masudi mentioned previously, the Arab Idrisi, writing about 1154, provides us with another detailed picture of the Pharos. He praised the amazing durability of the structure, the overall construction, and the technique used, writing that the minaret there had no equal in the world due to both its structure and durability. He called the stones used *sakhr* or *kedan*, that is, good house stones. The blocks were bound together with squared stones poured out of lead, allowing such close locking together that Idrisi called the entire structure inseparable in spite of the ocean waves. Some said the locking devices were lead clamps.

Idrisi stated that even the continuously endangered north side still stood. The ramp, as it proceeded through the tower, had rooms under it and was continuously illuminated by little windows facing the ocean on all sides. Thiersch quotes Idrisi as saying that the fire at the top was visible for 100 miles. It was seen as a radiating star at night and as smoke by day.

Adler tells us that Idrisi described the tower as Masudi did, as being in three parts, with two galleries, one around the octagonal story and the second around the cylinder-shaped upper story tapering at the top. Thiersch says that Idrisi saw a newly renovated tower. Due to storms, the upper cylinder and probably the middle octagon were missing. In place of the octagon was a square story upon which directly rested a chapel. Thiersch claims that Idrisi does not say a word about an octagon, describing only what sounds like a square second story over a square first story. He mentions no third story, no globe.

In the 1930s, a new description of the Pharos surfaced, dating back to the twelfth century. Don Miguel Asin y Palacios presented to the world the description of Ibn al-Shaikh, a Mussulman of Malaga, Spain, who resided permanently at Alexandria in 1165-66. This observer measured the inaccessible heights of the Pharos geometrically and made notes. He then wrote *Kitab Alif Ra*, a general knowledge work, which was eventually published in Cairo in 1870.

Lighthouse expert Douglas Bland Hague says the al-Shaikh description is by far the best survey of the building extant. Hague was born in 1917 and eventually became investigator on the staff of the Royal Commission on Ancient and Historical Monuments in Wales from 1948 to 1981. Besides his archaeological work on all kinds of

96 | A LIGHTHOUSE FOR ALEXANDRIA

structures, his specialty was researching the history and architecture of lighthouses in Britain. His books include *Lighthouses: Their Architecture, History and Archaeology* (1975), to which this current volume refers, and *Lighthouses of Wales*, published posthumously in 1994.

Ibn al-Shaikh stated that the height of the first square section, taken from the gallery that crowned its summit to its base, was 202 feet. The height of the walls of the octagon, measured from the gallery on its summit to the floor of the platform immediately beneath, was 98 feet. The third, cylindrical section, measured from the platform on its summit, was 26 feet. On the center of the highest platform was a small mosque with four doors, surmounted by a dome. The structure described here totaled 326 feet.

Thus, Hermann Thiersch's earlier-mentioned theory from his 1909 volume that the cylinder and octagon were largely destroyed by 1154 is contradicted by the description of Ibn al-Shaikh, written in 1165-1166. Don Miguel Asin y Palacios feels that, in spite of Thiersch's technical competence and all the documentary evidence he amassed, his theories are unconvincing and based on hearsay, not on an actual inspection of the Pharos by competent and trustworthy observers.

Pharos Arab period

THE LIGHTHOUSE DURING ISLAMIC TIMES

In 1167, while being governed by Saladin, Alexandria was besieged by the Crusader Amalric. Researcher Paul Lunde presents this statement by Andalusian traveler Ibn Jubair, writing around the year 1190:

> One of the greatest wonders that we saw in this city was the lighthouse which great and glorious God created by the hands of those who were forced to such labor...as a guide to voyagers, for without it they could not find the true course to Alexandria. It can be seen for more than 70 miles, and is of great antiquity. It is most strongly built in all directions and competes with the skies in height. Description of it falls short, the eyes fail to comprehend it, and words are inadequate, so vast is the spectacle. We measured one of the four sides and found it to be more than 50 arms lengths. It is said that in height it is more than 150 heights of a man. Its interior is an awe-inspiring sight in its amplitude, with stairways and entrances and numerous apartments, so that he who penetrates and wanders through its passages may be lost. In short, words fail to give a conception of it.

Economic historian Subhi Labib wrote in 1978 that during the later Arab period, entering the eastern harbor required careful navigation, with ships having to sail close to the Pharos and the western bank of the eastern harbor lest they hit submerged rocks. One could not avoid these rocks by sailing on the eastern side because of shallow water. Pilots and launches licensed by port authorities accompanied large ships to their anchorage. A wooden landing-stage connected the anchorage to the shore so that ships could be loaded and unloaded.

Johann Adler in 1901 presented the description of an Arab named Jaqut, who visited Alexandria in 1215 and again in 1227. He says that one of the pillars of the tower had collapsed but been repaired, perhaps by Melikes-Saliher-Raziq. It seems that extensive restoration occurred from 1193 to 1213. Abd el-Latif, writing at the end of the twelfth century, confirms this from personal observation.

He found at the ocean bank next to the city walls more than 400 pillars, broken in two or three pieces, of the same type of stone as Pompey's Pillar and about one-third to one-fourth as large as the latter. A governor during the time of Saladin had ordered the columns broken apart to use for protection against the waves. Adler thus surmises that the surf breakers Ammonios had repaired had again gone to ruin, rendering the Pharos vulnerable once again.

98 | A LIGHTHOUSE FOR ALEXANDRIA

Sais or footman by Leopold Carl Muller 1879 in Egypt book by Ebers

Jaqut described the Pharos as a high fortress on the ridge of a hill elevated in the ocean. He described the distance from the island to the mainland as an arrow-shot. Drinking water was pumped into the Pharos from one of its land sides. There were no large rooms, but only a staircase winding around an empty fountain. Jaqut visited the place where the mirror had been. Not a trace of it was left.

In summarizing Jaqut, Hermann Thiersch in 1909 stated that, when later Arabs cite different heights, or Jaqut, in the thirteenth century, speaks only of two stories, it is understandable, considering the damage and reconstruction efforts. He feels that, by that time, the octagon on the second level had completely disappeared and been replaced through renovation by a square top. Adler is again consistent in his disagreement. He says that even from Qazwini's statement in 1263, it seems the Pharos still had a three-part shape originating from the Byzantine restoration by Ammonios about the year 500.

Adler in 1901 mentioned the report of the Arab Ibn Abd el-Hakam in the time of Zaher Beibar, from 1260 to 1277, that one of the pillars threatened to totally collapse. Immediate repairs were ordered, with the top cupola or mosque also reinstalled. The frequently mentioned earthquake of 1302 ravaged the entire north coast of Africa and hit Alexandria especially hard, destroying the mosque. It was again reconstructed under the direction of Rokn el din Beibar El Gaschenkir.

As for maps, they rarely fail to show the Pharos of Alexandria, but it is always a fablized version. A map by Ebstorfen in 1284 shows it on a hill, as a pillar with red shaft, thick base, swollen neck, and cup-shaped top, out of which red flames rage. Researcher Thiersch feels that it is Pompey's Pillar that is probably depicted here. When Leo Africanus visited Egypt in 1517, he was told in Alexandria that the pillar existed first as a lighthouse in the harbor. After the destruction of the mirror at the top, the pillar was planted on the hill called Hammud es-Sauwari. Thus, fantasy took Pompey's Pillar, the second highest antique monument in the city, and made it into the Pharos, something it was not.

A 1303 map in the town of Montpelier, France, shows the Pharos destroyed. Ibn Battuta, on his first trip to Alexandria in 1326, says that he went to see the lighthouse and found one of its faces in ruins. He described it as a very high square building with its door above the level of the earth. Opposite the door, and at the same height, was a building with a plank bridge to the door. This provided the only means of entrance. Inside the door was a place for the lighthouse-keeper. Within the lighthouse were many rooms.

In 1324, Emir Buka ed-Din Baibars had ordered a restoration, but the decay that had occurred between 1303 and 1324 was no longer possible to halt. In 1349 A.D., Ibn Battuta once again visited Alexandria. This time, he found that the tower had fallen into such a condition of ruin that it was impossible to enter it or climb up to the door. Al-Malik an-Nasir had started to build a similar lighthouse alongside it but was prevented by death from completing the work. At the beginning of the fourteenth century, the Pharos disappears from illustrations.

In this Arab period, Hermann Thiersch, writing in 1909, keeps reemphasizing, on the one hand, the inner connection of the lighthouse with the religious precepts of Islam, and, on the other, the uninterrupted service of the lighthouse as a signal light. The Arabs all agree on the existence of a continuous guard and the maintenance of a prayer room (*kubba*, *masquad*, or small *moschee*) at the top of the lighthouse. Under the Arabs, the structure gained powerful religious significance as protector of the land.

On a particular Thursday each year all the inhabitants of Alexandria went out to the lighthouse to offer sacrifices, pray, celebrate, eat, and play games, returning home in the evening feeling they were safe from harm from the sea for the upcoming year. Thiersch mentions one Vezir Motewekki, who set the time of vespers at the moment when the sun set as seen from the top of the Pharos.

Egypt commerce expert Subhi Labib wrote in 1978 that, in the fourteenth century, the city was famous for its markets in spices, coral, silks, linen, slaves, money-changing and money-lending, fruits both fresh and dried, perfumes, sugared almonds and nuts, confectionaries, woods, waxes, and its many flea-markets or bazaars. The principal market of the period for Alexandria was the pepper trade, with Venetian vessels loading an average about 1,500,000 pounds of pepper per year.

100 | A LIGHTHOUSE FOR ALEXANDRIA

In 1365, Alexandria was partially destroyed during the invasion of Peter of Lusignan, the king of Cyprus. Writing in the *Dictionary of the Middle Ages*, medieval historian Boaz Shoshan states that the city never fully recovered from that raid. Shoshan received his doctorate in Near Eastern Studies from Princeton University in 1978 and is chairman of the Department of General History and Associate Professor of Middle East Studies at Ben Gurion University of the Negev in Israel, where he began teaching in 1978. His *Popular Culture in Medieval Cairo* was the first book-length study of popular culture in a medieval Islamic city, and his recent *Poetics of Islamic Historiography* studies Tabari, a classical Muslim historian.

In the fourteenth century, under Arab rule, Alexandria was considered only a *thagr* or frontier fortress. Gassir writes that nine doors were built through city walls. The Arabs kept the eastern harbor of the medieval seaport for Christian shipping and the western harbor for Muslim vessels. Also, the eastern or new port became little-used because it was exposed to the northerly gales and had limited space in which to anchor. Much of the population was destroyed by plague between the years 1347 and 1350, when 100 to 200 people died daily, the rate rising at the height of the plague to 700 citizens a day.

Alexandria experienced a brief revival in the late fourteenth and fifteenth centuries after the Crusades, when it once again served as a trade center. Goods from the Indian Ocean area were carried by Arab ships to Suez. There they were exchanged for European goods brought to Alexandria on Venetian vessels. By the year 1384, the population had once more rapidly increased to 60,000.

Alexandria and New Harbor 1762

The discovery of the southern sea route to India in the closing years of the fifteenth century dealt Alexandria a blow as a center of trade. The Cape of Good Hope was rounded in 1497 during the reign of Sultan El Ghouri. With the total decline of Egypt after its conquest by the Turkish Ottoman Empire in 1517, the city in effect disappeared. Shoshan quotes reports that, as of 1512, nearly 90% of Alexandria was in ruins.

Anthony DeCosson in 1935 emphasized that an important negative force striking Alexandria in the twelfth century was the silting up of the Canopic Nile and the channels which fed the lake. This cut off the fresh water supply to the Maryut western arm of Lake Mareotis and diminished cultivation in areas bordering the lake. The former lake now became a salty swamp or *sabbaka*.

By the end of the eighteenth century, it was so dry except at Nile flood-time that troops could cross it on foot. DeCosson says that Lake Mareotis was without water, that is, no longer a lake, for about 700 years, between the twelfth and nineteenth centuries, except for ocean flooding in 1801-1804 and 1807-1808. It was not until 1892 that it would become a lake once more, but without its western Abusir inlet. That was cut off from the main lake body by the Maryut railway embankment which had been constructed about 1858.

The 1892 flooding was done when area irrigation systems were reorganized, with the old lake basin of Mareotis changed into an area into which drainage canals could flow. In order to keep some water in the lake, pumps at Mex were kept constantly working. Various lake reclamation projects proposing the complete draining of Lake Mareotis have been discussed.

By the late eighteenth century, the harbor restricted for European vessels had been severely downgraded. G. Ebers wrote that when a gentleman by the name of Volney visited the city in 1782 during a seven-month stay in Ottoman Egypt, he discovered that a single windstorm had wrecked 42 ships against the harbor quays, threatening every ship with running aground. This Volney was the French historian, philosopher, and orientalist whose full name was Constantin-Francois de Chasseboeuf, Comte de Volney. His *Voyage en Egypte et en Syrie*, or *Travels in Syria and Egypt*, was published in 1787.

Another traveler reported that, in 1792, the gates of Alexandria had to be shut against possible Bedouin raids, after the herds and flocks that supplied the needs of the city were brought in each night. Georg Ebers wrote of this period decades later, in 1879, "The houses were low and squalid; nothing was to be seen in the market but dates and flat round cakes of bread, and the streets were choked by rubbish and ruins. The howl of the jackal and the screech of the owl disturbed the night." The life and wealth of Alexandria had vanished.

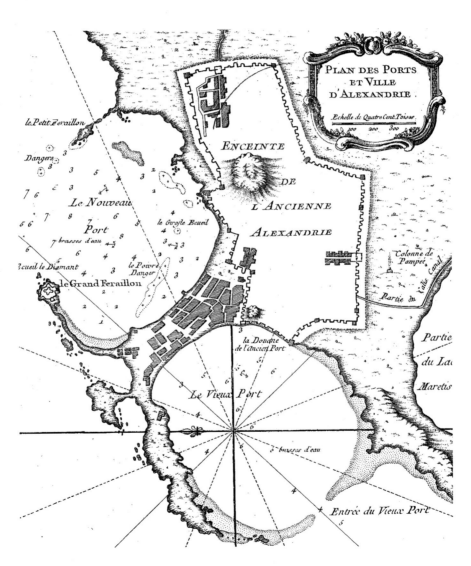

Map of Alexandria 1764, Jacques Nicolas Bellin, Paris

CHAPTER 14
NAPOLEON COMES TO ALEXANDRIA

We now come to the period of Napoleon. By the conquest of Egypt, the French ruler could cut England off from possession of India, dominate trade with the Orient, and gather an army of Asiatics with which to conquer the East, including India. A *New York Times* article on January 6, 2008, by Tom Reiss titled "Freedom at Gunpoint" called Napoleon's invasion of Egypt the first modern incursion by the West into the Middle East.

Bonaparte before the Sphinx 1867-8 by Jean-Leon Gerome

Admiral Brueys' squadron in Toulon of 40,000 soldiers and 10,000 sailors departed May 19, 1798. Friedrich Max Kircheisen finds it surprising that Napoleon's expedition to Egypt largely remained a secret since at least a dozen people knew about it. From studying letters of the period, it becomes obvious that hundreds more had guessed correctly that it was coming.

The expedition was led by the flagship *Orient*, ranked next to the Spanish man-of-war *Santissima Trinidad* as the finest vessel in the world. A violent storm had damaged Nelson's English fleet, forcing him to shelter on the south coast of Sardinia to repair his shattered vessels. This gave Napoleon a chance to sail his 400 ships to Egypt by way of Malta without being immediately pursued. After stopping in Malta to secure that island, the French fleet left June 19. Nelson got to Alexandria before the French, but then left for the Dardanelles to look for them. Many times between June 21 and 25, the opposing fleets were less than a day's sail apart, yet could not find each other.

On June 28, 1798, the French had the coast of Egypt in sight. On July 1, they could see Alexandria. Before landing, they learned that the English fleet had arrived off Alexandria some days before. Bonaparte then resolved to land immediately, even though the sea was extremely rough. The fleet did not enter the harbor of Alexandria, feeling a defense might be mounted. Also, the bay of Alexandria was very shallow. The warships anchored some distance from the coast, putting the troops ashore in boats.

Napoleon attempted his landing on the night of July 1st in the open near Marabout Fort at the extreme west end of the Alexandrian harbor on the bay of Agami, the site of the ancient fortress of Chersonesus. Here a promontory and island gave some shelter from the northwest wind at an inlet called the Creek of the Marabou.

That night, the wind blew violently and the sea broke heavily over reefs on the shore. The men had to row six or seven miles in open boats in a violent gale through tremendous surf. Bonaparte hit the shore before dawn, and his 4,300 men then marched five or six miles through the desert in three columns. They arrived before the walls of the old city at dawn. What Napoleon found was a dilapidated fishing village of 5,000 inhabitants. Three-fourths of the old city lay in ruins. An old wall flanked by towers enclosed the new and the old town.

After surrender negotiations failed, Bonaparte ordered an assault. Napoleon marched on the right with one column to the Rosetta Gate. Jean Baptiste Kleber marched in the center with the end column toward the Gate of the Catacombs. By mid-day, Alexandria had fallen, with only a handful of French troops killed or injured. Kleber suffered a wound to the head and saw no further action.

NAPOLEON COMES TO ALEXANDRIA | 105

James Matthew Thompson's 1951 book on Napoleon quotes Commissar Pierre Jaubert as writing within a week of the landing, "This city has nothing of the ancient Alexandria but the name...It is a mere heap of ruins, where you see a paltry hovel of mud and straw stuck against the magnificent fragments of a granite column." Thompson was born in 1878 and eventually went to Christ Church, Oxford, took priest's orders, and became associated with Magdalen College, where he was appointed dean of divinity. His career as an Oxford don soon became mired in controversy; he became increasingly liberal, arguing that the virgin birth and resurrection were inventions. His *French Revolution* was well received in 1943, followed by biographies of Napoleon in 1951 and Napoleon III in 1954. Some still consider his book on Napoleon the best one-volume study on the French leader.

After spending a week in the city, Bonaparte left to march on Cairo, leaving 6,500 men in Alexandria. Napoleon is alleged to have said as he approached the pyramids and Sphinx, "Soldiers, forty centuries are looking down on you."

Admiral François-Paul Brueys ordered the French fleet to anchor in Abukir Bay, since it was questionable whether the fleet's large ships could enter the port of Alexandria. In the famous Battle of the Nile naval fight of 1798 near the promontory of Abukir, Nelson destroyed Napoleon's fleet during the night of August 1-2. The sunken French vessels are still underwater, with their refloating being considered.

Only four French vessels managed to escape and take refuge in Malta. This defeat isolated Bonaparte's troops and brought about the end of the French campaign in Egypt, the disaster altering the entire outlook of Napoleon's expedition. At exile on Saint Helena, Napoleon wrote that the battle of Abukir had profound repercussions on the fate of the world.

Sea battle near Alexandria

106 | A LIGHTHOUSE FOR ALEXANDRIA

The Rosetta Stone was discovered by a French officer in 1798 in an old tower in the town of Rosetta on the Rosetta branch of the Nile River, 43 miles east of Alexandria. Although French experts studied it, only when Jean-François Champollion deciphered its hieroglyphs in 1820 was its mystery unlocked.

In 1801, in order to stop French forces from advancing, the British flooded the land near Abukir. The area remained flooded until 1804, when evaporation left large quantities of salt which the government then sold. The 1807 British expedition to occupy Egypt led by General A. Mackenzie Fraser advanced on Rosetta March 31, 1807, but had to withdraw when the city's population fought back. The land of the region was again flooded during this attack.

The long-awaited reconstruction of the city of Alexandria was begun by Pasha Mohammed Ali of Albania, the founder of modern Egypt, who ruled the land from his capital city of Alexandria. He wanted a deep port and naval station, and had the Mahmudiya Canal built to reconnect with the Nile, finishing it in 1820. He created the Ras-el-Tin Palace on the western part of Alexandria's Pharos Island as his favorite residence.

By 1825, the small Alexandrian population of 5,000 that Napoleon had found had risen to 16,000. By 1840 it totaled 60,000. Ancient Eunostos Harbor became the chief port and Alexandria became the true capitol of Egypt until Said Pasha died there in 1863. However, as late as 1843, the gates of Alexandria were still closed at night.

Visiting Alexandria in 1839, renowned artist David Roberts received an invitation from an attaché, one Colonel Campbell, to join him for breakfast and then accompany him for an interview with Pasha Mohammed Ali. Roberts later created a painting of the meeting titled *Interview with the Viceroy of Egypt at His Palace, Alexandria, May 12th*. It depicts officers in rich uniforms and the Pasha in fairly simple costume. The chamber to which the officers have been ushered has an excellent view of the harbor, including a fleet of twenty fully-equipped ships, the Arsenal, the docks, and numerous batteries. The American Historical Association used this painting on the cover of its October 2006 *Perspectives* magazine.

During this same period, Roberts did another painting titled *Alexandria—Where Ships Rest and Depart to the Other World*. He wrote at the time, "Though little can be seen of this ancient city from the sea, owing to the low land of the Delta, yet few spots are approached under deeper emotions than those excited by its historical associations with the ancient land of which it was the chief port."

NAPOLEON COMES TO ALEXANDRIA | 107

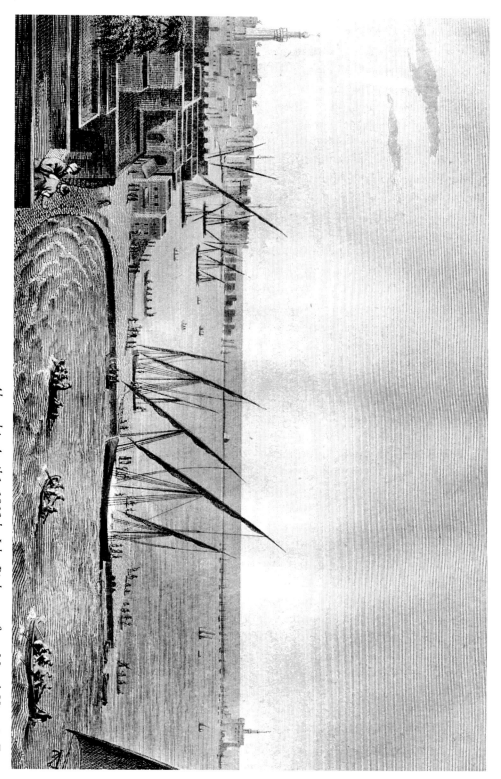

Alexandria April 1, 1813 by John Pinkerton, from Meyer's Views in Egypt

108 | A LIGHTHOUSE FOR ALEXANDRIA

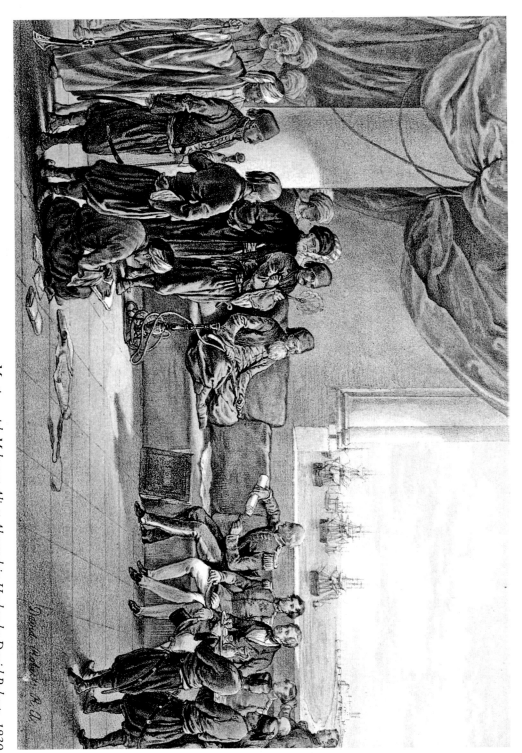

Meeting with Mehemet Ali at Alexandria Harbor by David Roberts, 1839

NAPOLEON COMES TO ALEXANDRIA | 109

Alexandria Harbor 1846 by W. H. Bartlett and R. Young, Fisher Son & Co.

110 | A LIGHTHOUSE FOR ALEXANDRIA

Pompey's Pillar at Alexandria 1848

Alexandria 1860, by J. Ramage, engraving by E. P. Brandard, pub. by William Mackenzie

112 | A LIGHTHOUSE FOR ALEXANDRIA

Cleopatra's Needle in Alexandria by David Roberts, 1839

NAPOLEON COMES TO ALEXANDRIA | 113

Cleopatra's Needle in Alexandria by Felix Bonfils, 1878

Square in Alexandria by B. Strassberger, 1879 book by G. Ebers

Roberts was excited that the city had been "chosen by the wisdom and power of the Macedonian conqueror." However, he was keenly aware of the poor condition of monuments in the area. After leaving Alexandria and returning to Cairo, David Roberts wrote to his daughter saying, "I have a tremendous file of excavations for temples and the great important temples of the Pharos."

Visiting Alexandria in 1841, Emma Roberts (not the daughter of artist David Roberts) wrote that Alexandria from the sea presented an imposing appearance with its long lines of handsome buildings, but added, "There is nothing, however, in the landing-place worthy of the approach to a place of importance; a confused crowd of camels, donkeys, and their drivers, congregated amidst heaps of rubbish." However, the city still had its two magnificent obelisks, one lying and the other standing, facing the Eastern harbor 150 feet from shore.

After the inauguration of the Suez Canal in 1869, Ismail Pasha, Khedive of Egypt, was talking with William Henry Hurlbert, an American who strongly believed in close American-Arab relations. As editor of the newspaper *The New York World* from 1876 to 1883, Hurlbert was aware that cotton-growing was severely depressed after the American Civil War; the country needed Egyptian cotton. Hurlbert suggested to the Pasha that a deal could be made. Egyptian cotton would be exported to the U.S. provided the remaining Alexandrian obelisk was sent in exchange. The deal cost philanthropist William Vanderbilt over $100,000. It obviously caused great controversy in Alexandria.

Egypt had already given Paris and London obelisks. The London needle erected on the banks of the Thames River in 1878 had a time capsule buried beneath it. Among items put into the capsule were photos of the twelve prettiest young women in London and the 26-word verse from *John 3:16* translated into 200 languages. Some enjoyed imagining that Moses himself had perhaps studied under the obelisk's shadow 3,500 years ago when it was in Egypt.

The famous Cleopatra's Needles had nothing of a personal nature to do with Cleopatra. The two were quarried in the fifteenth century B.C. under orders by Tuthmosis III. Legend had it that the ruler ordered his son lashed to the tip, so that workers would not dare to make an error. The red granite obelisks were covered in electrum, a naturally occurring alloy that was one part silver to four parts gold. A thousand years later, they were knocked down by Cambyses, son of Persian ruler Cyrus the Great, and reerected at Heliopolis.

Caesar Augustus conquered Egypt and in 13 B.C. had the pair deeply carved with hieroglyphics and placed at waterside in Alexandria in front of his Caesarium temple, the spot where Cleopatra and Antony had been lovers. Giant bronze crabs held up each base. The crabs were associated at the time with Roman mythology about the sun and worship of Apollo. Each crab weighed nearly a thousand pounds.

On February 22, 1881, the formal presentation of the gift to New York City from the government of Egypt took place in the Metropolitan Museum of Art's grand hall. The *New York World* on that day reported viewing through museum windows a towering shaft clear cut against a cloudless sky. In 1992, the Metropolitan Museum of Art opened its new Trustees Dining Room with splendid views of the obelisk as its dramatic center point.

While studying the sea route for departure of the needle from Egypt, American engineer Henry Gorringe found two of the ancient bronze crabs; they are today displayed at the Metropolitan Museum in New York City, as mentioned in Chapter 8. The Brooklyn Naval Yard cast replicas of the original four bronze crabs and foundation stones were laid in New York City's Central Park. Many feel that the obelisk, located behind the Metropolitan Museum, has today been largely forgotten. The hieroglyphics have been eroded by city exhaust fumes to the extent that they are nearly gone.

Writing just three years after the Central Park dedication ceremony in a book published by Dodd and Mead, Civil War Confederate General William Wing Loring called moving the New York obelisk from the land where it had been for 3,000 years a sad desecration and an act of selfish vanity, stating: "Now, even America violates a saddened shrine, and bears to her shores one of Egypt's altars." Born in 1818 in North Carolina, Loring moved with his family to St. Augustine, Florida, where, at age 14, he began his military career with the Florida Militia. He attended Georgetown University for one year, went on to study law, and was admitted to the Florida Bar in 1842. He served in the Florida House from 1843 to 1845 and was put in charge of the Oregon Territory. He fought with the South in the Civil War, then fought in Egypt for Khedive Ismail Pasha over nine years. He later returned to the United States and wrote a book about his experiences in Egypt to which this volume has referred.

By 1871, the population of Alexandria had risen to 220,000, of which 54,000 were foreigners. In May 1882, an Anglo-French fleet arrived to control unrest. The city was severely hit by a British naval bombardment. *Appleton's Annual Cyclopedia* of that year stated that in the European quarter at the eastern part of the city near the sea sat consulates and other public buildings, huge blocks of offices, and magnificent emporiums. Sumptuous mansions lined the streets eastward in the direction of Ramleh. In this cool and delightful suburb on the seashore, four miles from the city, the English all resided, some of them in splendid villas.

On June 11, 1882, an order was given by an Egyptian official to plunder and set ablaze this area. The riot led to the massacre of 400 Europeans, causing the British to occupy the entire country in August 1882.

Confederate General William Wing Loring wrote in 1884, "There is but little left of the past grandeur of the mighty city, only here and there the fragment of a column deeply imbedded in the earth." However, Loring quickly added, "The imagination readily carries one back to the days of the city's splendor described by the earlier writers."

Stated the *Encyclopedia Britannica* in 1891, "The general appearance of Alexandria is by no means striking; and from its situation its environs are sandy, flat, and sterile." At the Western Harbor, a breakwater was built 1871-1873 and was lengthened

Alexandria 1882 Grand Square after attack by British, Illustrated London News, *August 5, 1882*

118 | A LIGHTHOUSE FOR ALEXANDRIA

1906-1907 to make it two miles long. New harbor works were built from 1871-1878. A sea wall for the Eastern Harbor was built in 1905 and ran for three miles.

Creating this wall eliminated at the time a great deal of foul-smelling beach. In 1906, a new water supply was created; new drainage had been installed the previous year. In the early 1900s, the streets of the central part of Alexandria were paved with blocks of lava. Yet in spite of all this activity, power shifted again over the years back to Cairo.

CHAPTER 15
THE WEATHERING OF STONE

Besides the eroding forces of windstorms and heavy rain, modern researchers have discovered other destructive forces at work on a structure such as the Pharos of Alexandria. Major causes of weathering are water and temperature. Researcher Josef Riederer stated in 1978 that major studies in stone conservation concern mortar and plaster analysis, an analysis of salts, the determination of stone humidity, and a bacteriological analysis of the stone and mortar.

Decades ago, it was discovered that ancient wonders such as the Sphinx and the Great Pyramid have been decaying at an alarming rate. In a *Los Angeles Times* article on March 8, 1982, David Lamb discussed work at the time by Mark Lehner, who had just completed a two-year study identifying each structural element of the Sphinx. The 190-foot-long, 66-foot-tall statue had started to deteriorate as water seeped in from below, dissolving natural salt in the rock.

An Associated Press wire story carried in the *Miami Herald* on June 24, 1982, discussed the research of Dr. K. Lal Gauri concerning the decay of the Sphinx. The *New York Times* had previously discussed his work at the Sphinx site on December 26, 1979.

Gauri, an internationally-known expert on stone preservation, had worked on the Acropolis and the Taj Mahal. He obtained a Ph.D. in geology at the University of Bonn in Germany, did postdoctoral research at California Institute of Technology, and joined the University of Louisville in 1966, eventually becoming director of that school's Stone Conservation Research Laboratory until he retired as professor emeritus in 1998. He is a permanent member of the International Congress on Deterioration and Preservation of Stone Objects and was president of its Fourth Congress.

Gauri became involved in the Sphinx in 1980 after the American Research Center in Cairo learned of a plan to build a wind barrier around the Sphinx. Gauri concluded that stone to be used for the wall would add to the problem, and the idea was dropped. Sandstorms, wind, humidity, pollution, and a rising water table continue to erode the ancient monument.

In 1988, Joseph Davidovits, the French materials scientist, wrote that studies of the Sphinx's severe body erosion identified water as the damaging agent. Slow erosion occurs in limestone when water is absorbed and reacts with salts in the stone. Liquid pushes to the surface with a force of 1,400 pounds per square inch and the salt recrystallizes, causing the statue to crumble into rock chips.

A chemical analysis of the Sphinx has indicated that salt already in the limestone is causing the trouble. Gauri blamed harshly-alternating temperatures, with extremely hot days and cool nights. Water in the air condenses, is absorbed and dissolves the salt. When the salt crystallizes again, it puts added pressure on the monument, and pieces

The Sphinx

begin falling off. Poorer quality rock at the statue's base and paws has deteriorated more rapidly, with ancient repair workers covering the crumbling stone with masonry chopped from a nearby quarry.

The limestone of the Sphinx is 50 million years old and contains fossils of clams, corals, oysters and sponges. The monument was built by King Chephren, the Pharaoh Khafra, about 2,600 B.C. from solid limestone at the site. The first renovations were carried out by King Tutankhamen's great-great-grandfather when the Sphinx was already 1,200 years old. The chin, which fell off long ago, was brought to London, and the beard placed partly in the British Museum and partly in the Cairo Museum. In October 1981, a piece of the left hindquarter of the Sphinx fell off.

An August 5, 1982, story by David Ottaway in the *Washington Post* discussed the work of Lehner and Gauri that proposed a cure for the Sphinx's "salt cancer." Piece by piece, it would be wrapped in an impermeable bag. Air inside would be pumped out and water would then be drawn through the stone by a vacuum to either eliminate the salt or at least reduce it to acceptable levels.

K. Lal Gauri offered to develop technology specifically for the Sphinx. However, Egyptian archaeologists were not sure this was the best long-term answer. Saleh Ahmed Saleh believed that salt alone was not the problem, and, in fact, could work as a binder to give greater strength to limestone. Saleh instead focused on first lowering the high water table that was sitting 12 feet below the Sphinx. However, he was firm in his belief that each generation inevitably would leave its own "mark of time" on monuments and thereby reduce their lifetimes.

A 1989 *New Haven Register* article quoted Egyptian Minister of Culture Farouk Hosni as saying that the Sphinx was not in any danger of collapsing. However, months earlier, another chunk of rock fell from the statue's right shoulder. After patching the gap in white limestone, restorers encased a very weak section of the shoulder behind a limestone retaining wall and placed limestone blocks alongside the body as braces. Some critics at the time stated that the bright white limestone clashed against the ancient brown stone.

Antiquities officials have been trying to protect the relic as the ancient builders did, without using any cement. Sayed Tawfik (1936-1990), Chairman of the Egyptian Antiquities Organization for years, noted that the Sphinx's Arabic name is Abu el-Hawl, that is, Father of Terror. He admitted that experts remain terrified concerning how to properly preserve the landmark in the midst of major erosion problems.

Decades ago, UNESCO provided $100,000 for equipment to monitor harmful natural and man-made phenomena such as pollution and wind.

Gauri co-authored a book in 1999 on the conservation of carbonate stone, in which he included a discussion of his work on the Sphinx. He suggested in that book that anyone treating a carbonate structure, that is, one made out of limestone or marble, do seven things: make the treatment reversible; make sure the treatment reaches deep into the interior of the stone; not seal the surface to such an extent that the pores cannot breathe, trapping moisture inside; use material that does not absorb atmospheric gas; make sure only a minimum of treatment material is used; use a product that is not flammable; and use a material that does not require complex processes to apply.

In a 1978 Geological Society of America publication, Walter D. Keller called water "Public Enemy Number 1" of stone because it interacts with stone more than any other agent, dissolving, hydrolyzing, and hydrating. It enters by osmosis, gravity, capillary and siphon action to transport agents that oxidize and reduce rock and form salt. Water also carries bacteria and organic compounds into and out of the stone.

A highly-respected geologist for decades, Keller died in 2000 at age 101. After receiving an undergraduate degree in ceramic engineering from the Missouri School of Mines and a master's degree in geology from Harvard University, he began teaching at the University of Missouri in 1926. Besides publishing five books and over 200 papers, he won the national Neil Miner Award in 1967 for exceptional contributions to the teaching of geology and also received the Outstanding Educator in America Award. The university honored him for his contributions with the dedication of the W. D. Keller Geology Auditorium in 1981, and celebrated his hundredth birthday by presenting the geology department with the new $100,000 Walter Keller Opportunities for Excellence Endowment.

John Ashurst, author of the 1977 book *Stone in Building*, has offered that while pure water itself is virtually harmless to stone, it is at the same time the greatest enemy of natural stone in that it carries the main agents of decay. If stone could be kept perfectly dry, most of the causes of decay would be eliminated. An expert in stone decay and preservation, Ashurst was employed for twenty years as an architect in England's Ancient Monuments Division. He worked as principal architect for English Heritage, and then become professor of heritage conservation at Bournemouth University. From 1991 on, he worked in the private sector as a partner at Ingram

Consultancy, a firm specializing in conservation and repair of historic buildings. He was a vital member of the International Centre for the Study of the Preservation and Restoration of Cultural Property, teaching for years such subjects as "The Venice Stone Course." His *Conservation of Ruins* was published in 2007, just before his death in June 2008.

Ashurst says that, in high temperatures, on faces of stonework directly exposed to the sun, rapid evaporation occurs beneath the surface of the stone, depositing salts internally. Crystallization of soluble salts can set up sufficient forces to seriously damage most porous stone. After a day of hot sun, night-time radiation reverses the source of heat, so that a continual cycle of stress is set up between the surface and the core.

The abrasion of stone surfaces can occur even more in marine areas such as the Pharos of Alexandria, where high winds carry salt inland. However, true wind erosion is usually caused by rapid wetting and drying of wind-borne salt solutions. Repeated crystallization cycles in these conditions may cause what Ashurst calls very spectacular decay, occasionally aggravated by wind and sand scour.

Carbon dioxide, ever-present in the air dissolved in rainwater, will in time dissolve the calcium carbonate cementing together limestone so that cohesion is lost and the surface disintegrates. Where limestone is not steadily washed by rain, but only intermittently wetted, a hard impermeable skin of calcium sulphate will be formed, which eventually develops a surface "crazing" and may lead to blistering or exfoliation of the surface. Stone may also contain large quantities of soluble salts before quarrying. In limestone work, these may cause contamination by seawater during transportation.

Sulphur acids in the atmosphere and chlorides in sea spray also can cause salt contamination. Even the sand used for mortar and concrete is often salt-contaminated. As moisture evaporates from or near the surface, salts are readily conveyed from sand to the masonry.

The ground is also a tough enemy. All soils contain soluble salts. With sufficient moisture, their passage by capillary movement into porous stone is inevitable. Salts from the ground can travel to the first floor of a building. Lightning and atmospheric electricity currents can ionize these salts, thereby increasing their activity.

Writing in their 2007 book, *Building Stone Decay*, R. Prikryl and B. J. Smith emphasize that treating a stone structure's symptoms of decay may produce an initial short-lived improvement in condition or appearance, but can also allow potentially debilitating changes to continue while their worst effects are temporarily masked. They conclude that one needs a "complex stress history" over the life of the entire building to know how to effectively handle problems of decay.

A wire service news story appearing in the November 18, 1981, *Hartford Courant* mentioned that a few hundred of the Cheops Pyramid's 2,300,000 limestone blocks had been patched. Nassaf Mohamed Hassan, keeper of the pyramid, explained that the patch job would not have been necessary if the pyramid's hard white limestone outer casing had not been stolen over the past 1,000 years for use in building area mosques, churches, palaces, bridges, walls, irrigation canals, and houses. A 40-foot-high, 25-foot-thick apron of granite shielded it from the worst of the sandstorms. Patches were done through use of limestone blocks a quarter the size of the 2-1/2-ton originals. With a base of 13.1 acres, the Great Pyramid stood at 481.4 feet when it was built 4,600 years ago, but is today 31 feet shorter after losing about a dozen layers and its capstone.

A 1989 news story on the Great Pyramid appearing in the *Hartford Courant* reported it had reopened for the first time in 9 months. The Egyptian Antiquities Organization had pushed for the closing after discovering cracks in blocks lining interior passages and finding a half-inch layer of salt on inside walls. Zahi Hawass, then director general of the pyramids area, said that nothing had been done to restore the pyramid's interior since it was opened in the late 1830s. While removing salt from the limestone walls, restorers found weak and cracking rock throughout the pyramid. In the Grand Gallery, 500 limestone blocks were restored and 16 granite slabs reinforced with stainless steel bars.

According to a wire service story appearing in the October 19, 1983 *New Haven Journal Courier*, the Parthenon has also undergone restoration. Scientists focused on replacing the temple's rusted iron clamps and dowels with rustproof titanium. They also reassembled displaced marble blocks, and studied ways to prevent further damage from air pollution and earthquakes. Most of the lead-encased iron clamps and wooden pegs put in place when the temple was built in the 5th century B.C. were in good condition. However, iron used in restoration efforts a half-century ago had rusted and expanded, causing the marble to crack and crumble. Completed in 432 B.C., the Parthenon survived virtually intact until 1687 A.D., when a Venetian mortar was fired into it, setting off an explosion of the gunpowder stored there.

Preservation expert John Ashurst wrote in 1977 that stone preservation has had a long and disappointing history. Modern experts recently have begun favoring deep impregnation of treatment agents, feeling that shallow surface treatments actually only serve to accelerate decay.

Stonework decay expert Erhard Winkler noted in 1975 that conservators were not aware of the very complex internal travel routes of moisture nor ways to insulate against rising ground moisture, factors which were still unknown in the nineteenth century. Winkler earned his doctorate from the University of Vienna and became an internationally respected authority on the weathering properties of building and monumental stone. Traveling the world recording the deterioration of ancient temples, he was among the first scholars to identify air pollution as a major cause of historic building decay. Professor of civil engineering and geological sciences at the University of Notre Dame since 1948, he received an award in 2002 from the ASTM International testing standards association and was also honored in 2002 by the Geological Society of America's Engineering Geology Division with its Meritorious Service Award.

Sometimes, using an insulating surface barrier does more harm than good, since moisture acts from behind such insulation. This has been the case with the two famous obelisks taken from Alexandria. London's Cleopatra's Needle was treated with a mixture of Damar resin and wax dissolved in clear petroleum spirit in 1879, which has protected the monument. The sister monument in Central Park, New York, has done less well. Surface treatment on that obelisk was not started until ten years after its erection in New York, after high relative humidity had already penetrated the stone. Also, water-repellent coatings tend to discolor and to collect dirt. Furthermore, as the *World Monuments Fund Newsletter* of November 1985 pointed out, if damage is caused during the application of a product, it often cannot be reversed.

Writing in the 2007 publication *Building Stone Decay*, earth science experts C. Vazquez-Calvo, M. Alvarez de Buergo, and R. Fort say that some surface treatments with patinas have sometimes actually been beneficial. These experts say Egyptians in the second century B. C. used blood and animal glues, while Vitruvius in the first century B. C. mentioned the use of blood, eggs, albumen, animal glues, fig tree milk, wax, linseed oil and lard as organic additives. Pliny the Elder in the first century A. D. reported on the use of milk and saffron for plasters preparation.

One of the greatest changes in attitudes of twentieth-century researchers and preservationists is that monuments, sculptures, and buildings cannot be preserved by a single treatment but need regular maintenance. One of the main reasons for rapid stone decay in our time is that objects treated a few decades ago were left untended. Preservation expert Josef Riederer has written that the trend now is to develop products that can be reapplied after a certain time so that continuous protection is possible.

K. Lal Gauri in 1978 has summarized that actions taken by modern-day stone conservation experts involve cleaning, dampness control, consolidation, protection, and restoration of objects exposed to natural weathering. However, until more is known about all these complex problems, the *World Monuments Fund Newsletter* notes, "most conservators take the cautious approach of treating only with materials whose effects are reversible."

Writing in 2007, preservation experts R. Prikryl and B. J. Smith remind everyone that no stone lasts forever, and that using it in construction will invariably shorten its lifespan. However, they know that building owners think that using stone in a building "somehow immunizes it from even natural decay and renders it immutable.' When decay occurs, owners and laymen believe it is due to some mistake. Someone has to take blame and then immediately "cure" the building's ailment. Owners fail to accept that, as with all construction materials, stone has a design life.

Geology professors G. F. Andriani and N. Walsh emphasized in 2007 that particularly in coastal areas, salt weathering is the most important cause of stone decay, particularly where historic monuments and buildings are close to the coastline and partially or completely submerged by sea water.

A recent public television program that was part of the NOVA series provided an overview of Jean-Yves Empereur's special treatment process for blocks or statues taken out of the Alexandrian harbor in the last few years. There is a great deal of salt inside the skin of the blocks, which must be removed the same day the blocks come out of the water. Tanks are used that start with the same percentage of sodium as the seawater. The level of sodium is slowly reduced until the blocks have released all their interior salt. The salt removal process takes about six months, after which exposure to the open air does not harm them.

Franck Goddio, interviewed by Richard Fuchs in the May 4, 2007, issue of *Deutsche Welle*, discussed the problem of salt in items raised from Alexandria's harbor.

The salt removal process for a small artifact took a few days, whereas a statue of Hapi fifteen feet high required 18 months.

Goddio is discussed often as one proceeds through this book. In early years, he was a French statistician and financial advisor. He found an interesting niche as private businessman working with governments and non-profit foundations, but later broke away to pursue his passion of underwater exploration. In 1992, he began working with the Egyptian Supreme Council on remapping Alexandria's harbor. He also excavated numerous wrecks, including that of the British East India Company's *Royal Captain* and Bonaparte's sunken flagship *Orient*. He has since gone on to discover Cleopatra's Palace and two lost cities in Egypt.

The World Monuments Fund notes that, for architects, their response to salt and monument deterioration has been to choose materials that are more resistant to acid. They also have changed design concepts to eliminate cornices and moldings. Although intended by the original builders to protect buildings from erosion, these added features are now seen as problem areas for the collection of salt crusts.

Roman coin, illustration published by Milne 1841

CHAPTER 16
CLUES: ABUSIR, COINS, MOSAICS

The memory of the lighthouse of Alexandria still lives on in the city, thanks to a modern white marble carving that depicts Isis Pharia and the Pharos as one enters the gardens at the Kom-es-Shafur catacombs. There are other reminders. Twenty-eight miles southwest of Alexandria are the remains of the ancient city of Taposiris Magna, today called Abusir, on Lake Maryut. The town faces the lake, not the nearby ocean. Ancient Greek historian Callisthenes says that Alexander the Great visited Taposiris on his way to Siwa.

In Greek times, Taposiris Magna was involved with highly important trade at the western arm of Lake Mareotis, where goods moved to and from Libya and the interior of Egypt. There was a large and very important Ptolemaic Temple of Osiris there. The Temple of Osiris no longer exists, but its high, massive enclosure walls remain. Dating from the fourth century B.C., the enclosure is nearly 100 yards square with very thick walls. A Christian church replaced the Temple in 391 A.D. Since the wonders of ancient Alexandria have all gone, the Temple of Osiris at Abusir is the finest ancient monument left north of the Pyramids.

Above one large, ancient tomb in the city, a local resident built what most believe to be a replica of the Pharos, called the Abusir Tower. It appears as a stone structure 100 feet tall made of local limestone. An inner staircase provides access to the top. Many researchers feel that it was a Roman lighthouse. However, it probably did not serve coastal shipping, but lake shipping, namely at Binnen Lake and Mareotis Lake, over whose west end and dike the tower rose. Charts of the British Admiralty show the lighthouse tower as a landmark.

The structure has three levels: a square base, an octagon, and on the top, a sphere or cylinder. Hermann Thiersch in 1909 stated that the Abusir type of construction seems to date from the first half of the Ptolemaic period, which places it chronologically very near the Pharos. The Abusir Tower appears to have been modeled after the Pharos but built to one-tenth its size. It is therefore a very important structure for today's historians and archaeologists. Egypt's Supreme Council of Antiquities is today attempting to preserve the site.

Peter Fraser in 1972 called the Abusir Tower a large funerary monument closely resembling the Pharos. Thiersch, however, states that the structure has been unjustly considered a burial monument, with the tower actually having nothing to do with the rock grave at its base. Thiersch agrees with those who believe the structure was a functioning lighthouse.

With the loss of the Pharos as a landmark, mariners approaching Egypt picked up the tower at Abusir as their first landmark. It therefore became an important marking on all old maps published between 1500 and 1850, about which time the Ras-el-Tin lighthouse was finished on the western part of Pharos Island.

As for coins, the Pharos appears over and over on the bronze Roman coins of Alexandria from the reign of Domitian to that of Commodus, 95 A.D. to 190 A.D., providing a continuous record of coins to view, with a wide variety of depictions on the coins. Researcher Thiersch feels this is due in part to the decline of the art of coin-depicting, but more

Abusir Tower at Taposiris Magna, courtesy Amicale Alexandrie Hier et Aujourd'hui

CLUES: ABUSIR, COINS, MOSAICS | 131

Coin 150 A.D. by Donaldson in World's Lighthouses *by Stevenson*

importantly, to the linking with Isis that began to predominate on coins, leaving the lighthouse dwarf-like.

Johann Adler wrote in 1901 that there were three different types of coins. One shows Isis' fleeting Pharis, a barge or sailing vessel, hurrying to the right. Isis is holding in her hands an inflated sail. In front of her is a corner sketch of the Pharos. A second type is represented on a somewhat smaller coin. To the left is Pharos, with a departing commercial ship to the right. The third type of coin depicts the Pharos alone, with much more compact proportions.

The reverse sides of the first two types show a high, narrow tower with a considerably sloped pedestal and staircase leading to a high gate. The tower tapers towards the top, has broad, singular stones at the edges, and a surface extending three to five stories. Round windows are set in it. The top has a platform with tritons on the corners mounted on bearings, each blowing a buccine, an ancient trumpet-like instrument. In the middle is an open lantern. Atop it, according to Adler, rests a female figure with a scepter in her left hand. Adler accepts the idea that this is a colossal bronze statue of Isis Pharia crowning the Pharos.

Hermann Thiersch stated in 1909 that the best coins minted under Domitian show the tower in two parts. On a high square appears an octagon, with large tritons at the base. Above that is a sphere topped by a statue which Thiersch thinks may be Poseidon and his trident. The tower features a high-beamed door with a ramp leading up to it. As Isis takes over on the coins, the lighthouse loses its steepness, and takes on more and more of a sugar-loaf shape. By the end of the period of Commodus, next to the tower appears, not Isis, but instead, one of the great corn ships of Alexandria headed for Rome to feed the populace. Thiersch states that, unfortunately, this distorted coin is the basis for Adler's reconstruction of the tower. However, the coin is important, because it shows more clearly than earlier coins an upper third story.

Various art works have also been cited by researchers as important to a study of the Pharos. Perhaps the most famous of these is the painted glass beaker or vase found at Begram, Afghanistan, by French archaeologist Joseph Hackin. Results of a trip to Begram (the ancient city of Kapisa) accompanied by his wife were published in 1933, followed by extensive digging at Begram 1936-40. He lectured in 1933 at London's Royal Geographical Society concerning his travels through Persia and Afghanistan with the Citroen Trans-Asiatic Expedition. Statues studied by Hacklin were the same Buddha statues destroyed by the Taliban in 2001, creating an international furor. Besides the vase, Hacklin discovered at Begram beautiful ivory statuettes recently displayed at a Paris museum 2006-7. He and his wife were lost at sea in 1941 while on a diplomatic mission for the French underground opposing Nazi Germany.

On the Begram vase, a statue and two tritons are shown at the top. The statue appears to be holding an oar, and some scholars have assumed the figure is a heroic Ptolemy. Others assume it is Zeus Soter cradling a thunderbolt in his left arm. The vase clearly shows stonework and rectangular windows all the way up the sides.

Other representations of the Pharos in terracotta lamps and lamp-holders from Egypt take great care to show numerous windows on the structure's sides clear up to the lantern story. Some researchers have identified these as shields or bucklers hanging out on the tower's surface, but others say they are clearly windows.

As for other depictions, a famous one can be found in the village of Qasr Libya in current-day Libya, formerly Cyrenaica. Fifty square mosaic panels, moved from the church, are exhibited today in a small museum at Qasr Libya which houses the finest Byzantine mosaics in North Africa. Spaces in the East church floor from which the panels were removed can be clearly seen. One of the panels portrays the Pharos. To what extent the Pharos still retained its original ornamentation is uncertain. However, the depiction might not be a contemporary one, but artwork illustrating ancient knowledge. Of most interest in the mosaic of Cyrenaica is the statue at the top. Writing in 1961, Richard Goodchild feels it represents Helios.

Another mosaic depiction of Alexandria and the Pharos known as the Mosaic of Gerasa, in Palestine (modern-day Jordan), was identified in a 1938 publication by Carl H. Kraeling.

Still another depiction, a mid-fifth-century mosaic found in Israel in 1964, shows Ulysses and Sirens in the upper portion. Below is a reclining figure of Nilus, the river-god, holding a sacred ibis and looking out towards a small three-storied building above a pitched roof and colonnade. Beyond it is a stylized Nilometer marked off in cubits from 11 to 16, with 16 being the optimum height of a successful annual Nile flood. Above the tower is the word "Alexandria."

Hermann Thiersch stated in 1909 that the most famous copy of the Pharos of Alexandria was the lighthouse of Ostia near Rome, although it adds a fourth story which the original did not have. The depiction of the lighthouse of Ostia on the well-known relief from Terracina housed in Rome's Museo Torlonia is very instructive because Suetonius, a Roman historian and biographer of the Caesars, reports that this building erected by Claudius was a copy of the Pharos of Alexandria. At the time the relief of Terracina was done, the Pharos was still standing and in active use. The relief shows tall flames emerging from the top of the structure.

The Ostia lighthouse is also shown on a medallion of Emperor Commodus, who reigned 177-192 A.D. The medallion, now housed in the British Museum, shows the emperor welcoming the annual grain fleet from Egypt into the harbor at Ostia as he

Thirteenth century mosaic, Zen chapel, St. Mark's, Venice, from Thiersch book

stands before a three-tiered lighthouse. Clayton says that the medallion also shows the Greco-Egyptian god Jupiter-Serapis, wearing his corn modius to measure capacity on his head while steering one of the galleys.

Also, the thirteenth century mosaic in the Zen chapel of St. Mark's of Venice supposedly shows the Pharos of Alexandria and a ship. The Evangelist is sitting in the stern as he arrives in the city to found the Christian Coptic Church in Egypt. Lighthouse expert Douglas Bland Hague feels the artist was more familiar with numerous lighthouses around his native coast than with the Pharos, which by then only existed in truncated form.

Researcher Charles Picard says that another depiction of the Pharos of Alexandria is supposedly on the Gold Plate of Perm at the Museum of the Hermitage in Russia. It apparently shows a somewhat humorous depiction of engravers putting on Sostratus' inscription.

Of great interest is archaeological work recently done at Caesarea Maritima, a coastal city in Israel built by Herod the Great, king of Judaea from 40 to 4 B.C. Pontius Pilate, who ordered the execution of Christ, had his headquarters at Caesarea, a city that prospered for over 1,200 years. At the end of the thirteenth century A.D., Caesarea was abandoned and gradually slipped beneath advancing sand dunes. The site is located about 30 miles north of modern Tel Aviv, near the location of ancient Joppa.

Kenneth Holum, in his 1988 book, *King Herod's Dream*, reports Caesarea Maritima was named for the first Roman emperor, Caesar Augustus, with "Caesarea" coming from the family name of the Caesars; the harbor's name of Sebastos was the Greek translation of "Augustus." Holum received his Ph.D. from the University of Chicago in 1973, specializing in the antiquities of ancient Rome and Greece. Since 1989, he has directed the Combined Caesarea Expeditions, an international archaeological project working with Avner Raban. Besides his book *King Herod's Dream*, he has written two large collections of essays on Caesarea, published in 1999-2000. Since Raban died in 2004, Holum has been working on a four-volume study of their work. He is also writing a new book on the subject titled *Caesarea's Fortune*.

Caesarea was built on the site of Strato's Tower, a settlement established about 325 B.C. by Strato, king of the Phoenician city of Sidon. Although British explorers C. R. Conder and H. H. Kitchener visited the site in 1873 for six days and published the first scientific account of their findings, little took place there until the 1950s and 1960s.

Holum's book discusses in depth the Joint Expedition to Caesarea Maritima, which has been excavating the land site there since 1972, and the Caesarea Ancient Harbour Excavation Project, which has been exploring Caesarea's ancient port since 1980. A detailed exhibit on Caesarea's archaeological treasures sponsored by the Israel Department of Antiquities and Museums and the Smithsonian Institution's Traveling Exhibition Service was shown in several U.S. cities including Boston during 1989.

Technological breakthroughs in King Herod's time helped him create his city of Caesarea, including the impressive major harbor of Sebastos, in only thirteen years, from 22 B.C. to 10 or 9 B.C. The harbor included a lighthouse named Drusion and six colossal bronze statues, three on either side of the harbor entrance, to guard the passage and welcome sailors.

Researchers guess that the Drusion tower was 250 to 300 feet tall, and feel that they have found its remains in an area of massive stones at the west side of the channel entrance. The volume and size of these stones suggest a building of exceptional dimensions. The team also found two blocks that supported the statues at the right of the harbor entrance and discovered a huge foundation for the statues that stood on the left. However, no trace of statues or columns has been found.

A Reuters news service article of June 6, 2006, titled "Diving into History in King Herod's Harbor," discussed recent attempts to make Caesarea the first underwater archaeological museum in Israel. Metal poles with numbered signs marked 36 exhibits 20 feet below the Mediterranean. A ticket to view the site cost $2.50. As of that writing, hundreds of people had taken the 45- to 50-minute dive to visit the exhibit.

According to a June 8, 2006, article published in *News Depth*, DiveNews.com's online magazine, the park was inaugurated during the spring of 2006. The 25,000-square-foot park was divided into four tour routes along the ancient port: the port's entrance; lighthouse remains; remains of the piers, breakwaters, docking platforms; and remains of jewelry, statue bases, coins, and a shipwreck.

Said a 22-year-old diver to Reuters, "The visibility was low but that just made it more dramatic. You feel like you're in an ancient atmosphere and you feel the depth of the history of the place." Archaeologists claim that the Caesarea project is the world's first public underwater seaport exhibit.

Caesarea 2007 by Bukvoed in Wikimedia Commons

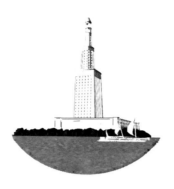

CHAPTER 17
FORT QAITBAY

After the Pharos had been destroyed by various earthquakes, the port of Alexandria was watched over from a knoll called Kom al-Nadura, where the arrival and departure of ships was noted. For closer supervision of the eastern harbor, a second lighthouse was built. Researcher Anthony DeCosson tells us that construction began in the time of Sultan Kalawun or his son, al-Nasir Muhammad b.

Fort Qaitbay in 1798, book by Thiersch

Kalawun, and was completed in 1365. This construction strengthened the eastern harbor, which was reserved for Christian shipping, with the western harbor restricted to Muslim vessels.

The ancient Pharos lighthouse had a resurrection of sorts in 1480 A.D. when Fort Qaitbay was built on its rubble. This fort served both a military and navigational role. Johann Adler reported in 1901 that it was built by the Egyptian Mameluke Sultan Qaitbay, who ruled from 1468 to 1496. Qaitbay visited the area between 1477 and 1478. He then ordered that a castle be built with four corner towers and a middle tower which was to carry a beacon. Stones from the old Pharos were used, and the building was completed in two years. Qaitbay used it as part of his coastal defense against the Turks, who were threatening Egypt.

Eventually, the Turks conquered Egypt in 1517. When their power declined in the early 1800s, Mohammed Ali (1805-1848) modernized the fort's defenses. No visitors were allowed there. E. M. Forster in *Alexandria* writes in 1922 that the fort thus took on the image of an impregnable and mysterious place.

Fort Qaitbay in American Architect and Building News, *May 15, 1886*

The fort went through various trials of history, including conquest by General Bonaparte in 1798 and a fierce bombardment of the city by the British in 1882. Visiting the site in 1882, archaeologist John Peters said the name and title of Qait-Bay were unmistakably legible on one of two quite decayed limestone tablets over the entrance gate. The fort has been repaired three times, by King Farouq in the 1940s, in 1982, and in 2000.

In the meantime, the old lighthouse built near the site of the ancient Pharos was deemed inadequate and a new lighthouse was built near Ras-el-Tin on Cape Eunostos in 1842. *Encyclopedia Britannica* of 1891 reported that this light had a one-minute

Fort Qaitbay Citadel sign

revolving light that could be seen 20 miles away.

Hermann Thiersch states that, in May of 1904, the toll authority of Alexandria was well on its way to having the Fort Qaitbay monument totally demolished. Only by the energetic intervention of the Cairo authorities, especially a Dr. Herz-Beys, was the core of the structure saved. Its renovation and future maintenance were taken over by the Committee of Conservation of Arab Monuments in Cairo. Researcher Thiersch reports, however, that the passageway and silhouette of the fort were gone forever.

Peter Fraser wrote in 1972 that the site on which Qaitbay stands is itself part of a much larger plateau, now largely submerged. This plateau was originally an island separated from the larger island of Pharos by a narrow channel through which ships could pass.

E. M. Forster says in *Alexandria,* in 1922 that inside the pentagon-shaped fort was a castle, whose foundations had a slightly different orientation from those of the Pharos. This was because the castle had to be adjusted to the points of the compass due to the mosque it contained, so that prayers could be performed facing east. In spite of the different orientation, the square castle stood on the exact site of the ancient Pharos.

A 2003 UNESCO report indicated that some studies on Fort Qaitbay have divided it into three areas: the fort itself as a 100-foot-square fortified building; the fortress that encloses the fort and is itself nearly completely encircled by a continuous wall; and a concrete

Fort Qaitbay Main Tower sign

platform around the Citadel on its eastern and northeastern sides. While the fort and fortress seem not to be immediately threatened by waves, the platform shows serious damage. Also, the concrete blocks forming a submerged breakwater a hundred feet out to sea have been found to provide no real protection.

Today on the second floor of the central fortress tower sits a model of the original fortress. Modern-day Fort Qaitbay, consisting of mostly white limestone, with a few decorative pieces in dark granite, sits smartly on the western end of Alexandria's Corniche, about which *New York Times* reporter Kareem Fahim wrote with amazement on December 17, 2007, "Fort Qaitbay feels like an Egyptian Coney Island, with pony rides for the kids and shisha tobacco pipes for their parents."

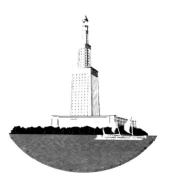

CHAPTER 18
MODERN-DAY ALEXANDRIA: BEAUTY AND HOPE VS. CHAOS

In 1980 Allen Drury wrote of Alexandria that its antiquities are Greek and Roman. Not only are its ties to ancient Egypt extremely tenuous, but its ties to Cairo and the rest of Egypt seem equally so. Drury notes that Alexandria sits on the Mediterranean shore, both physically and psychologically distant from the capital and the life of the 700-mile valley of the Nile.

Writer Michael Grant says that despite its contacts with the interior of Egypt by way of the Nile, "It never quite belonged to the country. The city was not so much its center as its superstructure. People spoke of traveling from Alexandria to Egypt. It was also the capital of an empire." The Ptolemies were not just kings of Egypt, but rulers over a vast area beyond.

Alexandria is situated at the western end of the Nile Delta, 110 miles northwest of Cairo and 12 miles west of the Canopic mouth of the Nile. It is located on Lake Mariyut, westernmost lagoon in the Nile delta. The sand spit of the lagoon consists of a low ridge of sand dunes stretching northeasterly for 50 kilometers to terminate at the promontory of Abukir. On this spit, together with some bordering alluvial land, today's Alexandria stretches between the sea and the salt lake.

Opposite the narrowest part of the sand spit are the remains of another largely submerged ridge of dunes, today appearing as isolated islets parallel to the shore about a mile out. Pharos is the largest of these, and it forms the basis for the port of Alexandria.

142 | A LIGHTHOUSE FOR ALEXANDRIA

Geographer Yehuda Karmon, born 1912 in Auschwitz, Poland, and writing in 1980, said that since the ocean currents of the southern Mediterranean flow from west to east, the silt of the delta is carried away from Alexandria toward the east, where it causes serious problems at the entrance to the Suez Canal and Port Said. Karmon emigrated to Palestine in 1938 and began a career in geography at age 38 at Hebrew University in Jerusalem. He received his Master's degree in 1953 for research on draining the Huleh swamps in Jordan, a paper that still angers Israeli ecologists. Dr. Karmon went on to serve as instructor of economic geography at Hebrew University, shifted his focus to regional studies of Nigeria and Ghana, then turned to urban issues and studies of world-wide ports, conducting field surveys of 250 harbors. He died in 1995.

The present city of Alexandria, called Al Iskandariya or Iskandariyah by today's Egyptians, really dates only from the nineteenth century. It has a shape 48 miles long but at points is as narrow as 1¾ miles. Alexandria has a population of 4.2 million, which traditionally rises to more than 5 million when it becomes a summer refuge.

Alexandria, one of the most ancient ports in the world still in use, is Egypt's chief port, handling 90% of the country's foreign trade, with over 4,000 ships a year entering the port. All of Egypt's cotton and a large part of its oil are exported through the city, as well as fruits and vegetables, perfumes, and some finished goods. The

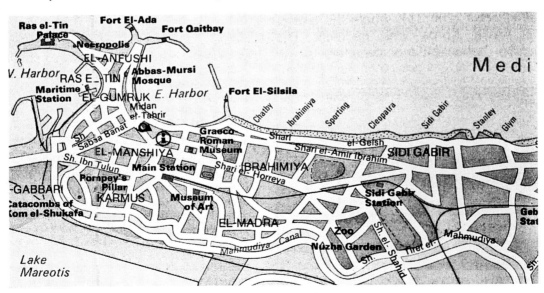

Modern map of Alexandria's eastern area

largest commodity imported through the harbor is grain. The city has always been oriented more toward the western Mediterranean than toward the east.

In ancient times the east basin was used as the main harbor, whereas, today, the main harbor is located in the western basin; the eastern harbor is now used just for fishing and yachting. The famous long walk along the Alexandrian seafront, the Corniche, extends from Ras-el-Tin on the west to Montazah on the east, a distance of 15 miles, then goes on to Abukir and Rosetta. It was built in 1934 at a cost of $1.5 million. There are two principal land routes to and from Alexandria, the Agricultural or Delta Road and the Desert Road.

Storms hit Alexandria for five- or six-day periods on the average of three times in December, twice in January, once in February and twice in March. The hot Egyptian summers are not felt too badly in Alexandria, where prevailing northwest winds from the sea blow for nine months of the year and the temperature seldom exceeds 85 degrees. In the winter, some rain falls, and throughout the year, the air can be damp with salt vapors from the sea.

The city has been slowly sinking into the sea for the last several hundred years. For many years now in the summer, potentially beautiful city beaches have been overused and polluted, with untreated sewage flowing into the Mediterranean. However, there are excellent beaches 50 miles east or west of the city proper. Some consider the beaches between Alexandria and the Libyan border some of the finest on the Mediterranean.

El Alamein, an unknown village before World War II, became famous when the British 8th Army, retreating from Rommel's forces, halted there and, under Montgomery, waged a battle as Rommel prepared to break through to Alexandria. The British pushed Rommel back and pursued him to Tunisia before invading Sicily and then Italy. After the war, thousands of mines placed in the desert by both sides remained hidden in the sands. Researcher Fouad Gassir estimates that 24 million mines were planted in the Western Desert.

An interesting sidelight to Rommel and war is related in David Fisher's 2004 book titled *The War Magician,* wherein he recounts the story of Jasper Maskelyne. Famous in the 1930s as a stage magician, Maskelyne used his skills of illusion to help the British military in World War II. He toured the Nile Basin with his show many years earlier and spoke some Arabic. His father had served in Egypt during World War

I. Fisher says that Maskelyne attempted to hide Alexandria Harbor from Nazi bombers in 1941 using the magic of camouflage to make the port appear to be one mile west of where it actually was. The success of this illusion is hard to evaluate, but it makes for a very interesting story.

Borg El Arab, a small village near El Alamein, was much more famous. Forty feet above sea level, it was the site of a small lighthouse used to guide ships and a source for fresh water to supply caravans traveling the northern seashore route. The famous Wadi el Natrun monasteries still exist 73 miles from Alexandria along the Desert Road between Alexandria and Cairo. Tradition says that Jesus and the Holy Family lived in this desert area after fleeing Palestine to escape Herod's persecution.

Refugees leave Alexandria, Illustrated London News, *July 8, 1882*

Years ago, foreigners from twenty countries made up the population of Alexandria, and English, French, Greek, Italian, Hebrew, Armenian, Turkish, and Arabic were all spoken there. Writer Hamza Hendawi says that popular songs from the 1940s told of the cool Alexandrian sea breeze, pretty women, and love in the air. In 1952, after the revolution for independence, 750,000 foreigners were expelled by nationalist Egyptians. Writing about Alexandria in 1981, A. Hoyt Hobbs said, "the realist today sees a rundown beachside city, though the romantic senses levantine and oriental mysteries."

Imperial Air's flying boat Caledonia over Alexandria, Aeroplane *magazine,*   March 3, 1937

In the 1950s and 1960s, Nasser's nationalistic policies caused much of the city's expatriate community to leave Alexandria. Later, many Alexandrians left for other countries in the oil-rich region; returning years later, they brought Islamic conservatism with them. Very conservative poor people from rural areas in Egypt have moved to Alexandria over the years for jobs at the port and in the city's chemical and steel industries.

Writing about Alexandria in 1971, Fouad Gassir considered Alexandria to be an enchanting city. It was clean, pleasant, still young and beautiful, in his eyes still "The Pearl of the Mediterranean."

Dr. Edmund Keeley, an expert on the famous early twentieth-century Alexandrian poet Constantine P. Cavafy, said that Cavafy saw Alexandria as "a city of the imagination; a city that satisfies the mind's eye first of all." Born in Damascus, Syria in 1928 the son of an American diplomat, Edmund "Mike" Leroy Keeley was an author, translator of works of Greek poetry, educator, critic, and administrator. He lived in Greece from ages 8 to 11, graduated from Princeton University, became a Fulbright Scholar and a Woodrow Wilson Fellow, and then obtained his doctorate in comparative literature from Oxford University in 1952. He began teaching at Princeton in 1954, then taught there as full professor from 1970 until he retired in 1993. Among his many translations of Greek was *C. P. Cavafy*, which was nominated for a National Book Award in Translation in 1973.

Keeley noted that for any visitor to Alexandria, it was hard to keep one's eye in the mind. Visiting the city in the spring of 1973, Keeley wrote of the ugly reality he was seeing:

> Today's Alexandria strikes one first of all as squalid. If you walk along the esplanade leading to where the wondrous ancient Pharos used to stand (now Fort Kayet Bey, grotesquely restored as a museum celebrating the Egyptian navy), you will encounter odors and sights that will amaze you. All conflict between illusion and reality vanishes in the filth and stench of narrow unwashed streets overflowing with the murky drift of the poor.

Added Allen Drury in a 1980 book describing his Egyptian journeys, "The Alexandria waterfront, that famed corniche which may once, in its heyday as a playground for Europe's wealthy, have been a gracious and beautiful promenade, is now a cluster of rundown apartment houses and dying hotels."

Stephan Schwartz, a psychic research team leader who visited the city in the 1980s, wrote:

> There is a never-ending quality to Egyptian street noise, a sound compounded of constantly blowing car horns, radios, blaring Arabic

music, market haggling and, five times a day, dozens of overlapping calls to prayer broadcast over the loudspeakers of the minarets dotting the city's skyline. Once I had welcomed all this as "white noise." Now, under stress, I was worried about this cacophony.

Schwartz also mentions traveling at speeds of five to fifteen miles per hour on streets with no lanes, no signals, and an interweaving of animal carts.

Even Confederate soldier William Loring, writing in 1885, echoed this theme by stating of Alexandria:

> The traveller, unaccustomed to the din of a people unlike any he has encountered before, is delighted to get away from the noise and turmoil. He congratulates himself on this, his first visit to Egypt, on having made his way safely through the greatest confusion of tongues and the most dissonant screeching and yelling with which his ear has ever been assailed. Proceeding further his amusement increases as he passes through the narrow Arab streets lined with small shops, and his joy is complete when he finds himself quietly seated at his fine European hotel, where he can breathe freely and leisurely retemper his nerves.

Fatemah Farag described some of Alexandria's modern-day problems in a June 2001 article in *Al-Ahram*. She wrote of a population projected to reach 4.6 million by 2017, with one in three residents today living in one of the city's 57 shantytowns; 355,000 cars were using streets designed for 100,000. Pollution hovered over the city, with illegal high-rise buildings on the corniche preventing ocean breezes from purifying inner-city air. Areas of King Maryout, Khalig Al-Max and Abukir were identified as international pollution areas by the 1997 Barcelona report, which blamed the city for causing 30% of the Mediterranean's pollution.

Farag reported that forty percent of Alexandria's garbage was not being collected. A CNN September 4, 2000, story reported that Alexandria's Governor Mohammed Abdel Salam Mahgoub had just signed a 15-year, $445.6 million contract with CGEA Onyx, a French company, to collect and treat one million tons of solid waste a year. The project included collection of trash from factories, homes, streets and beaches and the construction of a medical waste incinerator and leak-proof landfills. Money for the contract would be obtained from higher electricity rates charged to residents.

Fatemah Farag quoted one cab driver as saying:

> The Alexandria of my childhood was beautiful. I remember that when it rained, the streets shone and you would swear that someone had polished them by hand. Today, when it rains, the city becomes a dirty swamp. But I see things getting a bit better and I hope that after having reached the dumps we will be able to pull the city together. I want my children to have the opportunity of seeing at least a bit of the city of my childhood.

Writing in 1984, Neil Pierce said that planners hoped to set up a "green-belt limit" to stop residential and industrial growth that threatened the scarce fertile lands of the Nile River Delta which were needed to feed the growing city. Instead, development was to be pushed toward a large chalky desert area to the west of Alexandria. Historic preservation, beach erosion, and water pollution were then also on the planners' agendas.

Instead of remaining gloomy, one delights in steadfastly believing that a description of the area by researcher James Matthew Thompson in 1951 still applies to Alexandria as well:

> Few Europeans approach the North African coast for the first time without excitement and emotion. The brilliance of the sky, the exhilarating dryness of the air, the sharp contrasts of sunlight and shadow, the rare green of the date-palms, standing out against the dull gold of the desert—all are strange to Western experience; but behind the newness is a suggestion of a world incredibly old, mysterious and rather terrifying.

Egyptian writer Naguib Mahfouz called Alexandria "nostalgia steeped in honey and tears," while Lawrence Durrell labeled it "the capital of memories."

A tremendous boost to the image and future of Alexandria has been provided by the building of the new Library of Alexandria. UNESCO worked hard for many long years to bring about its return. It launched its Revival of Alexandria Library campaign with its Aswan Declaration, which had the backing of many heads of state.

Amadou-Mahtar M'Bow, then Director General of UNESCO, issued this appeal on October 22, 1987:

> The Egyptian government has done all it can to provide the best possible conditions for the implementation of this project. A Higher National Council of the Library of Alexandria has been set up under the patronage of the President of the Arab Republic of Egypt. In order that this exceptional undertaking should have its proper world-wide dimension, however, the Egyptian Government plans to involve the entire international community therein. For this reason it has asked UNESCO to support its action, in particular by means of an appeal to universal solidarity. The Executive Board of the Organization thus invited me, at its 126th session, to launch such an appeal. I therefore call on the governments of all States, international governmental and non-governmental organizations, public and private institutions, funding agencies, librarians and archivists, and last but not least, the peoples of all countries to participate, by means of voluntary contributions in cash, equipment or services, in the immense effort undertaken by the Egyptian Government to reconstruct and equip the Library of Alexandria, constitute and preserve its collections and train the requisite personnel.

M'Bow's UNESCO statement continued with this added plea for help:

> I call on all intellectuals, artists and writers, historians and sociologists, and on all those whose work it is to inform journalists, columnists, professionals of the press, radio, television and cinema, to help to develop an awareness by the public in all countries of the universal dimension of the project for the revival of the Library of Alexandria, and to encourage them to contribute to its implementation. I especially invite the publishers of literary, scientific and artistic books

Carl Sagan's version of ancient Library of Alexandria prepared for TV's Cosmos series

and periodicals the world over to send two copies of each of their publications to the Library of Alexandria, beginning on 1, January, 1988.

Federico Mayor, at the time Director General of UNESCO, wrote in 1989 that the reason for building the structure was not to attempt the reconstruction of an ancient historical monument but, instead, to revive in a modern way a unique world heritage in the cultural history of mankind. It was being designed "to bear witness to the deep roots of Egyptian civilization and be a pearl in the crown of the culture of tomorrow." According to planners, "The site of one of the most ancient libraries will soon be the site of one of the most modern."

The international committee led by UNESCO had the support of the Egyptian government and was sponsored by President Francois Mitterrand of France, Egyptian President Hosni Mubarak and his wife, Suzanne, Queen Sofia of Spain, Princess Caroline of Monaco, and Queen Noor of Jordan, among others. The new library was built near its original site.

The collection was started with a donation from the Egyptian Book Organization of 76,000 rare Arabic, Persian, and Turkish documents preserved on microfilm. The library's initial focus was to be on the Mediterranean region, the Arab world, and, of course, on Alexandria, but it would also be a center for studying ancient civilizations of the Mediterranean and the entire world.

A special flyer for the May 8, 1991, National Online Meeting in New York City announced that the aim of the library was to revive Alexandria as an intellectual center of learning in science, arts, and culture by creating a public research library and museum complex. Stated the flyer, "The goal is not so much to construct the new library in the image of the old, but rather to give Alexandria back the glory it had in ancient times by creating a public research institution that will become famous throughout the world for the quality of its services and the wealth of its resources."

Construction started in May 1995, but the planned library inauguration of 1999 had to be repeatedly postponed. The new library and conference center was built on important historical sites where some say too limited archaeological exploration took place before beginning the building process.

The Bibliotheca Alexandrina was finished July 2001, at a cost of about $230 million U.S. dollars, and finally had its official opening in October 2002. Wrote Scott Macleod in his June 12, 2000, story for *Time Europe*, "the 11-story library gives the impression that the cloistered temple of Euclid and Archimedes is reemerging from the earth."

Hosni Mubarak and his wife, Suzanne, who had long been ardent advocates of the library, opened the specialized Antiquities Museum of the Bibliotheca Alexandrina on October 16, 2002. Mrs. Mubarak had praised the library in speeches delivered around the world, and exuded in London that it would have the highest technology and provide Internet accessibility to all. Asked if that meant access would be free of censorship, Suzanne poignantly replied, "Inshallah," meaning, "God willing."

The new Bibliotheca Alexandrina when opened added 200,000 new volumes and 1,500 journal titles to material already collected. The complex is to eventually house four million volumes, a science and calligraphy museum, a planetarium, a music library, a center for book and manuscript preservation, an international school for information studies, and very modern communications technology permitting access to computer networks and online information systems through over 2,000 workstations in the library.

Official friends groups around the world have been raising money and collecting books for the library for many years. One group, Baltimore Friends of the Bibliotheca Alexandrina, has been especially enthusiastic and supportive, undoubtedly because Baltimore is a sister city to both Luxor and Alexandria. The Baltimore Friends planned a trip to Egypt in October 2008 with an itinerary including two days in Alexandria, one day devoted to visiting the Alexandria National Museum, Qaitbay Fort, and the Roman Amphitheater, the next spent at the Bibliotheca Alexandrina complex.

UNESCO designated Alexandria "World Book Capital City 2002" as an acknowledgment of the best program dedicated to books and reading. The award came from UNESCO working with the International Publishers Associations, the International Federation of Library Associations and Institutions, and the International Booksellers Federation. The 2002 award from UNESCO was largely in honor of the dedication that year of the Bibliotheca Alexandrina.

This unique, highly impressive structure won the 2004 Aga Khan Award for Architecture. Designed as a tilting disc that starts 60 feet below ground and then rises out of the earth, it has seven levels above-ground and four below. The complex includes a reading room that seats 2,000, six specialty sub-libraries, three museums, seven research centers, three permanent galleries, a planetarium, plaza, offices and cafeteria.

The exterior walls are covered with 4,000 granite blocks carved with letters from the world's alphabets. The building uses a great deal of indirect natural light streaming in through glazed panels on the roof. A pedestrian bridge connects the library to the University of Alexandria and to the coastal road.

Some feel that the $230 million Bibliotheca Alexandrina has failed in its goal of reviving the city's rich cultural and intellectual past. A February 13, 1990, *New York Times* story by Alan Cowell titled "Egypt Asks Help for New Alexandria Library" conveyed a harsh view of the modern city:

> Alexandria these days is a tawdry place, a rundown port on a polluted sea, and Egypt itself has problems that occlude historical greatness. It is $55 billion in debt, it cannot feed itself, its population is growing too fast to house or school, and more than half its 55 million people cannot read or write.

A sobering article in the *Miami Herald* of October 23, 2005, reported on the worst Muslim-Christian violence in Alexandria in five years. A day after 5,000 Muslim rioters attacked two Alexandrian Christian neighborhoods, four were dead and 90 injured. The violence followed a week of protests after DVDs were circulated of a stage play two years before at a city Christian Coptic church. Some said the DVDs were released by hard-line Islamists to hurt a Coptic candidate in upcoming elections.

An equally sobering article by Daniel Williams published in the *Washington Post* of May 13, 2006, bore the title, "In Egypt, an Old Beacon of Tolerance Flickers." The article discussed tensions between Coptic Christians and Moslems in Alexandria. The previous month, a man drove to three Coptic churches and stabbed several worshippers, killing an old man. The incident triggered three days of fighting in the streets of the city. Wrote Williams, "The city's celebrated tolerance has been more legend than reality for 50 years," starting with the 1956 Suez War.

Continued Williams in his description of Alexandria:

> Almost all that remained was a kind of archaeology of sophistication. The faded Cecil Hotel, with its cafes and wrought-iron elevator, sits on the waterfront drive still known by its French name, the Corniche. Ruined palaces of aristocrats crumble in their lush gardens. Nearly

empty churches—Greek and Armenian Orthodox, Catholic and Anglican—nestle among a forest of minarets and mosques. The old synagogue sits under guard, unused.

Hamza Hendawi wrote in the *Charleston* (West Virginia) *Gazette* on June 10, 2007, that most of Alexandria's bars, restaurants, and nightclubs are no longer in business. Their owners have returned to Europe for good. Only a few elderly Greeks, Cypriots, Italians, French and Armenians remain out of the diverse population that Hendawi says once made Alexandria Egypt's most cosmopolitan city. Tourism is way down.

Says Hendawi, "The city's move toward Islamist fundamentalism has driven away the wealthy and secular middle-class Egyptians who once flocked to Alexandria in the summer for its beaches and nightlife." To quote a 29-year-old resident, "You are lonely in Alexandria if you're not religious."

But there are other descriptions that point hopefully to a picture of Alexandria that all desire to continually see. Deb Halpern, writing in the *Tampa Tribune* on September 2, 2001, calls it much underrated as a tourist destination and said that the city provides a nice break from the hot and crowded desert locations of most of Egypt's major monuments. She added:

> The most wonderful thing about Alexandria is when you've had enough of history, there is the Mediterranean to enjoy. All along the Corniche, the main thoroughfare that hugs the sea, small cafes prepare delicious seafood. Meals tend to be prepared simply and served with a wonderful sesame paste called tahina. These cafes are an excellent place to enjoy shisha, the flavored tobacco Egyptians like to smoke through beautifully crafted water pipes.

Writing in the May 26-June 1, 2005, issue of *Al-Ahram Weekly*, Rasha Sadek enthused about "the romantic ambiance of the Corniche, greenery of Montazah, historical aroma of the Roman Amphitheater, Kom Al Shokafa catacombs and Pompey's Pillar as well as the cultural influence of the Bibliotheca Alexandrina." The writer noted they were all one Alexandria, of which E. M. Forster said, "The best way of seeing Alexandria is to wander aimlessly."

Port of Alexandria 1920

Kareem Fahim, in his *New York Times* article of December 16, 2007, called Alexandria "a faded metropolis that is rising again from the sea, one replicated landmark at a time." One symbol of new elegance is the Four Seasons Hotel Alexandria, which opened in July 2007 with 118 luxurious rooms and nine restaurants on the site of Egypt's once-famous San Stefano Hotel.

Some experts consider a recent find of ancient lecture halls in Alexandria important for the city's image. Discovered by Warsaw University's Grzegorz Majcherek of the Polish-Egyptian Archaeology Mission, they show university intellectual life continuing long into the Arab era after Rome's decline.

Besides the tremendous boost provided by the new library, another great cause for optimism is recent development at the port and harbors of Alexandria. The Alexandria Port Authority (APA) has worked with its affiliate, the El-Dekheila Port Authority, to implement its master plan for 2015. This seeks to accommodate future growth of the port and revive the international role of the city of Alexandria and its great port. Its goal is to place the harbor back on the map of global navigation as one of the largest ports on the Mediterranean Sea.

The APA delights on its Internet site in presenting updated news of cruise ship arrivals, with their welcome delivery of tourists. *El Gamhoria* on May 27, 2007, reported the arrival of two tourist ships from Panama, the *Morgan Julia* and the *Legend of the Seas*, carrying a combined 4,225 passengers. The Port Authority has developed a program for tourists that includes viewing of historical monuments, cultural sights, the library, and commercial markets.

The Alexandria Port Authority also reported that, in April 2007, Egyptian President Hosni Mubarak visited the port, accompanied by the prime minister and the ministers of defense, housing, tourism, employment, and domestic development. The president officially inaugurated the site, opened the port museum, visited a new tourist passenger terminal and commercial center, and inspected a new railway station that will service passenger ships. The train depot will allow tourists to visit archaeological sites in Giza and return the same day. The Port Authority delights in telling people that the $1.5 billion expense of improving the port comes from port resources, at no cost to the state.

The April 2007 tourist center opening at the port coincided with the arrival of a huge Italian cruise ship carrying 3,600 passengers. In 2005, the number of passenger ships arriving at Alexandria was 102, carrying 101,000 tourists. In 2006, the number of visiting cruise ships increased to 141, carrying 135,000 tourists, with a further increase in 2007 to 300,000.

Quay of the Grands Couriers, Alexandria

Unfortunately, bad weather with wind speeds up to 70 miles an hour prevented the largest tourist ship in the world, *Queen Mary 2*, carrying 4,500 tourists, from entering the port on one voyage in 2007. After a six-hour try, the captain decided to continue on to ports in Greece, forcing the cancellation of celebrations in the port.

As for general cargo and container transport, the *EuroMed Transport Project Diagnostic Study* of December 2004 noted that the port of Alexandria handled 32,852,000 tons of imports and exports during the year 2002. The number of vessels calling at Alexandria for that same year was 4,400.

Another report by EuroMed Transport dated February 2005 said that 3,800 vessels called at Alexandria between October 1, 2003, and September 30, 2004, 1900 of them greater than 5,000 gross tons. The December 2004 report stated that the port of Alexandria together with Dekheila Port several miles to its west handles about 65% to 70% of Egyptian's seaborne trade, in the form of containers, general cargo, grain, and petroleum.

The Alexandria Port Authority quoted statistics from *El-Ahkbar* newspaper on January 15, 2007, that showed the importance of the harbor for Alexandria's well-being. Over 30,000 people visit the port daily, not counting 52,000 employees who work at the harbor in ministries such as customs, exports and imports, and security.

Highlighting another city improvement, a *USAID/Egypt* report by the United States Agency for International Development discussed the creation of a one-stop customs shop in Alexandria. The March/April 2005 online publication *EG Link* reported that the Alexandria Modern Customs Center was created to help businesses move goods through the border more quickly. A well-trained staff of customs officials was trying hard to reduce the time it took to clear goods through the port from days and weeks to hours, even for complicated transactions. As an example, the number of signatures required to clear a shipment has been reduced from 35 to three or four.

There are still other ongoing improvements in Alexandria. An April 11, 2006, article by Simon Ingram written for UNICEF tells of the group's work in Egypt trying to improve child labor conditions. It studied a 14-year-old boy, Ahmed, who worked 12 hours a day in a small ironing and dry-cleaning shop. He was employed by a lawyer. On Sundays, Ahmed went to work late, having spent most of his day at the Marine Scouts Association club on Alexandria's waterfront.

Under a 1993 agreement with UNICEF, the Marine Scouts tries to make sure that working children like Ahmed receive health care and are protected from abuse. Out of such youth centers spread across Alexandria, social workers from the Scouts visit child workers in their workplaces. Literacy and art classes are taught in the clubs combined with sessions of football, table tennis, and judo. Life and social skills are also taught to help keep children out of trouble.

Michael Haag, speaking in Greece in 2007 shortly after the release of his book, *Alexandria: City of Memory*, stated that the first time he ever saw Alexandria, it was from a plane and it was at night. He saw only black land, black sea, black sky.

> Then suddenly I saw the city – a brilliant and glittering necklace of a city – and it had exactly the same shape as the ancient city in the maps. Looking down from the plane, I realised that Alexander, or Cleopatra, could recognise their city even today. Its form is unique, and it is enduring. And that I think is one reason why Alexandria has made such an impression on modern writers – Alexandria reminds us of the flux and the constancies of history.

Haag also spoke that day of the haunting quality of Alexandria. "Alexandria is all intimidation: here is where Alexander lay entombed; here Cleopatra and Antony loved; here the Library; the Serapeum...and there is almost nothing physically there. If more of the city survived it would be less haunting."

Edmund Keeley, who was quoted earlier describing the city in harsh terms, breathes out a comment that, in the city's recent troubling times, is worthy of remembering again and again:

> "The mystery of modern Alexandria seems to be not in what it actually is or was at any given moment but in its power to stimulate—as perhaps no other city in this century—the creation of poetic cities cast in its image, cities that imitate it as it can be, or even ought to be, in its essence."

Keeley calls this quality, this ancient city's power to inspire municipal emulation the world over, "this godlike attribute of Alexandria."

*Alexandria's breakwater from Fort Qaitbay, 2006.
Ahmed Dokmak, Wikipedia Commons*

CHAPTER 19
EMPEREUR, GODDIO, AND UNESCO GO UNDERWATER

In the late 1890s, Abbe Suard conducted one-day boat trips for tourists to view the submerged statues and buildings of Alexandria. The highlight of these trips was a visit to the Pharos site, where divers with ropes and harpoons tried to lift pieces of marble and stone up for tourists to see. Writing about remains beneath the ocean, Honor Frost stated in 1975 that, in the nineteenth century, the remains were still so obvious that tours were listed as: "Embarkation on a fishing boat with one or two divers, a sound, ropes and harpoons. From the harbor mouth to Diamond Rock (the Pharos area), soundings and dives, harpoonings of pieces of marble and numismatic stones."

Edgar Banks says that, in 1898-99, a German expedition searched the ocean for the foundation of the Pharos but had no luck. In 1910, Gaston Jondet, chief engineer of the Alexandrian Department of Ports and Lighthouses, discovered the Old Port of Pharos, finding huge breakwaters and statues twenty-five feet beneath the ocean. The discovery of the breakwater of a pre-Alexandrian harbor to the north and west of the Ras-el-Tin promontory was a shock to everyone. Until then, there was a tremendous lack of any real historical evidence that such structures had ever existed.

Concerning above-ground remains, writer E. M. Forster states in his 1922 *Alexandria* that about thirty broken columns of red Aswan granite, two or three pieces of fine speckled granite, and one piece of marble were built into the masonry of Fort Qaitbay's wall or found lying on the beach. These were from the Pharos, and may have stood in the colonnade of its surrounding court.

A 1934 letter-writer to the *Egyptian Gazette* summarized the concerns of many both past and present when he stated:

> I am really worried about the repairing of many important monuments of Greater Alexandria that are in the open. Parts of the Temple of Osiris at Abusir are in a dangerous condition. It is obvious that the impressive Ptolemaic beacon near the temple is disintegrating rapidly. The greatest thing in Alexandria is the Pharos...Almost certainly, stones of the original Pharos exist in position...Apart from its own value therefore, as largely a mediaeval monument, Fort Qaitbay is of priceless value as indicating and preserving a structure which the ancients considered as of such transcendent importance that they put only six other things in the world in the same class.

Diver and customs house official Kamel Abul-Saadat of Alexandria has only recently been recognized as the pioneer of underwater diving in Alexandria. For years, his diving work was lonely, self-motivated, and self-financed. One paper published in his honor after an April 1997 UNESCO workshop was titled "Recuperating an Alexandrian Pioneer in Submarine Archaeology."

In 1961, he found large statues on the sea bed in shallow waters at the entrance to Alexandria Harbor. In 1962, he convinced the Egyptian Navy to raise a broken female figure, measuring 23 feet in length, from waters twenty feet deep off the Qaitbay Fortress. The female statue, probably a third century B.C. statue of a queen portrayed as Isis, weighed 25 tons and is now in the Serapion Gardens.

Honor Frost said in 1975 that this statue was possibly from the original Pharos, although perhaps it also could have been from a temple located elsewhere on the island of Pharos. Frogmen lifted another very tall statue from the same underwater area in December 1963, which towards the end of 1966, was moved to Serapeum Hill. Some at the time believed that this huge statue was from the temple of Isis Pharia that was located near the Pharos on the island.

In 1968, the Egyptian government, in cooperation with UNESCO, decided to evaluate the site using experts. It invited University of Paris geologist Vladimir Nesteroff and British archaeologist Honor Frost to study the Pharos site in the shallow water off Fort Qaitbay. The area where the remains lie, starboard of all ships entering

Honor Frost 1962 triangulating with surveyor's tape sixteenth century wreck, photo by Frederic Dumas

the harbor and thus a logical place to put significant plaques and inscriptions, has survived undisturbed since the lighthouse fell.

Six dives by Frost in October and November of that year showed remains to be from a highly decorated structure, with two female and probably two male pillar-statues 35 feet in height that would have stood on 10-foot plinths. Also found were a detached Isis Hathor crown six feet high, two sets of sphinxes, a piece of stone with an inscribed Roman numeral one-and-a-half feet high, and pieces of masonry up to 20 feet long. Frost felt at the time that a complete survey of the area could result in finding one hundred times more fragments.

In her dives, Frost found no white marble but did find black marble. Most of the larger pieces discovered were of Aswan granite. Frost predicted that after the collapse of a colossal building that had rested on just a small rock, its remains should be spread over a large area. This was found to be the case.

Frost stated that the foundations must have been at water's edge, adding that one side of the Pharos appears to have collapsed into the sea, and to have remained exactly where it fell. Frost emphasized that sufficient evidence remained in the sea to occupy scholars for a considerable time. Following her work in 1968, she made a preliminary map that included 17 sunken monuments next to the fort.

During a 2006 television program on the History Channel titled *Deep Sea Detectives: Pharos and Alexandria*, a great deal of the program discussed modern earthquake research. John Swain, professor of physics at Northeastern University in Boston, stated that damaging effects of an earthquake hitting the Pharos would have come not just from the quake but from stored kinetic energy at the top of the building, just as with the destroyed Twin Towers in New York City's 911 tragedy. Two Egyptologists affiliated with the Bibliotheca Alexandria were interviewed on the show as they studied a large chart labeled "The Fall of the Pharos."

Concerning finds of statues, four sphinxes, columns, and a Roman IV from an inscription, writer Douglas Hague said in 1975 that these were almost certainly remains of the Pharos. Although they did not assist in making a reconstruction of the tower, they did give a vivid impression of its quality and grandeur.

A 1974 article in *Nautical Archaeology* reported many sculptures in the sea surrounding the fort, possibly from the Pharos. Subsequent researchers surmised that one side of the lighthouse collapsed into the sea. In 1979, Italians Bruno Vailati and Paolo Curto led an expedition that for some reason convinced them that Alexander the Great was buried under the lighthouse. Vailati was an Italian television producer and an amateur oceanographer who had led a major exploration of the *Andrea Doria* shipwreck.

The Mobius Group, Stephan Schwartz's psychic archaeology team, dove off the Pharos area in the early 1980s and saw several sphinxes and a statue in granite nearly 15 feet long which was assumed to be a statue of Isis from the temple that many experts believe stood next to the Pharos. The statue was similar to one raised some years earlier by an Egyptian diving team. Schwartz described his attempts in the fascinating book *Alexandria Project* published in 1983.

After being at the site for only a few minutes, his team encountered a wave of sewage sweeping in and was forced to leave. The spot was one of the major sewer runoffs of Alexandria. Schwartz mentioned in accounts of the incident that Honor Frost had a similar problem years earlier while exploring this spot.

Schwartz's group eventually spent 43 hours of actual dive time at the Pharos site, with up to six divers in the water at a time, working at an average depth of from 20 to 35 feet. While his group was diving, large cement blocks were brought to the area by barge and dropped in the antiquities zone to either extend or build up the breakwater. Said Schwartz, "The effects of this construction on antiquities was devastating." However, the block-dumping had one good effect. Right after it happened, a bad storm hit Alexandria for two days, causing the cement blocks to move. Six feet of silt on the bottom shifted, lowering the seabed and exposing new artifacts.

Stephen Schwartz leader of Mobius Group's psychic archaeology dives

In the 1980s, jurisdiction of underwater sites moved from the military to the Ministry of Culture, largely due to pressure by Dr. Ahmed Kadry, president of the Egyptian Ministry of Antiquities. In 1984, Jacques Dumas, president of the Confederation Mondiale des Activities Subaquatiques or World Confederation for Underwater Activities, launched a campaign to search for *Orient*, the flagship of Bonaparte's fleet which had sunk in the Bay of Abukir. Prince Napoleon Bonaparte sponsored the group's underwater activities.

In April 1986, an agreement was signed by Egypt's Supreme Council of Antiquities president Ahmed Kadry and Electricite de France. That company set up a laboratory in the center of Alexandria and eventually perfected techniques to preserve metallic objects found underwater. EDF started its work by restoring objects from *Patriote*, the largest of the civilian ships in Bonaparte's fleet that had run aground nine miles west of Alexandria.

The Supreme Council of Antiquities in the early 1990s decided that action had to be taken to save Fort Qaitbay Citadel from erosion by the sea. During 1992 and 1993, approximately 180 blocks of from seven to twenty tons each were dropped to the ocean floor on the fort's exposed northeast perimeter. Unfortunately, they again fell on ruins of the ancient lighthouse.

An underwater film crew headed by Egyptian film director Asma El-Bakri set out in March 1994 to film fallen columns and sculptures near Fort Qaitbay. Diver and researcher Jean-Yves Empereur, director of the Centre d'Etudes Alexandrines which he had founded in 1989, joined her team as an advisor. Empereur stated in a March 1999 article for *Archaeology* magazine that the day they began filming, there was hardly a ripple on the sea, the wind was from the south, and visibility at the site was unusually good. During filming, El-Bakri noticed damage being caused by more huge blocks being dumped. She complained to the Supreme Council and the Egyptian press, forcing the government to immediately halt the project.

The Council consulted with the Institut Francais d'Archaeologie Orientale and with Empereur. Empereur was told he could survey the site for a month, and obtained $100,000 from the French government for this purpose.

Empereur, a Greek classical scholar and archaeologist, was not strictly speaking an Egyptologist. He had been secretary-general of the French School of Archaeology in Athens. Over a twelve-year period, he studied inscriptions at Delphi and worked on excavations at Argos, Delos and Thasos, where he started underwater explorations.

Empereur had spent five years investigating Alexandria's land sites. His heart continually sank whenever a new building was constructed on Alexandrian land. In every instance, 33 feet of Mameluke, Fatimid, Byzantine, Roman, and Greek history were disturbed or destroyed forever. One of the most beautiful items ever unearthed in Alexandria was a mosaic of Medusa from the second century A.D.,

Empereur teaching at Fort Qaitbay 2002, courtesy httpjdalbera.free.fr

discovered in 1994 by Empereur just after developers had torn down the historic Diana Theater of the 1930s in downtown Alexandria.

In May 1994, the Marine Policy Center of the Woods Hole Oceanographic Institution organized a one-day symposium titled "Alexandria, the Land-Sea Relationship, Marine Archaeology, and Coastal Development," convened by James M. Broadus and Nils Tongring. The minutes of the meeting were sent to the Archaeological Society of Alexandria in July 1994. They were also discussed in a December 7-8, 1994, symposium in Alexandria, and further reviewed at the April 3-4, 1996, annual meeting of the Archaeological Society of Alexandria.

In Fall 1994, an Egyptian-French team of divers studied underwater remains for six weeks and found 70-ton blocks at a depth of 26 feet, a second layer of blocks ten feet below that, and a third layer another ten feet down. Some of these blocks were 20 feet long and 8 feet wide, and were believed to be part of the remains of the ancient Pharos.

Fragments of a large statue were found and brought up in 1994. From its base to the statue's huge head, it may have originally stood over forty feet high. Empereur concluded it was Ptolemy II Philadelphus. An Isis statue of similar colossal size had been found by Kamel Abul-Saadat and raised by the Egyptian Navy in 1962. Honor Frost wrote in 1975 that these two huge statues had lain parallel to one another while underwater. Frost and Jean-Yves Empereur concluded that the royal couple stood at the foot of the Pharos when it was first built. The remains of two other such couples have now been found.

Besides these tall statue pairs, a series of huge white-stoned granite blocks were discovered, each about thirty feet long, each weighing 75 tons. Two dozen of these stand in a line over 100 feet in length at the foot of Qaitbay running northwest. Jean-Yves Empereur found thirty pieces of massive size, some 35 feet long and weighing 75 tons, laid out in an underwater line as if falling from a great height. Empereur leans strongly towards attributing them to the lighthouse. Also, he believes that it was a statue of Zeus that stood atop the Pharos.

Empereur's team stopped diving in November 1994 due to rain and heavy waves. It was decided that if they did not soon find definitive proof that the blocks were from the Pharos, the government would resume its project of dropping concrete blocks over the ruins to protect Mameluke Fort Qaitbay. Obviously frustrated, Jean-Yves Empereur said in 1995, "Why should we choose between the Mameluke fort and the Greek antiquities? We have to protect both the ancient and the medieval monuments."

Empereur's team restudied the area in May 1995, and, in the fall of 1995, Empereur's privately-funded French-Egyptian team of thirty divers began work documenting the entire Pharos site. Thirty-five pieces were salvaged and restored. Some were put on display in Alexandria's Kom El-Dekkah archaeological gardens. Others, after a soaking process to remove salt, were put on display in the fall of 1996 in the Qaitbay maritime museum.

Said Empereur:

> Obviously, we can never reconstruct the lighthouse from the objects the archaeologists have found so far, but the desk-top work now underway allows us to hope that soon we shall have a more precise image of this tower, thus refining and connecting the image given to us by Hermann Thiersch at the beginning of this [the twentieth] century.

Block Identification Sheet

Location: Qaitbay   **No. 1027**

Date: 10/2/95	Illustrator: John Smith	Lifted: NO Moved: YES

Beside Block No.	Orientation:	Max Depth	Min Depth
1634	north-south	15 feet	15 feet

√ Complete Element or
__ Fragment

Material: Granite
Type of Block: Slab
Color: Red
Inscription: None
Dimensions: <u>18 ft 3 in., 9 ft 6 in and 3 ft 2 in</u>

Markings
√ Fastening Marks   No. <u>1</u>
__ Cut Marks   No. __
__ Lifting Marks   No. __
__ Assembly Marks   No. __

Estimated weight: 2.5 tons

Comments: Flat block with semi-circular hole carved onto surface. Possibly intended for a door hinge.

Figure 23 Identification sheet based on CEA's ID forms as presented by NOVA.

Pharos Block 1027 ID Sheet, courtesy Kim Williams

Empereur noted that the lighthouse was a mix of Greek and Pharaonic styles far more than had previously been expected.

He added that 1998 underwater investigations have led him to believe that the site has subsided since antiquity, perhaps twenty feet, meaning that a good part of the east side of the fort was at one time above sea level. Nearly all blocks discovered have been of Aswan granite; those of marble and limestone had long ago disappeared into lime kilns or were used in newer buildings.

Progress has been made on raising the 180 concrete blocks inappropriately dropped in 1992 and 1993 on the underwater archaeological site. In 1996, ten were raised in a search for the missing legs and feet of the huge statue of Ptolemy. Forty-five blocks were raised in February 1998, and the remaining ones were brought up in January 2001. This cleared the site for serious exploration. The Supreme Council of Antiquities had the damaged fortress platform sections and bedrock cavities studied and photographed by divers in 1999. A thick concrete revetment was extended over the platform.

Among the 3,100 pieces now identified underwater at the Pharos site are 28 sphinxes bearing insignia of Pharaohs from the nineteenth to the sixth centuries B.C. As for obelisks, there are three from the fourteenth century B.C. and one from the third century B.C. Columns and granite blocks of over 70 tons each have been identified. Empereur believes that few of the several thousand pieces found at the lighthouse site are from the Pharos. However, he is certain that a dozen or so 70-ton pieces belonged to the ancient wonder.

On November 18, 1997, PBS's *Nova* series aired an episode on public television titled *Treasures of the Sunken City*, a wonderful documentary on the underwater search for remains of the Pharos in Alexandria. That show has been repeated several times, as recently as February 27, 2007. One of the divers, Jean-Pierre Corteggiani, was shown stunned by the disorder he saw across five acres of seabed. "It's a kind of huge chaos…it was a strange impression because the water is almost never very, very clear…probably the first impression was, I understand nothing."

The *Nova* show reported that some thought the hundreds of blocks were dumped into the harbor during the Middle Ages to blockade it from invading Crusaders. Others believe they are from a different ancient structure than the Pharos. Each block was lifted with parachute-shaped balloons.

Empereur was quoted in *Life* magazine's April 1996 issue as saying, "At last we can put our finger on the myth. We can touch the lighthouse." He added in a 1998 issue of *Time*, "Alexandria was a beacon of Western civilization. But unlike Rome or Athens, it has been forgotten."

Added the Egyptian government's antiquities chief in 1998, "We have so many gaps in the history of Alexandria. We are starting to fill them in." Ahmed Abdel Fattah, director of Alexandria's Greco-Roman Museum, stated that same year, "We are recovering Alexandria from beneath the water and the earth. It has been buried long enough." Fathi Saleh's foreword to UNESCO's *Sourcebook 2* published in 2000 called Alexandria's Eastern Harbor one of the most fascinating underwater sites in the world. Saleh added, "We are witnessing the uncovering of the monumental ancient Lighthouse of Alexandria."

The colossus of Ptolemy and a bust of a Ptolemaic queen represented as Isis, together with an obelisk from the time of Seti I, were put on display in mid-1998 at *La Gloire d'Alexandrie* exhibit at the Petit Palais in Paris. The display brought together over 200 pieces from museums throughout the world and was the first major exhibit of Hellenistic Alexandria ever presented outside Egypt.

By 2008, 3,200 blocks had been registered, and Isabelle Hairy was leading an operation by Jean-Yves Empereur's team to chart another 5,000 sunken blocks. Hopes were that these building elements lying on the seabed could help graphically reconstruct some of the ancient monuments. Blocks now identified as belonging to the doorway of the Pharos will hopefully be removed from the water, undergo desalination, and be reassembled by Empereur's team, led by Yvan Vigouroux. Egypt's Supreme Council of Antiquities has asked Empereur to use 2008 to also study the Hellenistic tombs of Anfoushi on the ancient island of Pharos. A rising water table is gradually flooding its painted scenes.

From April 7 to 11, 1997, the University of Alexandria, the Supreme Council of Antiquities (under the country's Council of Culture), and UNESCO co-sponsored an International Workshop on Submarine Archaeology and Coastal Management in the city of Alexandria. Over a hundred experts from Egypt and abroad took part in the gathering, with seventy representatives of the worldwide media present. It was abundantly clear to all present that the city was in severe need of a master plan to both preserve its ancient cultural heritage and yet assure its continuing social and economic development. Also, the Supreme Council in 1997 created a department for submarine archaeology.

Drawing of underwater wreck site from 1963 Frost book

The "Alexandria Declaration" by Professor Hassan El-Banna Awad on behalf of workshop participants during the closing session on April 10, 1997 is worth repeating:

> The significance of Alexandria in history has made the threat to its land and marine archaeological sites a matter of urgent concern to Egypt and the world. Recommendations dealing with the erosion under the Qaitbay Fortress and long-term preservation and management of the cultural assets of Alexandria have been made by the scientific community attending the International Workshop on Submarine Archaeology and Coastal Management. With the co-operation of the world community, we believe that Egypt will be able to succeed in the stated goals of preserving the cultural heritage of the City of Alexandria as part of the heritage of all humanity.

Three important underwater sites of Alexandria are currently of high interest: Ras-el-Tin's ancient harbor on the western side of Pharos Island, the Eastern Harbor, and Abukir Bay. Ibtehal Y. El-Bastawissi of Alexandria University's engineering department stated in an April 1997 conference paper that these three areas were of great significance, not only to the city but also to human knowledge of history, geography, geology, oceanography, and climatology.

UNESCO's 2003 report focuses on three important and more specific archaeological sites, all located close to each other in the Eastern Harbor: Qaitbay Citadel, the remains of the Pharos just offshore of the Citadel, and the ruins of the Ptolemaic Royal Quarters.

Sewage patterns in the Eastern Harbor have been generally seen as the greatest obstacle to developing any archaeological museum. Northerly winds move contaminated water from the Qaitbay outfall to the Pharos site. The April 1997 gathering recognized the erosion of Fort Qaitbay and heavy pollution of coastal waters from city sewage as major problems. More than 50 million cubic meters of untreated sewage and industrial wastewater were being discharged each year from Alexandria into the Mediterranean. A *New York Times* article on October 29, 1997, by reporter Douglas Jehl carried the graphic title, "Alexandria Journal: Down Among the Sewage, Cleopatra's Storied City."

At the 1997 meeting, Youssef Halim of the Faculty of Science, Alexandria University, reported that over a million cubic meters of mixed sewage water were being drained into the Eastern and Western harbors each day, one third of it with no treatment at all. The Qaitbay outfall was releasing 200,000 cubic meters of wastewater per day, and the Eastern Harbor had seven outfalls, causing its water to remain permanently turbid with very poor underwater visibility. Two-thirds of the city's wastewater was being released into Lake Mariout and then pumped into El Mex Bay, west of the city. On the east side of Alexandria, two million cubic meters of industrial wastewater were being dumped into Abukir Bay each day.

Sewage drained into Lake Mariout and then out into the sea west of Alexandria at El Mex. The Qaitbay outfall was a few hundred meters west of the Pharos site. The smaller outfall of El-Silsilah was on the eastern side of the peninsula. Both outfalls were outside of the Eastern Harbor, but a third outfall occasionally drifted into the Harbor. These outfalls came into being sometime after 1960.

In 1999, further studies were made to better plan solutions to Alexandria's wastewater problem. Douglas Nakashima in UNESCO's *Coastal Management Sourcebook 2* published in 2000 said that today's Alexandria was being confronted and confounded everywhere by the archaeological remains of its remarkable past, and noted that the dismal condition of coastal waters was defacing its underwater archaeological sites.

Sewage has caused a decline in Alexandrian tourism for years. In 1985, the summer peak of tourists plunged from the then usual high of 2 million to about 500,000. The *New York Times* on September 11, 1985, pinpointed sewage as the main culprit in the decline.

Wealthy members of Alexandrian society, especially members of the Alexandria Yacht Club, protested so strongly that year that a major shuffle in the Egyptian cabinet took place. Many children swimming in the area developed unusual skin rashes and intestinal illnesses that had never been seen before. Egyptians at that time looked to the United States for major funding of wastewater projects, to the tune of perhaps $1.5 billion.

That hope has been fulfilled. By 2010, all of Alexandria's wastewater will be treated when the new Western Treatment Plant is finished. Since 1987, when 14 outfalls were disposing raw sewage along the beaches of Alexandria into the Mediterranean Sea, the U.S. Agency for International Development (USAID) has invested $425 million in the Alexandria Wastewater System Expansion Phase I Project. Under the plan, 130 miles of sewer pipe, six major pumping stations, two state-of-the-art treatment plants, and a sludge disposal facility have been constructed.

USAID has invested an additional $113 million for Phase II, a project to expand the plants and pumping stations to handle population growth through the year 2010. Cases of waterborne diseases such as typhoid and hepatitis and infant mortality rates have notably decreased as sewage treatment steadily improves. With the closure of the Qaitbay sewage outfall in 2003 after 23 years of work, it could finally be said that Alexandria had stopped dumping untreated sewage into the Mediterranean.

From 2003 to the present, the three main sewers with outlets near archaeological sites have been closed. The understanding is that they are only to be opened if the governor of Alexandria decides there is an impending emergency due to flooding by rainwater. New studies are underway to separate

USAID's Andrew Natsios and Pope Shenouda, Jan. 2002 at Egypt's Grand Cathedral

out rainwater and use it for watering woodlands southwest of Alexandria with help from the International Monetary Fund.

USAID has also contributed $134 million in electrical power and $10 million in telecommunications for Alexandria. Other American funds have been used to promote better education and help small- and medium-sized business enterprises through the Alexandrian Businessmen's Association. As these projects were being completed, USAID Egyptian Director William Pearson bid farewell to Alexandria to assume new duties in Washington, D.C. As he left, success with new sewage plans finally brought Alexandria into compliance with terms of the Mediterranean Sea Protocol.

Modern Alexandria has other problems. Reports of strong erosion along the main axis of the Eastern Harbor, at a rate of 13 centimeters per year, leaves deposits of 5 centimeters annually. Much of this eroded material has been escaping into the harbor to settle in the vicinity of the Pharos site. In September 1997, experts came up with a plan of action to stabilize erosion at the Citadel without damaging the underwater Pharos site. In September 1998, a second group visited the fort and recommended that Qaitbay and all Eastern Harbor sites be developed into underwater archaeological parks and museums, with nomination for World Heritage status.

A workshop was convened November 20-21, 1999, at Alexandria University to study progress in developing submarine archaeological sites at the Qaitbay Citadel and the Eastern Harbor. That report concluded that Lake Mariout was also a significant historical site and recommended that all wastewater be diverted from the lake. Also recommended was the immediate cessation of any reclamation and landfill work there. The workshop recommended the site also be nominated to the World Heritage List. Also working for years on extensive area dives has been a French-Egyptian team under the leadership of Franck Goddio, who used his group's series of dives in Alexandria to make an outline map of the Ancient Harbor. Goddio has worked for two decades at more than fifty underwater sites. The November/December 2006 issue of *Archaeology* magazine, in an article by Mark Rose, says that many academics criticize Goddio's work for yielding more exhibitions and coffee-table books than serious research. However, no one can criticize Franck Goddio's impressive results. Perhaps he is correct on his website when he says that he is "probably the most successful marine archaeologist in the world."

In 1998, after six long years of searching, Franck Goddio found Cleopatra's palace underwater in Alexandria's Eastern Harbor. On October 29, 1998, a team lead by

Goddio raised from the site a granite sphinx carved to the likeness of Ptolemy XII, Cleopatra's father. The find was bolted into a steel frame underwater and then winched up onto the deck of *Princess Dudu*, a research vessel. Also raised was a first century A.D. statue of the Great High Priest of Isis holding an urn, perhaps part of an Isis sanctuary on Antirrhodos Island. Remains were also found of what could be Cleopatra's royal barge.

Goddio says, "It's rather fantastic because it explains the ancient world. Everything that was described by Plutarch and the ancient authors about where Cleopatra was reigning and living on this island with Julius Caesar and Mark Antony can be beautifully understood now from the map that we have achieved."

Archaeology magazine's online database reported on April 24, 2008, an important *AKI Adnkronos International Egypt* story out of Cairo. Zahi Hawass had just revealed that archaeologists planned to uncover the tomb of Antony and Cleopatra later in 2008. They were going to test the theory that the two were buried together inside a temple at Taposiris Magna 18 miles from Alexandria. The tomb has been underwater for years, but archaeologists have decided to drain it and then investigate. Researchers recently uncovered at the site a 400-foot-long tunnel with many rooms. However, a follow-up article in a June 2008 issue of *Al-Ahram Weekly* quoted Hawass as stating that international media reports were mistaken. "We have found nothing that indicates the presence of Cleopatra's or Antony's tomb." Further excavation at the site was put on hold due to the summer heat until November, when radar was to be used to search for hidden chambers.

Goddio's studies in 1999 proved that existing maps of Alexandria were incorrect. The first map of the topography of Alexandria's Eastern Harbor was created by Mahmud Bey el-Falaki in 1866 based on ancient texts. From Goddio's geophysical data, a new topographical map was created and presented April 10, 2001, at the British Museum's exhibition, *Cleopatra of Egypt: From History to Myth*. This new map was remarkably different from previous maps, both ancient and modern.

To achieve the mapping, the team used nuclear resonance magnetometers to create a magnetic profile of the bottom and also made use of sonar scanning to create a more detailed map. Using the image, divers quickly made major finds. The royal barge was found in a private royal harbor. Latex molds were used to make prints of underwater hieroglyphics and Greek inscriptions because it was so hard to read them underwater.

On June 2, 2003, Goddio and Oxford University announced the creation of the new Oxford Centre for Maritime Archaeology. The university, Goddio, the Hilti Foundation, and the Institut Europeen d'Archaeologie Sous-Marine signed an agreement to establish the Center within Oxford University's Archaeology Department. Stated Oxford classical archaeologist Barry Cunliffe, "We were blown over by the quality of Franck's underwater field work. It was an extremely smart piece of archaeology, well-ordered and observed."

Goddio will oversee underwater exploration by Oxford graduate students, who will work with professors to help analyze data. The Hilti Foundation of Liechtenstein has supported Goddio for years. It was this group that put up the initial $300,000 for the Oxford Centre. The Hilti Foundation belongs to the Martin Hilti Family Trust, a shareholder in Liechtenstein-based Hilti AG, a leading supplier of equipment for the building industry, whose sales are at 3 billion Swiss francs and employees number 14,600.

Said Michael Hilti, president of his foundation, "When we started supporting Franck Goddio, we did not imagine he would discover objects of such unmatched historical value." As the research missions have now reached a new level of complexity, the support of Oxford scholars and institutions is very welcome.

Goddio is excellent at underwater data collection, but still remains a non-scientist. Many argue that only trained archaeologists should be doing this work. Therefore, everyone applauds the non-credentialed Goddio's linking up with a major university for his research. High-level underwater exploration is estimated by some to cost in excess of $1 million a month. In the final analysis, many agree with Oxford University's Cunliffe, that the cost of doing such work is almost prohibitive unless you have the backing of a large foundation.

In 2003, a statement on Cape Lochias (El-Silsilah), across the harbor from the site of the ancient Pharos, said that the layout plan of the Royal Quarters and its monuments, harbors and shipyards on Cape Lochias attests to the majestic setting of Portus Magnus (the Eastern Harbor; the Western Harbor was known as Portus Eunostos) and its glorious past. Over 1,000 artifacts from the royal buildings have been located on the harbor bed. A Greek-Egyptian research team led by Harry Tzalas, president of the Hellenic Institute for the Preservation of Nautical Tradition, has recently finished its tenth underwater survey of the El-Silsilah area.

The Greek mission's area is the shore of Ramleh from the eastern boundary of Portus Magnus to the Peninsula of Montazah, the possible site of the ancient small city of Taposiris. The Romans called this area Mare Eleusinium. Eleusis was later named Juliopolis and then Nicopolis. Fifteen to twenty divers and scientists have done seven diving campaigns of four weeks' work each.

Before urban development hit the area from Lochias to Montazah, one could see the remains of numerous burial grounds, military installations, villas, residences, shrines and small monuments including the Tomb of Stratonice and the Martyrium of St. Mark. Tzalas concluded in a 2000 preliminary report that at least 15 years of hard work were needed to complete a survey of this area.

A UNESCO workshop in Alexandria July 3-6, 2006, titled "Underwater Museum in Alexandria" was opened by Zahi Hawass of the Supreme Council of Antiquities, who called such a museum a beautiful dream for the city. He revealed that he had decided four years before to stop removing all ancient objects from the seabed except for small artifacts such as coins that would be easy to steal. Ali Radwan, head of the General Union of Arab Archaeologists, felt that it was Alexandria's obligation to establish an offshore submarine museum in Alexandria to protect its submerged antiquities.

This workshop revealed great differences of opinion among 28 Egyptian and international experts concerning the notion of such a museum. An *Al-Ahram Weekly* article by Nevine El-Aref dated July 13, 2006, summarized the meeting. Ibrahim Darwish, Alexandria's archaeological museums director and one of the founders of underwater archaeology, said that the city's Eastern Harbor was the area most deserving of a submerged museum. He noted that it was a closed bay protected from waves, and emphasized that it tells the story of a long history of activity that for hundreds of years has inspired the world. Darwish, however, urged caution in setting up such a museum, saying that the really worthwhile items had already been taken up and that the remainder of artifacts still submerged was rubble that only experts would find interesting.

But one such expert, Abdel Moneim, stated at the conference that such a museum would become one of the world's modern wonders. It could possibly have three floors, the first one holding objects previously raised from all over Alexandria, not just from the Eastern Harbor. The second would contain within aquariums important items still submerged. The third he envisioned as a Plexiglas underwater tunnel.

Francoise Rivier, UNESCO's assistant director, spoke at the June 2006 conference and reviewed her group's recent efforts to protect Alexandria's monuments, especially submerged ones. She referred to previous attempts by UNESCO between 1994 and 2001 to establish an underwater museum at the site.

Doreya Said, general director of Alexandria's archaeological sites and museums, had stated in a 2005 *Christian Science Monitor* article that there were no lighthouse remains left, only ancient objects brought to Alexandria from other parts of Egypt. She backed plans to remove these from the sea floor and place them in Alexandria's new maritime museum. As for more concrete blocks being dropped on the site, Egyptian filmmaker El-Bakri warned, "If they start again I'm going to start another scandal."

Gaballa Ali Gaballah, secretary-general of Egypt's Supreme Council of Antiquities, has stated that he hopes the entire submerged area of the harbor becomes a museum with glass-walled viewing tunnels. Others have favored glass-bottomed boats ferrying tourists from site to site. Another suggestion is to have a floating submarine that would take visitors to the Eastern Harbor, Qaitbay Fort, El-Silsilah and Abukir Bay. This would avoid any problems with a glass tunnel that could be costly, dangerous in case of an earthquake, difficult to maintain, and would take a tourist to only one site.

Other experts at the conference were not keen on the idea of a floating museum provided by means of a glass boat or submarine. They felt such methods could pose a threat to submerged treasures by altering the topography of the area as a craft maneuvered. Diving into wrecks should probably also be sharply curtailed, and boats should be forbidden to travel inside the bay because engines could hit a submerged object.

One far-fetched proposal was to completely drain the Eastern Harbor. However, with the rapidly increasing pace of development in Alexandria, many recognized that notions of parks, museums, and draining might prove difficult to accomplish.

Professors from faculties of science at both Alexandria and Cairo Universities have reported results of studies of the Eastern Harbor, concluding that the bay has been badly exploited. In one such occurrence, part of the harbor's shoreline was filled in. They have recommended that all work in the area cease until the completion of a master plan for the harbor site as a whole. Professor Abdel-Moneim said that a museum would rescue the harbor and put an end to its legendary problems. After a museum was built, city officials would have to be vigilant and protect the purity of the harbor's water.

Continuing the debate, a two-day seminar titled "The Future of Sunken Antiquities" was held by the Supreme Council of Culture on March 20-21, 2007, at the Opera House grounds in Cairo. Maged Ahmed reported in the *Daily Star Egypt* of March 31, 2007, that artifacts from the ancient kingdom of Alexandria and Abukir were discussed. The total number of artifacts recovered from the ancient port of Alexandria has now been put at 6,000.

Writing in the May 26-June 1, 2005, *Al-Ahram Weekly*, Rasha Sadek all but swooned while describing her wonderful underwater adventure in Alexandria's Eastern Harbor. She was taken out to harbor dive sites by businessman Ashraf Sabri's Alexandria Dive. Sadek plunged down to the site of huge Pharos blocks. In what she described as a highly moving experience, she actually touched them.

Geologist Jean-Daniel Stanley of the Smithsonian Institution in Washington, D.C., and Franck Goddio have been studying the submerged cities of Herakleion, Canopus, and Menouthis, all in Abukir Bay. Some have called Goddio's Herakleion work the most exciting find in the history of marine archaeology. Stated Goddio, "We have found an intact city, frozen in time."

This city flourished until Alexander the Great founded Alexandria in 331 B.C. Herodotus, writing in 450 B.C. about his visit to Egypt, said that Herakleion had a temple dedicated to Hercules. Ruins of the city have now been found by Goddio four miles from land.

Goddio also discovered that the cities of Herakleion and Thonis, described in Greek and Egyptian texts, were the same place. Canopus was known in legend to be where the goddess Isis found the fourteenth and last part of god-king Osiris' body, which his jealous brother Seth had ordered dismembered and scattered throughout Egypt. Legend said that Isis assembled the pieces and put them in a vase at Canopus.

A flood destroyed Herakleion in the eighth century A.D. Thonis-Herakleion controlled trade in the area before trading ships ventured further upriver to Naukratis. A tomb dedicated to Amun-Gereb or Heracles has been found in the area.

Jean-Daniel Stanley of the Smithsonian, studying Alexandrian harbor floor cores, reports finding evidence of city engineers fighting the gradual submersion of the shoreline for hundreds of years. The Herakleion, Canopus, and Menouthis areas received large amounts of sediment from the Nile that eventually compacted and sank.

A slow rise in sea level over the centuries contributed to the disappearance of Alexandria's shoreline. Severe Nile flooding in 741 and 742 A.D., as well as earthquakes during that period, were also involved, causing sudden movements of water and sediment.

Writing in *Science* magazine in 2005, Andrew Lawler stated that new data suggested that environmental disasters played an important role in ancient

Alexandria's downfall, rather than just religious and political turmoil. Lawler suggested that the fate of Alexandria could provide a warning for today's fast-growing cities built on deltas. Since 1994, Lawler has been senior writer at *Science Magazine*. He graduated from the University of North Carolina at Chapel Hill, concentrating on geography and anthropology. He was founding editor for *Space Station News* in 1987 and wrote over a period of five years for *Space News*. As a freelance writer, he has compiled articles for such magazines as *Smithsonian*, *National Geographic*, and *Archaeology*, and writes provocative articles on human life and earth's future in forward-looking *Sun Magazine*.

An August 27, 2007, MSNBC story by Anna Johnson of the Associated Press was titled "Rising Seas Washing Away Egypt's Nile Delta." It discussed the World Bank's portrayal of Egypt as particularly vulnerable to the effects of global warming and facing catastrophic consequences. Since the Aswan Dam was constructed in 1970, nutrient sediment from the Nile's flooding no longer replenishes the delta. Add in threats of global warming and the effects on Egypt could be devastating.

Scientists predict that the Mediterranean and other seas across the world will rise between one and three feet by the end of the century. Over the last decade, the Mediterranean has been moving upward about .08 inches annually. The threatened three-foot rise would force 10% of Egypt's population out of their homes, and destroy nearly half of Egypt's crops, such as bananas, wheat, and rice now grown in the delta.

Also, salt water from the Mediterranean would contaminate fresh water that is now brought in from the Nile for irrigation. Anna Johnson reports that authorities in Alexandria are spending $300 million to build concrete walls to protect Mediterranean beaches, and sand is being dumped to help replenish the shrinkage of these beaches. Said one Egyptian authority, "After this we will request that the world help. We have to protect ourselves. But it costs so much."

The Herakleion treasures of Goddio were displayed at the *Egypt's Sunken Treasures* exhibit in Berlin's Martin-Gropius-Bau Museum starting May 11, 2006, and at the Grand Palais in Paris starting November 20, 2006. Revenue from the exhibit was earmarked to help finance an 18-month study administered by the Ministry of Culture to develop a step-by-step action plan.

An article in the December 14-20, 2006 *Al-Ahram Weekly* discussed the exhibit in Paris, which attracted 450,000 visitors when it was opened in December 2006 by French President Jacques Chirac and Egyptian President Hosni Mubarak at the Grand Palais. It featured 500 objects recently discovered by Franck Goddio's team. These had been submerged in Egyptian waters after sudden changes hit Egypt's north coast from 600-800 A.D.

At Paris, wave sounds were played in the background, while the shiny black floor looked like a seabed. An attempt was made to take visitors back to ancient times when Alexandria, Canopus and Herakleion were the main commercial centers of Egypt. Gereon Sieverrich, director of the Martin Gropius-Bau Museum in Berlin, said that this was an archaeological discovery on a par with that of Pompeii.

After Berlin, *Egypt's Sunken Treasures* moved to Bonn, Germany, to be shown April 5, 2007, through January 27, 2008. A Bonn museum brochure stated, "The exhibition *Egypt's Sunken Treasures* restores them [Alexandria, Canopus and Herakleion] to the light of day without, however, stripping them of their mystique."

Franck Goddio, in his interview with Richard Fuchs published in the May 4, 2007, issue of *Deutsche Welle*, stated that the objects then on exhibit in Bonn had all been found next to each other, having waited in the same place for thousands of years. He described them as literally living together: "In the exhibit you can see that they speak to each other."

From April 16 through September 28, 2008, the exhibit was displayed in Madrid at the Antiguo Matadero de Legazpi, a 43,000-square-foot area in the city's former

Goddio exhibit 2006 at Grand Palais, courtesy Patrick Debetencourt

slaughterhouse. Egyptian Culture Minister Farouk Hosni claimed that the artifacts for the Madrid exhibit had been insured for a total of $41,692,000.

The spectacularly lighted exhibit showcased Franck Goddio's work at ancient Herakleion, Canopus, and part of the submerged port of Alexandria. It also offered what the Egyptian government's official website called spectacular insight into the fascinating work of divers and marine archaeologists. After Madrid, the artifacts will travel to Turin, Italy, Japan and America before they return back in Egypt to their new permanent home in the Alexandria Museum.

Spain's King Juan Carlos and his wife Queen Sofia opened the exhibit. For years, she had an important role in bringing the Bibliotheca Alexandrina into existence. In the April 24-30, 2008, issue of *Al-Ahram Weekly*, writer Nevine El-Aref noted that the queen paused as she stood before a black diorite statue of Isis, eyes speaking to inlaid eyes as one royal leader to another. Franck Goddio stood next to Queen Sofia, explaining everything. The Queen told the visiting Egyptian delegation that she had always loved Egypt, having spent part of her youth in Alexandria at school while her parents were exiled in Egypt. She added, "I consider myself half Egyptian."

The National Museum of Alexandria, newly opened in 2004, includes finds by Goddio, among them his discoveries at the site of Herakleion and the figure of Cleopatra's father. The museum is a 1929 Italian-style mansion on Fouad Street, purchased from the American consulate in 1997. Other Goddio finds are displayed in the Antiquities Museum of the Bibliotheca Alexandrina. In April 2006, Franck Goddio resumed work at the site of the sunken Timonium in Portus Magnus. During 2007, his team studied a strange 100-foot-wide cavity in the middle of the building's basement.

The Geological Society of America's August 2007 issue of *GSA Today* reported on underwater studies at Alexandria by Jean-Daniel Stanley of the Smithsonian Institution's National Museum of Natural History. The GSA report was discussed in Smithsonian.com's August 2007 online issue under the title, "Underwater World; New Evidence Reveals a City Beneath Ancient Alexandria."

The team was attempting to study the history of Rhacotis, a settlement established before the fourth century B.C., assumed to be buried under the modern city of Alexandria, but for which there is no proof. While there are many references to Rhacotis in ancient writings, little detail is given. Working with a team of geologists, anthropologists, and geochemists, Stanley in 2001 collected seven underwater sediment core samples measuring three inches wide and 6 to 18 feet long from the Eastern Harbor, at depths of up to 20 feet.

These cores were studied for five critical indicators of human activity: ceramics; rock fragments derived from Middle and Upper Egypt; and significant amounts of lead, heavy minerals and organic matter. Stanley concluded that not only was there evidence of human activity before Alexander the Great at the site, but that activity may well go back 700 years, that is, to 1,000 B.C.

CHAPTER 20
PIERRE CARDIN'S DREAM

A *Der Spiegel* article of 1990 mentioned that a syndicate of Egyptian and Finnish companies planned to build a new Pharos in Alexandria based on reconstruction drawings of German archaeologist and researcher Hermann Thiersch. Plans were to use the tower as a five-star hotel and conference center.

Strong opposition came from orthodox Muslims, especially from Mohammed Sadik Mohammed, a powerful member of the Alexandrian city parliament and also director of housing for the city. He felt that recreating the Pharos would be a blasphemous glorification of the *Dschahilija*, The Time of Unknowing or Ignorance. However, he agreed reluctantly to accept a new tower that would not be any higher than the Islamic Qaitbay Fortress, which is about 100 feet in height. Plans for the structure were scrapped.

Then came startling news. The *Times* on September 15, 1998, reported that Pierre Cardin, 76, famous head of a cosmetics, food and fashion empire and also a UNESCO peace ambassador, had just received permission from the Egyptian Government to build a lighthouse in Alexandria's harbor. It would be on a jetty jutting out 450 feet into the bay. The site would be next to the new Bibliotheca Alexandrina. An official at the Supreme Council of Antiquities said that after months of negotiations, Alexandrian Governor Abdel-Salam Mahgoub had agreed to allocate an area 1,500 feet long and 600 feet wide. There was allegedly no fear of disturbing any archaeological remains at the eastern harbor of Alexandria.

The project apparently had the backing of UNESCO, the Council of Europe, and several French companies. The Centre National d'Art et de Technologie de Reims or National Centre for Art and Technology was assigned by Cardin the process of constructing a contemporary 480-foot-high obelisk. The new lighthouse would measure twenty-seven feet along each side of its base and taper to eighteen feet with a pyramid at the top. It was expected to be finished by June 2000 and to be dedicated at the dawn of the new millennium, something that sadly never happened.

The new lighthouse was to be designed by French lighting engineer Jacques Darolles, director of the Centre at Reims. It would be made out of special concrete that could withstand earth tremors and tidal waves. It would be covered in mirrored glass more than an inch thick. During the day it would reflect the sun's light just as the ancient Pharos' mirror had done centuries before.

It would also have more than 16,000 computer-controlled fluorescent lights the length of the tower. They would light up the structure in laser lights of blue, red, green and pink, making it visible 37 miles out at sea. Also, laser beams would move throughout the harbor to illuminate Alexandria's monuments.

The outside of the tower was to be inscribed with lettering in Greek, Latin and Arabic, as well as Egyptian hieroglyphics, to reflect the four civilizations that contributed their riches to Alexandria. Darolles said that the column would be a gift to Egypt, which had given to France the obelisk standing in the Place de la Concorde. The glass covering would have the appearance of a mirror during the day and a needle of light upon nightfall.

The lighthouse compound would also include an archaeological research center and an amphitheater. Attached to the lighthouse would be a hall fitted with giant television screens. Here, visitors would be able to watch the latest Egyptian archaeological discoveries.

Pierre Cardin came to Lisbon's Expo '98 World Fair to present the plan and unveil a four-foot model of the lighthouse. When asked by a reporter why he had come up with the idea, Cardin replied that he believed it was a way to work for peace in the world. He added that the tower would symbolize the start of the third millennium just as the Eiffel Tower had symbolized the beginning of the twentieth century. He wanted the lighthouse to serve as a symbol of light. His project would make people dream about the past and the future.

Financing would be coordinated by the Fondation Internationale, the Pierre Cardin International Foundation for Culture and Peace. It would finance part of the total $70 to $86 million. The rest of the money would come from people around the world. They would pay $30 per share in the enterprise. Shares would be offered to public investors under the name, Alexandria Twentieth Century Project.

Somehow, Cardin's project never reached fruition. If one asks UNESCO officials what became of it, they will say they have never heard of the plan.

There is no lighthouse yet listed on UNESCO's list of World Heritage Sites, but two lighthouses are part of structures now listed. One is the Queen's Tower of Castle Kronborg in Denmark, which has been used as a lighthouse since 1767 and has been listed as a World Heritage Site since 2000. The other lighthouse on a heritage site is Point de Galle, located on the site of the former Galle fort in Sri Lanka. First occupied by the Portuguese in 1505, Galle was captured by the Dutch in 1640; a lighthouse was later built. The British took over the site in 1796 and changed the location of the lighthouse. The current structure there was built in 1939.

The *World Lighthouse Society Newsletter* of Autumn 2006 reported that during the inaugural meetings of the society at Gatwick, United Kingdom, it was suggested by the chairman that one of the group's goals should be to put a lighthouse on the UNESCO World Heritage list.

Cairo minaret after Pharos, Saudi Aramco World - *PADIA*

CHAPTER 21
MILE-HIGH SKYSCRAPERS

How would the ancient Lighthouse of Alexandria measure up against modern-era skyscrapers? Although historical purists would argue that you cannot compare a unique classical structure such as the Pharos with anything, the comparison begs to be made. Dreams of tall structures were definitely in the minds of the ancients. Labib Habachi, former chief inspector of antiquities in Egypt, fittingly published a book in 1977 titled *The Obelisks of Egypt* with the subtitle, *Skyscrapers of the Past*.

Habachi stated at the book's end, "Queen Hatshepsut wrote that the tops of her obelisks penetrated the sky, and Tuthmosis II claimed that his mingled with the sky." History Channel commentators on the *Mega Machines* episode of the *Ancient Discoveries* television series shown in 2008 said of the Pharos, "It truly was an ancient skyscraper."

Let us consider modern tall buildings. To first consider the world's recent unoccupied towers, the guy-wired Warszawa Radio Mast at Konstantynow near Gabin and Plock in Poland was 2,120 feet, 8 inches high or four-tenths of a mile, supported by 15 steel guy ropes until its collapse in 1991. That collapse had KVLY-TV's 2,063-foot-high guy-wired mast in North Dakota built in 1963 retake its spot as the world's tallest supported structure. Completed in 1974, the Warszawa mast was so high that anyone falling off the top would reach terminal velocity before hitting the ground. It recaptured the tallest structure record for Europe after the Chrysler Building surpassed the Eiffel Tower in 1929. Finished in 1889, the Eiffel Tower was 985 feet, 11 inches high, now extended by a television antenna to 1,052 feet, 4 inches.

To show the fragile nature of such structures, we note that a $7 million, 1,971-foot-high commercial broadcast tower in Missouri City, Texas, collapsed when a steel antenna being placed on top of the tower fell, snapping a guy wire and causing the tower to twist and then topple in December 1982.

Considering a much newer, simple, uninhabited tower, Japanese experts announced plans in 2006 for the New Tokyo Tower, a 2,013-foot-high broadcast tower due to be completed in 2011. If built, it will exceed what has long been the world's current tallest self-supporting structure, the $44 million CN Tower in Metro Center, Toronto, Canada, which stands 1,815 feet, 5 inches high, and was finished in 1975. The Japanese tower would replace a 1,090-foot-high one erected in 1958 that currently is visited by 2.5 million tourists annually.

Moving past simple unoccupied towers, one considers actual inhabitable structures that we call skyscrapers. Plans for these buildings several decades ago seemed to float aimlessly about and never materialize. There were tentative plans in England in 1981 for a 1,825-foot, 139-story office building in Meyseyside County. A *Chicago Tribune* article by Michael Millenson published October 27, 1981, stated that on the drawing boards of architects Skidmore, Owings & Merrill that year was a design for a 169-story skyscraper to be built in Chicago, 2,300 feet in height—or close to half a mile. Its estimated cost then was $1.25 billion.

According to an Associated Press story published in the *Hartford Courant* of August 1, 1984, developer Donald Trump wanted to build a $1 billion, 150-story, 1,940-foot tapered tower possibly to be called "Television City" on a 26-acre New York City landfill still to be created. The site at present lies beneath the East River and nothing has happened there to date.

In 1989, Miglin-Beitler Developments Inc., a major Chicago developer of offices, announced it planned to build a slender 125-story, 1,914-foot-high downtown skyscraper designed by architect Cesar Pelli of New Haven, Connecticut. A Beitler spokesman said then about building the world's tallest building that it was the dream of every developer. The structure was to be built on a one-acre parcel about three blocks from the Sears Tower, and would move past the Sears structure to become the tallest building in the world, even though the new skyscraper would contain only about one-third the rentable space of the bulkier Sears giant.

Proposed as a very narrow white tower growing even narrower to a point at the top, it was canceled with the crash of the United States real estate market during the first Gulf War. Engineers and architects for this building were shortly thereafter hired to build the twin Petronas Towers in Kuala Lumpur.

We might also mention a much older structure more in the fashion of the Pharos of Alexandria: Philadelphia's City Hall, built between 1871 and 1901, which stands 548 feet high and is considered the tallest building in the world in which the bearing walls have no steel skeleton. To compensate, the white marble walls at the base are 22 feet thick.

Now that the twenty-first century has arrived, tall buildings are suddenly going up like new toys. The tallest one in existence, Taipei 101, named for its 101 floors, was opened during 2004 in the city of Taipei, Taiwan, at a height of 1,671 feet. A ceremony to attach the 197-foot-high top spire took place October 18, 2003. Taipei 101 has offices for 12,500 people and the Taiwan Stock Exchange, at a cost of at least $1.7 billion. Elevators in the structure travel at 37 miles per hour and go from ground level to the ninetieth floor in under 39 seconds.

A big challenge with Taipei 101 was to make it strong enough to withstand area typhoons and earthquakes. It is supposed to be able to withstand an earthquake above 7 on the Richter scale, which happens once every 2,500 years in the area. In March 2002, when the tower was just half-built, it survived a 6.8-level earthquake that toppled two cranes and killed five workers. The structure was also built to withstand a one-in-a-hundred-year storm.

Skyscrapers ranked second and third in the record books are the twin Petronas Towers opened in 1998, each 1,483 feet with 88 floors. A steel sky bridge open to the public connects them between the forty-first and forty-second floors.

Next is the world's former tallest building, the Sears Tower in Chicago. Finished in 1974, that 108-story office building is 1,451 feet tall; with two radio antennae, it stands 1,707 feet in height. Fifth on the world list is the Jin Mao Tower in Shanghai, built in 1999 at 1,380 feet with 88 floors. The Empire State Building, built in 1931, is ninth on the current world list at 1,250 feet with 102 floors.

A nice surprise on visiting the Empire State Building's 34th Street lobby is to see a colorful panel depicting the Pharos. Large stained glass panels portraying the traditional Seven Wonders of the World were added in July, 1963. Called "softly lit

188 | A LIGHTHOUSE FOR ALEXANDRIA

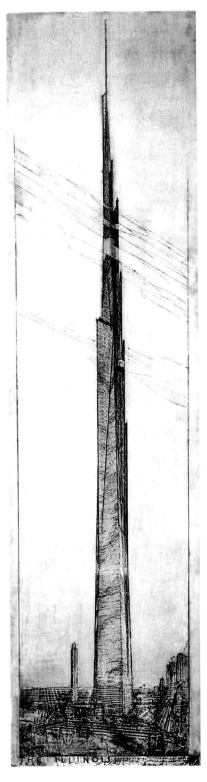

Frank Lloyd Wright mile-high proposed "Illinois" skyscraper

illuminated panels" rather than stained glass, the 5-foot-wide, 7-foot-high creations are made of crystal resin and stained glass. The work of husband and wife Roy and Renee Sparkia (she now uses her maiden name of Nemerov), the panels were commissioned by Laurence Wein, one of the building's owners. An eighth panel showing the Empire State Building, presumably as one of the world's wonders, is included in the display.

Skyscrapers now in the planning or building stages are The Pinnacle, planned at 2,460 feet, Burj Dubai at 2,313 feet with 160 floors to be completed in 2008 or 2009, the Chicago Spire at 2,000 feet, and the Golden Dome Dubai at 1,476 feet. Also proposed is the Shanghai World Financial Centre, planned to be 1,614 feet high.

A possible winner in future competitions for world's tallest building is a 3,284-foot-high proposed skyscraper in Kuwait planned as part of a new city development project called Madinat al-Hareer or City of Silk. However, it may take twenty-five years to complete the complex, which includes an Olympic stadium.

Construction on Dubai's The Pinnacle, also called Palm Tower and located on Palm Jumeirah island, started 2005 with a completion date of 2008. It will be a cluster of three towers around a hollow circular interior. Six sky-bridges will join the towers.

Burj Dubai (*burj* is Arabic for tower; Dubai is the second largest of the United Arab Emirates) is part of Dubai-based Emaar Properties' flagship project called Downtown Burj Dubai, a 500-acre development which includes commercial, residential, hospitality, retail, and leisure amenities. The tower, now the world's tallest man-made structure, was the brainchild of architect Adrian Smith of Skidmore, Owings & Merrill, the Chicago-based firm which has been in business since 1936. They also designed that city's Sears Tower, which opened in 1973.

It is unclear what the final height Burj Dubai will be when completed. The constant readjusting of the peak height is a frequent occurrence during the planning of modern skyscrapers. When finished, Burj Dubai will hold the record for all four categories recognized by New York City's Council on Tall Buildings and Urban Habitat: tallest structure, roof, antenna or spire, and occupied floor.

The scheduled opening of Burj Dubai was revised in June 2008, with a new goal of September 2009 on account of increase of the height and enhancement of interior finishes. The super-tall tower will house the Armani Hotel and Armani Residences and will have an observation deck on the 124th floor.

On July 21, 2007, Burj Dubai reached 1,680 feet, surpassing Taiwan's Taipei 101 as the world's tallest building. Shortly thereafter, it surpassed Toronto's 1,815-foot CN Tower that had been the world's tallest freestanding structure for 31 years. In April 2008, Burj Dubai reached 2,063.6 feet to surpass the KVLY-TV mast in North Dakota and become the world's tallest man-made structure of any kind.

World Islands was another plan announced for Dubai in September 2003. Three hundred man-made islands are being created to resemble in total a map of the continents of the world. Stores, resorts, restaurants, apartments, and homes were planned throughout the islands. A well-known individual who has purchased one of the islands is Sir Richard Branson.

Three man-made Palm Islands, called Palm Jumeirah, Palm Jebel Ali, and Palm Deira, are also being created in Dubai. Construction on Jumeirah began June 2001. Shaped as a date palm tree with a crown of seventeen fronds, it will include a crescent island serving as a breakwater. Palm Jumeirah will offer 25 international hotels, including Trump Plaza and Marina Residences. Trump Tower Dubai, also referred to as Palm Trump International Hotel and Tower, is considered the luxury centerpiece of the area. When complete in 2009, it will be 48 stories high and offer the mix of a 300-room five-star hotel and 360 residential apartments.

Located on the crescent of Palm Jumeirah will be the 380-room Lighthouse Hotel and Residence. According to one real estate description, it will capture the light of the rising sun and beam it into the complex's interior. In the evening, the roof will be lighted and an art of light will be projected across the Arabian Gulf.

The residential section will consist of two hundred two-, three-, and four-bedroom apartments having 99-year leases. The Lighthouse Hotel and Residence was originally scheduled for completion December 2007. However, even though all units have long been sold out, construction on the building has often stopped for months at a time. Work on it has recently resumed.

Dubai has not cornered the market on new and ever-taller skyscrapers. Another interesting skyscraper was presented in an Associated Press wire story on November 28, 2006, out of Paris, picked up by ABC News. Called Phare or Lighthouse and designed by American architect Thom Mayne, it is to be completed by 2012 in the Paris business suburb of La Defense, the location of many of France's major corporations. The 984-foot-high curving tower is to include a wind farm to help generate its own heating and cooling.

For replacement structures to commemorate New York City's Twin Towers, destroyed by terrorist-highjacked airliners on September 11, 2001, Berlin-based architect Daniel Libeskind entered the fierce design competition with his plan of a 1,776-foot-high skyscraper. Another proposed design for the site was a 2,100-foot World Cultural Center. Libeskind won the competition and is masterminding the planning of the 911 commemorative. Skidmore, Owings & Merrill was awarded architectural design control for Libeskind's Freedom Tower.

Chicago Tribune writer Michael Millenson reported on October 27, 1981, that, in October 1956, architect Frank Lloyd Wright rocked the architectural world with drawings of a 528-story building, exactly one mile high, to be located on Chicago's lakefront. Wright never actually planned on building the "Illinois," as he called it. It was one of his ways of celebrating Frank Lloyd Wright Day, which had just been proclaimed by Mayor Richard J. Daley. But dreams have a way of growing.

On April 20, 2007, the Chicago city planning board approved plans by Spanish-born architect, artist, sculptor, and engineer Santiago Calatrava for his Chicago Spire, a twisting 2,000-foot, 150-story tower on the waterfront that would become the western world's tallest building and the world's tallest residential skyscraper when it is completed. Sporting a twist in the exterior designed to help deflect wind, it is to be built on a peninsula, with the Chicago River on the south and Lake Michigan to the east, with Lake Shore Drive cutting through the peninsula. The beautiful structure is referred to as seven-sided, but it is hard to identify any sides at all amidst the twists.

Typical of how buildings go through changes in the construction phase, the Chicago Spire was originally to be topped by a 400-foot-high broadcast antenna, but now the extra 400 feet will be all occupied building. It was initially planned for a full 360-degree twist to the exterior, but now will only twist 270 degrees on the way up to its 2,000-foot apex. The base of the tower is now 35 feet wider than planned. It is being constructed by Shelbourne Development Limited under its chairman, developer Garrett Kelleher.

Calatrava in 2005 said that Chicago is a North American Indian name, and that his mind therefore conjures up pictures of Native Americans arriving at the lake and making a fire that creates a column of smoke going up in the air, with his skyscraper resembling that column. Some describe it as a drill bit, a blade of grass, or a tall twisting tree. Others have compared it to a lighthouse, which could one day turn out to be its nickname due to the location. Calatrava has sometimes called his Spire "a vertical city."

One presentation event by Calatrava was a slide show set to Dvorak's Ninth Symphony *From the New World* played by the Chicago Symphony Orchestra. The Calatrava name is the prime mover selling apartments in the Spire. He is well-known and respected for projects such as the Athens Olympic Sports Complex and Tenerife Opera House. Among current projects, he is planning New York City's World Trade Center transportation hub to be built at Ground Zero.

Initially, a hotel was planned for the first 20 floors of Chicago Spire; the remainder of the building would be comprised of up to 300 luxury condominiums. However, hotel plans have been dropped, as its location is considered too far from the city's main area. The skyscraper is now slated to offer 3 million square feet of completely residential space. The original 300 exclusive condos are now 1,193 apartments. Those on the fiftieth floor and above will have unrestricted views. New plans call for a 56-foot-tall lobby with glass walls that will offer a clear view through the base on all sides.

Within three months of its announcement, 800 people called wanting to buy in the building. Apartment prices range from $750,000 to $40 million. Real estate experts place the cost of the spire at $1.2 billion. Perhaps due to the severe housing recession in the United States, its proposed 2009 completion date has been pushed back to early 2012. In a stirring four-page ad in the May 2008 issue of *Architectural Digest*, Calatrava and Spire salespeople called this collection of unique and extraordinary condominium residences "the most significant development in the world." The ad boasted that among the one- to four-bedroom "homes," no two units were alike. This author was told that, several days after *Architectural Digest* arrived in homes, Shelbourne Development Limited's Chicago realty office was bombarded with phone calls.

Lorna Blackwood in her October 5, 2007 *Times* article reported that Chicago's downtown area alone has 13,000 apartments due for completion by 2010. Competition for sales is coming from two other partial residential buildings now under construction—the 1,362-foot Trump International Hotel and Tower, and the 1,047-foot Waterview Tower and Shangri La Hotel.

Cecilia Chow and Nova Theresianto reported in *The Edge – Singapore* on March 17, 2008 that 800 people turned up recently for a private investors' Chicago Spire presentation in Singapore. A draw for Asian residents was the very cheap value of the dollar in 2008. Other cities next on the sales tour were Hong Kong, Kuala Lumpur, Shanghai and Beijing, followed by offerings in fifteen other cities in Africa, the Middle East, and Europe. Half the buyers at Chicago Spire are expected to be from other than America.

Plate 1
Chicago Spire, September 2007. Courtesy Shelbourne Development and Santiago Calatrava.

Plate 2
Burj Dubai at over 160 floors, June 2008. Courtesy Emaar Properties.

Plate 3
Burj Dubai, March 2008, by Aheilner at Wikimedia Commons.

Plate 4
Louisiana State Capitol Building, by Pattie Steib, March, 2006, featurepics.com

Plate 5
George Washington Masonic National Memorial, Alexandria, VA, 1995, by Ben Schumin.

Plate 6
Traveler's Tower, Hartford, CT. Flickr.com

Plate 7
Luxor light, Las Vegas, by Wes Keller, Pbbase.com

Plate 8
The 911 tribute in lights Sept. 11, 2006.
Denise Gould, U.S. Air Force.

Plate 9
Alexandria Planetarium. p.vtourist.com

Plate 10
Bibliotheca Alexandrina, 2006, back view.

Plate 11
Bibliotheca Alexandrina dome. ©Christian Richters, Aga Khan Trust for Culture.

Plate 12
Bibliotheca Alexandrina letter wall. ©Christian Richters, Aga Khan Trust for Culture.

Plate 13
Bibliotheca Alexandrina from across harbor.
©Christian Richters, Aga Khan Trust for Culture.

Plate 14
Logo of the Baltimore Friends of the Bibliotheca Alexandrina

Plate 15
Bibliotheca Alexandrina, interior. ©Christian Richters, Aga Khan Trust for Culture.

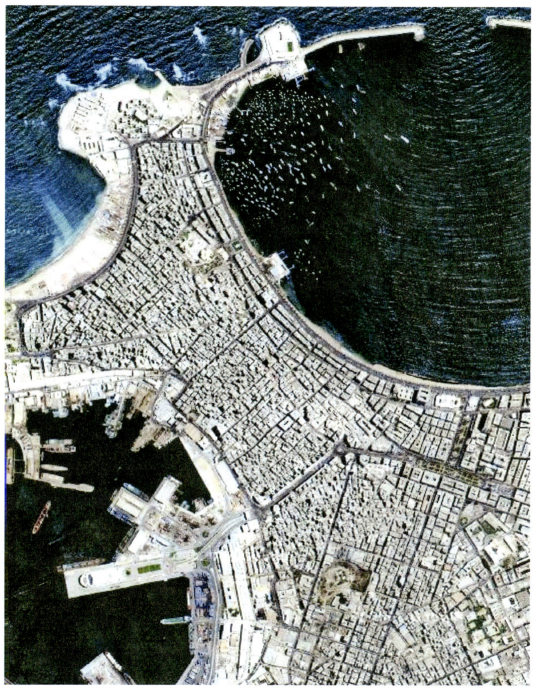

Plate 16
Lighthouse of Alexandria site, Google satellite view.

Plate 17
Tom and Rose Clarie at Montazah Palace. Alexandria, December 1987.

Plate 18
Maze of commercial signs in Alexandria, 2007.

COLOR PLATES | 207

Plate 19
Marketplace in Alexandria, 2007.

Plate 20
Fort Qaitbay, women and surf.

Plate 21
Our Saviour's Church, Copenhagen, by Squirmelia, 2006, Flikr.com

Plate 22
Pharos reconstruction, Changsha, China, 2005,
by Dawidbernard, Wikimedia Commons.

Plate 23
Eilean Glas, Scotland, by Michael Grimsdale,
Saudi Aramco World/*PADIA*.

210 | A LIGHTHOUSE FOR ALEXANDRIA

Plate 24
Pharos harbor in Roman times, by Michael Grimsdale, 1994, Saudi Aramco World/PADIA.

Plate 25
*Arab astronomers atop Pharos, by Michael Grimsdale,
1982,* Saudi Aramco World/*PADIA.*

Plate 26
Fort Qaitbay, by T. Peter Limber, Saudi Aramco World/*PADIA*.

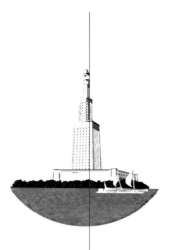

CHAPTER 22
LEGACY: WONDER OF THE WORLD AND MORE

Though the light of the Pharos of Alexandria went out centuries ago, it still shines down through the ages in five important ways: as one of the Seven Wonders of the Ancient World; as an engineering feat; as an architectural model for lighthouses; as an architectural model for minarets, churches and skyscrapers; and as the supreme symbol signifying the greatness of the city of Alexandria itself.

The list of wonders was pegged at the number seven because of the great symbolism attached to that number in ancient times as a holy number. Traditionally accepted as the seven wonders of the classical world are these structures: the Pyramids of Egypt; the Hanging Gardens of Babylon; the Statue of Zeus in Olympia; the Temple of Artemis at Ephesus; the Mausoleum at Halicarnassus; the Colossus of Rhodes; and, finally, the Lighthouse of Alexandria.

Some wonder how a forgotten eighth marvel could have been left off the traditional list. Greek historian Herodotus as well as others also raved about the Egyptian Labyrinth, 1,300 years old at the time he visited it in the fifth century B.C. A vast structure seven days' journey from the Pyramids at Giza traveling up the Nile, the Labyrinth sat on the shores of a very large body of water called Lake Moeris, which Herodotus described in circumference "equal to the whole seaboard of Egypt."

The temple was described as being divided into twelve huge courtyards and a large pyramid decorated with huge statues, all connected by an underground passage. Greek geographer Strabo, the only other writer who actually visited the Labyrinth,

214 | A LIGHTHOUSE FOR ALEXANDRIA

claimed that no one could find his way in or out without a guide. Modern experts believe the structure was the mortuary temple of Amenemhet III, but Herodotus claimed the site was the work of twelve kings, the last of whom was Psammetichus.

The list of ancient wonders has changed back and forth through the centuries. Some lists used to include both the Hanging Gardens and the Walls of Babylon, grabbing two precious slots quickly. A nineteenth century list of the Seven Ancient Wonders published in *Banner of Liberty*, a Middletown, New York newspaper of August 31, 1859, included the Colossus of Rhodes, the Pyramids, the Pharos, and the Temple of Artemis (Diana), but dropped the gardens, Zeus and the Mausoleum, replacing them with the Labyrinth of Psammetichus (Egyptian Labyrinth), the Aqueducts of Rome, and the Walls of Babylon.

Many claim that the basic list was compiled by Philo of Byzantium in the second century B.C. and that his constitutes the oldest list of wonders known. Others dispute

Seven Wonders, Magyar Posta, L. Dudas c. Janas

this, but Tony Perrottet in the June 2004 issue of *Smithsonian* indicates that Philo did compile such a list. It was perhaps based on an earlier one by Callimachus of Cyrene (305-240 B.C.), an Alexandrian scholar writing an essay on wonders. It does seem clear that one of the earliest lists of wonders was compiled about 100 B.C. by Antipater of Sidon. Gregory of Tours created another classic wonder list in the 6th century A.D. Writing in the 10th century A.D., Arab historian Masudi listed the lighthouse as one of the wonders of the world.

Although there were many beautiful buildings in the ancient world, the list by Antipater mentions Greek structures all built within a few centuries of the rule of Alexander the Great. All existed in countries where Alexander was victorious. Writer Charles Walker states, "This would suggest that this ancient list was in some way concerned with applauding the magnificence of this great Macedonian, or providing a sort of advertising campaign for the Greek nation."

Some believe that the list of wonders was compiled as a must-see travel list for ancient holiday-takers. However, each of these structures must have been remarkable indeed to be part of such a short list limited to seven great marvels of construction.

Johann Adler wrote in 1901 that, due to the boldness of its design and the magnificence of its completely unique appearance, the Pharos of Alexandria was from a very early time considered among the Seven Wonders of the World. For many centuries, ancient geographers and historians included it on various lists of the wonders. Don Miguel Asin y Palacios designates it the "Third" Wonder of the World but some researchers such as Paul Lunde call it the "Seventh," saying it made the list later to replace the deletion of the "Walls of Babylon." Mid-second century A.D. writer Lucian calls it one of the greatest and most splendid works in the world.

Recently the exciting notion of the creation of a new Wonders of the World list was put forward. Swiss Canadian Bernard Weber, explorer, aviator, filmmaker and museum curator, has come up with something that might have some lasting value. In 2001, he set up the New Seven Wonders Foundation in Zurich, with a website of *new7wonders.com*.

Its purpose is to protect humankind's heritage across the globe and to warn people about the threat of famous man-made structures decaying and disappearing. Weber's goal is to bring emotions to the man-made monuments, and his slogan is "Our

Seven Wonders Certificate, www.new7wonders.com

heritage is our future." Voting on a new World Wonders list started in 2001. A list of 177 nominees was cut to 77 and then to 21 finalists by late 2005.

To quality for the wonders list, a structure had to be man-made and date from the start of humanity to the year 2000. A person's first seven votes were free, after which it cost $2 to vote. Early profits would be used to restore Afghanistan's Buddhas of Bamiyan, destroyed by the Taliban in 2000. The World Monuments Fund's *Icon* of

Spring 2007 delighted in stating that eight of the 21 finalists had been the subject of previous WMF-sponsored conservation efforts.

Zahi Hawass, director general of Egypt's Supreme Council of Antiquities, had been steadfastly opposed to seeing the Giza Pyramid nominated for the listing, saying that only archaeologists or UNESCO have true expertise in these matters. To short-circuit this criticism, the New7Wonders Foundation designated the Pyramids of Giza as an Honorary New7Wonders Candidate on which no one could vote, calling it a shared world culture and heritage site.

On July 7, 2007, at ceremonies before 50,000 at a soccer stadium in Lisbon, Portugal, the choices by 100 million Internet and cell phone users were announced. The Seven New Wonders selected were the Great Wall of China, Rome's Coliseum, India's Taj Mahal, Mexico's Chichen Itza Mayan Pyramid, Jordan's Petra, Peru's Machu Picchu, and Brazil's Statue of Christ the Redeemer. The fourteen losers out of the final 21 were the Eiffel Tower, Easter Island, the Statue of Liberty, the Acropolis, Russia's Kremlin and St. Basil's Cathedral, Australia's Sydney Opera House, Cambodia's Angkor, Spain's Alhambra, Turkey's Hagia Sophia, Japan's Kiyomizu Temple, Germany's Neuschwanstein Castle, Britain's Stonehenge, and Mali's Timbuktu.

The city of Dubai, not to be outdone by Weber's new wonders of the world list, has itself planned a new $1.5 billion creation called Falcon City of Wonders. The 100-acre development will be built within a 3-billion-square-foot "retail mega project" called Dubailand, now under development. Dubailand will be by far the largest theme and amusement park in the world.

Falcon City will be shaped like a falcon, and contain life-size replicas of seven wonders of the world: The Lighthouse at Alexandria, The Great Pyramid at Giza, the Hanging Gardens of Babylon, the Taj Mahal, the Great Wall of China, the Eiffel Tower, and the Leaning Tower of Pisa. Besides wonders, the Falcon City development will offer residential apartments, villas, malls, hotels, restaurants, health clubs, schools and parks. Dubailand will not be completed until perhaps 2020.

Dubai's wonders remind us that it is time to look at the Pharos as an engineering feat. No other lighthouse in history has rivaled it in size or in its 1,500 years of service. D. Alan Stevenson says that it must have been of vast size and not merely the largest building in Alexandria. He feels that its endurance as a great mass of stone for 1,600 years suggests that it may have been a structure even larger than the dimensions given by various authorities.

Writing in 1975, Douglas Hague says that the importance of such an immense building cannot be over-estimated. It was the tallest roofed structure ever built, until eclipsed by steel-framed skyscrapers at the beginning of the twentieth century.

The History Channel's *Ancient Discoveries* series aired its *Mega Machines* episode April 2008 in the United States. That show stated the Pharos lasted so long due to the care with which it was built. It called the structure "propaganda in stone," because of the way it portrayed the Ptolemies as rulers able to do things of which no one else was capable. *Mega Machines* commentators said that, by using its steam-producing furnaces and mirrors, all sorts of moving figures, sirens and flashing beams were created, making the Pharos what some call "a multi-faceted weapon" of which Archimedes himself would have been proud. Summarized the History Channel show, "The Pharos lighthouse was a magnificent structure and a mega-machine, the largest and most complex machine in antiquity."

There are those who do favor downgrading its status as both wonder and engineering feat. Peter Fraser wrote in 1972 that the Pharos is not regularly included in the earlier lists of the Seven Wonders, but is discussed, indicating that it was considered unique in its class. Others argue that it may have been smaller than we think, since it did not last.

Author E. M. Forster writes in his classic 1923 work, *Pharos and Pharillon*:

> Perhaps it was merely very large; reconstructions strike a chill, and the minaret, its modern descendant, is not supremely beautiful. Something very large to which people got used—a Liberty Statue, an Eiffel Tower? The possibility must be faced, and is not excluded by the ecstasies of the poets.

Writer Paul Lunde also asks if the wonders could measure up to today's structures. He questions, for example, if the Colossus of Rhodes would measure up to the Statue of Liberty. Says Lunde, "The answer, cruelly, may be, with the exception of the Lighthouse at Pharos and the Pyramids, they don't come off too well."

Bruce J. Graham, considered one of America's leading designers of high-rise buildings, addressed some of these issues in a 1988 essay titled "Tall Buildings as Symbols." Born 1925 in Bogota, Colombia, to American parents, he received his architecture degree from the University of Pennsylvania in 1948 and has worked most of his life for Chicago's Skidmore, Owings and Merrill, the largest and most famous architectural firm in the United States. His words speak of having quality in structures:

> What *is* important is how poetic and beautiful is the large or the small. Responsible architects must respond to the totality of human experience, from the most basic human needs to the highest human aspirations. In all of their elements, both large and small, beautiful cities should reflect the richness of human activity.

William Ellis states in his 1989 *National Geographic* article on skyscrapers, "And when it is finished and there are souls awash in the pride of it all, the tower then stands as a monument in the service of a bank or an oil company or perhaps a maker of soap." Ellis says of modern skyscrapers that they are too bulky and do not fit comfortably into their sites.

Researcher Paul Lunde notes that the seven wonders were far more wondrous than today's Superdomes and Pentagons. "While some of the wonders won fame because of their sheer size and magnificence, others did so because they were particularly beautiful or had endured a long time." For example, the Statue of Zeus by Phidias, the greatest sculptor of that time, was only 30 feet high, but the entire surface was made of ivory and gold, and it stood for nearly 900 years.

It would be wrong to attribute the design and construction of the Lighthouse of Alexandria solely to practical, mechanical needs. In his book on tall buildings, skyscraper designer Bruce Graham states:

> Evidence of human traditional reverence for grand structures still remains in Egypt, Mesopotamia, and the Far East, where towers have functioned as stairways to God in a literal sense. In western culture, the mythical Tower of Babel is a familiar symbol of both man's innate power over nature and God's innate power over man.

Also, we would do well to remember that the Pharos of Alexandria was built in a vulnerable location with a durability that allowed it to last a millennium and a half. Our wonders of today have a long way to go before they reach that time sphere of endurance.

Honor Frost in 1975 called building at water's edge a form of "architectural brinkmanship" dictated by local geography. She marveled at the building of a great tower on a rock so small that it had to be artificially reinforced. None of this took into consideration the structure's giant crabs, the famous mirror, and the functioning tritons, which might make it an engineering feat in any era.

As for its importance as a lighthouse model, researcher Hermann Thiersch says that this was the first lighthouse of the world, a completely new type of building. He claims that there has never been a lighthouse of significance for which the Pharos was not the model. As an antique lighthouse, Thiersch states that it was the first and last of its kind. None of its fellow antique lighthouses survived as it did. It above all passed on to later generations the concept of marine observation on a gigantic scale.

John Lawton in 1990 mentioned that the lighthouse of Alexandria was the inspiration for the Egyptian-style keepers' cottages at various places, such as at Noss Head, Eilean Glas on the island of Scalpay in Scotland; in the Outer Hebrides; and at Ardnamuchan, the western-most point on the Scottish mainland. Born 1949 in England, Lawton became a television documentary producer, specializing in films about American cities. He has also written a highly-acclaimed series of Frederick Troy mysteries set in Scotland Yard. He was raised in Derbyshire in the Pennine Mountain area of northern England, where he makes his home today.

Alan Stevenson, a relative of the author cited in this volume, designed the keepers' cottages in the 1830s and 1840s, planning a low, oblong building with a facade as a series of four pylon-shaped structures typical of ancient Egyptian architecture. The nineteenth-century Scottish lighthouse at Cromarty on the Black Isle also has classic Egyptian features. Lawton notes as well that six ships called *Pharos* have served as lightships, tenders, and flagships in Scotland's fleet for supplying island lighthouses over the past 200 years.

Concerning other influences on lighthouse-like structures, feature story writer Fred Allen in his 1986 article for *Aramco World Magazine* says he believes that the Statue of

Liberty was designed by French sculptor Auguste Bartholdi as a modern-day colossus based on Egypt's past wonders. In 1867, Bartholdi went to see Ismail Pasha, viceroy of Egypt, who was visiting Paris at the Universal Exposition. Bartholdi proposed that a colossal statue be erected at the entrance to the Suez Canal then nearing completion. The statue, to be called Egypt (or Progress) Carrying the Light to Asia, was in the form of an Egyptian female peasant or *fellah* holding a torch up high to symbolize Pasha's efforts to modernize Egypt. The statue was also to serve as a lighthouse, recalling the pharaonic Lighthouse of Alexandria.

Eventually, the viceroy said that he could not afford the new Colossus. Bartholdi later insisted his Suez project was totally ended then, and that its similarity to the Statue of Liberty was just a coincidence. But says researcher Fred Allen, "this clearly was not the case." In both the Suez Progress sculpture and the New York Liberty sculpture, the lighthouse beacon was not planned for the torch, but was to radiate from the forehead of the figure. The torch was to be purely symbolic.

In considering the Pharos of Alexandria as an architectural model for some minarets and churches, John Feeney writes in 1985 for *Aramco World Magazine* that the minarets of Egypt are a direct imitation of the ancient Pharos, in structure and in their very name. The Arabs called the Pharos *al-manara*, the place of fire. Thiersch notes, however, that this is only valid for Egypt. Persian, Turkish, North African, and Syrian towers have completely different roots.

One Arab author, Abd el-Wahid Marrakuschi, writes that when Sultan Abu Jasuf Jakud al-Mansur founded the city of Ribbat near Schella on the Atlantic Ocean, he built a very large moschee with a very high minaret in the form of Pharos of Alexandria. This was the later form of the Pharos in the thirteenth century. It had a high square tower with a low square top, which served as the model for the more westward-situated minarets.

In considering the Giraldo of Seville, one of the best-known towers in Spain, one moves to European soil. Belfries appeared at the same time as minarets appeared, but their origin remains in the dark. One sees the succession of square, octagon, and globe, but, more often, an even simpler form: a high, narrow square with a low square or octagon on top. Thiersch says that we therefore have the old known forms, undeniably further extensions of Pharos, both in the minaret's earlier and later states.

To sea-going Italian Republicans, the Pharos was certainly known. It was they who first introduced the lighthouse into Europe, at Pisa with its "Faro" on Melorca in

1157 A.D., at Magnale near Livorno in 1163 A.D., and at Genoa with its lighthouse of 1139 A.D. which was restored in 1543 A.D.

Hermann Thiersch reports that one tower at Venice that seems to have had a very special relationship to Alexandria was the campanile at San Marco. We no longer know its upper part. However, its complete appearance with a very large lower foundation dating from the ninth century and the general design inside, complete with air shaft and entrance ramp, remind one of the Pharos. This campanile was the main signal on the Adriatic. The most honored relic in the church, the bones of St. Mark, had been brought to Venice from Alexandria. The Pharos, then, was an important influence on later minaret and church architecture.

The ancient Pharos of Alexandria has inspired numerous constructions, both old and new. The tower of Our Saviour's Church in Copenhagen looks very much like the fanciful imagination of the Pharos presented earlier in this book, taken from Georg Ebers' nineteenth century book on Egypt. This church was consecrated in 1696. Its tower, completed 50 years later, was designed after Rome's university chapel of St. Ivo.

The George Washington Masonic National Memorial in Alexandria, Virginia, was completed in 1932 and dedicated to the memory of George Washington. It was created in likeness to the Lighthouse of Alexandria both due to the town's name and because of Masonic interest in great buildings of the ancient world. The tower is capped with a flame-like symbol to honor the Pharos of Alexandria.

Concerning the Pharos' representing the crowning achievement of the city of Alexandria, tall buildings expert Bruce Graham says that every tower has to relate to its people and to the unique character and psyche of each city. E. M. Forster in his 1922 *Alexandria* suggested that perhaps the greatest importance of the Pharos was to the city itself: "To the imagination of contemporaries, the Pharos became Alexandria and Alexandria became the Pharos. Never, in the history of architecture, has a secular building been thus worshipped and taken on a spiritual life of its own." He emphasizes that the Pharos was the greatest practical achievement of the Alexandrian mind. It was the outward expression of mathematical studies carried on in the Mouseion.

Johann Adler feels that through the Pharos, Alexandria reached the pinnacle of an almost one hundred-year period of development. He is astounded at the daring quality of this act of erecting a massive tower 450 to 600 feet in height at the edge of the ocean. He deduced that it could only have originated in a place that was governed autocratically with statesmanlike intelligence, with the necessary advisory helpers and workers, plus enormous financial resources.

During a 2006 television show on the History Channel titled *Deep Sea Detectives: Pharos and Alexandria*, one commentator stated, "The great lighthouse of Alexandria is a symbol of a great cosmopolitan civilization at the very roots of our cities today." Speaking on the same program, classics professor Joseph Manning of Stanford University said, "The more we reconstruct Alexandria, the more we reconstruct ourselves."

In his research at Massachusetts Institute of Technology during the 1950s, Kevin Lynch found that the perceptions and memories of people in an urban environment are basically shaped by five elements: paths, edges (such as rivers and railways), districts, nodes (such as crossroads), and landmarks. One likes to think that the Pharos molded the perceptions of urban dwellers of Alexandria through all five of these basic elements.

Discussing Caesarea Maritima in 1988, Kenneth Holum said that, to the residents of the city, the linkage between city and harbor was intimate and enduring. It undoubtedly was the same with Alexandria. Adler wrote in 1901 that, little by little, the Pharos became for Alexandria what the pyramids of Memphis had become for all of Egypt and the walls and hanging gardens became for Babylon. What better symbol to convey the spirit that was Alexandria's than a shining light?

Wrote Peter Clayton in 1988, "These two institutions at Alexandria, the Museum and the Library, were a metaphorical beacon in the ancient world of learning; the literal beacon was to be supplied by the Pharos." Paul Lunde in 1980 quoted twelfth-century observer Ibn Jubair after he saw the Pharos as marveling, "Description of it falls short, the eyes fail to comprehend it, and words are inadequate, so vast is the spectacle."

In the breathtaking new spirit embodied in the renewal of the Alexandrian Library, in-depth archaeological work is now taking place both in Alexandria as a whole and near the Pharos site in particular. As these labors continue and grow, we assume that what researcher Kenneth Holum said in 1988 concerning Caesarea Maritima will be applicable to Alexandria as well: "This beautiful seaside resort...is proving to be a brimming repository, filled with insights about the human past."

In these days of pre-fabricated, starkly functional, depressing office towers, times of avalanche debt and zero-based budgeting, it is thrilling to ponder the Pharos as an ancient structure built not just to fulfill a function but also to give daily pleasure and meaning. It was sculpture erected to create an uplifting symbol of man's perhaps foolish striving for greatness.

Is it wrong always to dream that lofty, meaningful structures such as the Pharos of Alexandria may yet someday return to grace our planet? Or, have we simply turned a corner, with the hour now late, oh, so very late, with just no time or space left for any more beacons of light?

BIBLIOGRAPHY

"Acid Rain 'Sleeper.'" *World Monuments Fund Newsletter* Nov. 1985: 4.

Adams, W. H. Davenport. *Lighthouses and Lightships: A Descriptive and Historical Account of Their Mode of Construction and Organization.* New York: Charles Scribner and Co., 1870.

Adler, F. von. *Der Pharos von Alexandria.* Berlin: Verlag von Wilhelm Ernst und Sohn, 1901.

"Alexandria." *Encyclopedia Britannica.* Chicago: The Werner Company, 1893 [reprint; orig. pub. c. 1891]: 493-497.

"Alexandria Looks to French Company to Clean Up City." CNN.com: Archives.cnn.com/2000/WORLD/meast/09/04/egypt.cleaning.ap; 4 Sept 2000.

"Alexandria." *The World: Its Cities and Peoples,* vol.1. 7 vols. London & New York: Cassell & Co. Ltd., 1887.

Allen, Fred. "The New Colossus." *Aramco World Magazine* 37:5 Sept.-Oct. 1986: 2-7.

"Ancient Sphinx Safe, but in Rocky Condition." *New Haven Register* 31 March 1989.

Appleton's Annual Cyclopaedia and Register of World Events 1882. New York: D. Appleton & Co., 1883.

Ashurst, John and Francis G. Dimes. *Stone in Building; Its Use and Potential Today.* London: Architectural Press Ltd., 1977.

Asin, Don Miguel de and Don M. Lopez Otero. "Pharos of Alexandria." *Proceedings of the British Academy* 1933: 277-292.

Atlas of Ancient and Classical Geography. New York: E.P. Dutton & Co., 1933 [reprint; orig. pub. c. 1907].

Banks, Edgar J. "Seven Wonders of the Ancient World; VII—the Seventh Wonder: the Lighthouse of Alexandria." *Art and Archaeology* 6 1917: 77-81.

Battuta, Ibn. *Travels in Asia and Africa, 1325-1354.* Trans. and ed. H. A. R. Gibb. London: Routledge & Kegan Paul Ltd., 1929.

Beaver, Patrick. *History of Lighthouses.* Secaucus, NJ: Citadel Press, 1973 [reprint; orig. pub. c. 1971].

Bell, H. Idris. *Egypt from Alexander the Great to the Arab Conquest.* Oxford: Clarendon Press, 1948.

Bickerman, Elias J. *The Jews in the Greek Age.* Cambridge, MA: Harvard University Press, 1988.

Caesar, Julius. *War Commentaries of Caesar.* Trans. Rex Warner. New York: New American Library, 1960.

Carroll, David. *Wonders of the World.* New York: Bantam Books, 1976.

Clayton, Peter A. and Martin J. Price. *The Seven Wonders of the Ancient World.* London: Routledge, 1988.

Cleopatra's World: Alexandria Revealed. Videotape [2 hours]. History Channel/A&E Home Video, 1996 [DVD c.2006].

Daniel, Suzanne. "Greek: the Septuagint." *Encyclopedia Judaica,* vol. 4. 16 vols. Jerusalem: Encyclopedia Judaica, 1971.

Davidovits, Joseph, and Margie Morris. *The Pyramids; an Enigma Solved*. New York: Hippocrene, 1988.

DeCosson, Anthony. *Mareotis, Being a Short Account of the History and Ancient Monuments of the North-western Desert of Egypt and of Lake Mareotis*. London: Country Life Ltd., 1935.

Deep Sea Detectives: Pharaoh's Lost Treasure [Pharos of Alexandria]. DVD [50 minutes]. The History Channel/A&E Television Networks, 2006.

della Dora, Veronica. "The Rhetoric of Nostalgia: Postcolonial Alexandria Between Uncanny Memories and Global Geographies." *Cultural Geographies* 13 2006: 207-238.

Diodorus. *Diodorus of Sicily*, vol. VIII [Books XVI 66-95 and XVII]. Trans. C. Bradford Welles. Cambridge, MA: Harvard University Press, 1963.

Drury, Allen. *Egypt, the Eternal Smile: Reflections on a Journey*. Garden City, NY: Doubleday & Company Inc., 1980.

Ebers, G. "Ancient Alexandria." *Egypt: Descriptive, Historical, and Picturesque*, vol. 1. Trans. Clara Bell of *Aegypten in Bild und Wort*. New York/London: Cassell & Company, 1879: 1-30.

_____. "Modern Alexandria." *Egypt: Descriptive, Historical, and Picturesque*, vol. 1. Trans. Clara Bell of *Aegypten in Bild und Wort*. New York/London: Cassell & Company, 1879: 31-58.

"Egyptians Repair, Reopen Great Pyramid of Cheops." *Hartford Courant* 1989.

El-Aref, Nevine. "Archaeologist with a Mission" [Jean-Yves Empereur]. *Al-Ahram Weekly* 9-15 Oct. 2003.

_____. "Designer Lighthouse for Alexandria." *Al-Ahram Weekly* 390 Aug. 13-19, 1998.

_____. "Paris Plunges into Egyptology: An Exhibit of Historic Treasures That Lay for Centuries on the Mediterranean Seabed is Now on the Second Leg of Its European Tour." *Al Ahram Weekly* 14-20 Dec. 2006.

_____. "Under the Waves: Will Egypt Built the [Nation's] First Offshore Underwater Museum?" *Al-Ahram Weekly* 13 July 2006.

El-Baz, Farouk. "Finding a Pharaoh's Funeral Bark." *National Geographic* Sept. 1987: 513-533.

Ellis, William S. "Skyscraper: Above the Crowd." *National Geographic* Feb. 1989: 143-174.

Empereur, Jean-Yves. *Alexandria, Jewel of Egypt.* New York: Harry N. Abrams, Inc. (Discovery Books), 2002 [reprint; orig. pub. 2001].

_____. *Underwater Archaeological Investigation of the Ancient Pharos.* [Coastal Man Sourcebooks 2.] Paris: UNESCO, 2000.

Fahim, Kareem. "A City of Legend Embarks on a New Journey." *New York Times* 16 Dec. 2007.

Farag, Fatemah. "Alexandria of the Heart's Mind." *Al Ahram* 7-13 June 2001.

Feeney, John. "The Minarets of Cairo." *Aramco World Magazine* Nov.-Dec. 1985: 10-23.

Forster, E. M. *Alexandria: A History and A Guide.* 3rd ed. [1st ed., 1922; 2nd ed., 1938.] Garden City, NY: Doubleday, 1961.

_____. *Pharos and Pharillon.* 2nd ed. Richmond, Surrey, England: Hogarth Press, 1923.

Franklin, Stephen. "The New Old Alexandria: Rolling Back the Centuries in Egypt's Second City." *Chicago Tribune* 28 Oct. 2007.

Fraser, P. M. *Ptolemaic Alexandria.* 3 vols. London: Oxford University Press, 1972.

Frost, Honor. "Pharos Site, Alexandria, Egypt." *International Journal of Nautical Archaeology* 4 1975: 126-130.

Gambino, Megan. "Underwater World: New Evidence Reveals a City Beneath Ancient Alexandria." *Smithsonian* 1 Aug. 2007 [online edition only]: <http://www.smithsonianmag.com/history-archaeology/archaeology/10025011.html>.

Gassir, Fouad, ed. and trans. *Vacation in Alexandria: Touristic Sites*. Alexandria, Egypt: Archaeological Society of Alexandria, 1971.

Gauch, Sarah. "Diving for Sunken Treasure—of Stone." *Christian Science Monitor* 87:105 26 April 1995: 14.

Gauri, K. Lal and Jayanta K. Bandyopadhyay. *Carbonate Stone: Chemical Behavior, Durability, and Conservation*. New York: John Wiley and Sons, Inc., 1999.

Gauri, K. Lal. "Conservation of Stone: a Literature Review." *Decay and Preservation of Stone*. Ed. Erhard M. Winkler. Boulder, Colorado: Geological Society of America, 1978: 101-104.

Georgiades, Patrice. *Les Secrets du Phare d'Alexandrie*. Alexandria, Egypt: Centre Cultural Hellenique and L'Atelier, 1978.

Goddio, Franck, and Manfred Clauss, eds. *Egypt's Sunken Treasures* [published in conjunction with exhibit in Berlin 13 May-4 Sept. 2006]. Munich and Berlin: Prestel/Martin-Gropius-Bau, 2006.

Goodchild, R. G. "Helios on the Pharos." *Antiquaries Journal* 41 1961: 218-223.

Graham, Bruce J. "Tall Buildings as Symbols." *Second Century of the Skyscraper*. Ed. Lynn S. Beedle. New York: Van Nostrand Reinhold, 1988: 117-148.

Grant, Michael. "Alexandria." *A Guide to the Ancient World: a Dictionary of Classical Place Names*. New York: H. W. Wilson Co., 1986: 22-25.

"Greek Pharos." *Bulletin of the Beaux-Arts Institute of Design* 11 1934: 14-16.

Hague, Douglas B. and Rosemary Christie. *Lighthouses: Their Architecture, History and Archaeology*. Llandysul, Dyfed, England: Gomer Press, 1975.

Halim, Youssef and Fatma Abou Shouk. *Human Impacts on Alexandria's Marine Environment*. [Coastal Management Sourcebook 2.] Paris: UNESCO, 2000.

Halpern, Deb. "Alexandria Shines as Egypt's Mediterranean Oasis." *The Tampa Tribune* 2 Sept. 2001.

Hendawi, Hamza. "Center of Ancient Enlightenment Turns Islamist." *Charleston Gazette* [WV] 10 June 2007: 12A.

Hobbs, A. Hoyt and Joy Adzigian. *A Complete Guide to Egypt and the Archaeological Sites*. New York: William Morrow & Co., 1981.

Holum, Kenneth G. et al. *King Herod's Dream: Caesarea on the Sea*. New York: Norton, 1988.

Homer. *Odyssey*. Trans. Richmond Lattimore. New York: Harper & Row, 1967.

International Workshop on Submarine Archaeology and Coastal Management, April 7-11, 1997. [Coastal Region and Small Island Papers 14.] Paris: UNESCO, 1997.

Karmon, Yehuda. *Ports Around the World*. New York: Crown Publishers, 1980.

Keeley, Edmund. *Cavafy's Alexandria; Study of a Myth in Progress*. Cambridge, MA: Harvard University Press, 1976.

Keller, W. D. "Progress and Problems in Rock Weathering." *Decay and Preservation of Stone*. Ed. Erhard M. Winkler. Boulder, Colorado: Geological Society of America, 1978: 37-46.

Kircheisen, F. M. *Napoleon*. New York: Harcourt, Brace and Co., 1932.

Labib, Subhi. "Al-Iskandariyya." *The Encyclopedia of Islam,* vol. 4 [new edition]. Leiden, The Netherlands: E.J. Brill, 1978: 132-137.

La Riche, William. *Alexandria, the Sunken City*. London: Weidenfeld & Nicolson/Orion Publishing Group, 1996.

Lawler, Andrew. "Ancient Alexandria Emerges, by Land and by Sea." *Science* 307:5713 25 Feb. 2005: 1192-1194.

Lawler, Andrew. "Raising Alexandria." *Smithsonian* 38:1 April 2007: 48-57.

Lawton, John. "Scotland's Egyptian Lights." *Aramco World* 41:5 Sept.-Oct. 1990: 13-15.

Limber, T. Peter. "Beacon Across the Ages." *Aramco World* 45:2 March-April 1994.

Loring, William W. "Chapter 1, Alexandria." *A Confederate Soldier in Egypt*. New York: Dodd, Mead, 1884.

Lucian. *Works of Lucian*. 8 vols. Trans. K. Kilburn. Cambridge, MA: Harvard University Press, 1959.

Lunde, Paul. "The Seven Wonders." *Aramco World Magazine* 31:3 May-June 1980: 14-27.

Macleod, Scott. "Alexandria Rising." *Time* 151:24 15 June 1998.

_____. "Recreating a Jewel: Egypt Has Built an Updated Version of the Fabled Bibliotheca Alexandrina, but Its Commitment to Intellectual Freedom Remains an Open Question." *Time* 155:23 12 June 2000.

Maged, Ahmed. "What to Do with our Submarine Treasures." *Daily Star Egypt* 31 March 2007.

Mahaffy, J. P. *Empire of the Ptolemies*. London: Macmillan & Co., 1895.

Marlowe, John. *Golden Age of Alexandria*. London: Victor Gollancz, 1971.

Matheny, Ray T. "An Early Maya Metropolis Uncovered: El Mirador." *National Geographic* Sept. 1987: 317-333.

Millenson, Michael. "Chicago Developers Plan 2,300-Foot Skyscraper." *Hartford Courant* 27 Oct. 1981: A6.

Morcos, Selim, Nils Tongring, Youssef Halim, Mostafa El-Abbadi and Hassan Awad. *Towards Integrated Management of Alexandria's Coastal Heritage.* [Coastal Region and Small Island Papers 14.] Paris: UNESCO, 2003.

"New 125-Story Skyscraper Would Dwarf Sears Tower." *Hartford Courant* 24 May 1989: F6:3.

NOVA—Treasures of the Sunken City: The Riches of Alexandria. Videotape [60 minutes]. Boston: WGBH-TV/Gedeon, 1997.

Perrottet, Tony. "Journey to the Seven Wonders." *Smithsonian* 35:3 June 2004.

Peters, John P. "Castle of Pharos." *American Architect and Building News* 12 1882: 101-102.

Picard, Charles. "Sur Quelques Representations Nouvelles du Phare d'Alexandrie et sur l'Origine Alexandrine des Paysages Portuaires." *Bulletin de Correspondance Hellenique* 76 1952: 61-95.

Pierce, Neal. "Saving Egypt's Cities." *Hartford Courant* Nov. 25, 1984: D4+.

Pliny. *Natural History.* 10 vols. Trans. H. Rackham. Cambridge, MA: Harvard University Press, 1947.

Plutarch. *The Age of Alexander: Nine Greek Lives by Plutarch.* Trans. Ian Scott-Kilvert. New York: Penguin Books, 1973.

Pollard, Justin and Howard Reid. *The Rise and Fall of Alexandria, Birthplace of the Modern Mind.* New York: Viking Penguin, 2006.

Prikryl, R. and B. J. Smith, eds. *Building Stone Decay: From Diagnosis to Conservation* [Geological Society Special Publication no. 271]. London: Geological Society of London, 2007.

Radka, Larry Brian, ed. *The Electric Mirror on the Pharos Lighthouse and Other Ancient Lighting.* Parkersburg, WV: Einhorn Press, 2006.

Rappoport, S. *History of Egypt from 330 B.C. to the Present Time*. 3 vols. London: Grolier Society, 1904.

Renault, Mary. *The Nature of Alexander*. New York: Pantheon, 1975.

Rice, E. E. *The Grand Procession of Ptolemy Philadelphus*. New York: Oxford University Press, 1983.

Riederer, Josef. "Recent Advances in Stone Conservation in Germany." *Decay and Preservation of Stone*. Ed. Erhard M. Winkler. Boulder, Colorado: Geological Society of America, 1978: 89-94.

Sadek, Rasha. "Passion Under Water." *Al Ahram Weekly* 744 26 May-1 June 2005.

Schwartz, Stephan A. *A Preliminary Survey of the Eastern Harbor Alexandria, Egypt Including a Comparison of Side Scan Sonar and Remote Viewing*. Mobius Group, 1980.

_____. *Alexandria Project*. New York: Delacorte Press, 1983.

Shoshan, Boaz. "Alexandria." *Dictionary of the Middle Ages,* vol. 1. Ed. Joseph R. Strayer. New York: Scribner's, 1982.

Soren, David. "The Day the World Ended at Kourion: Reconstructing an Ancient Earthquake." *National Geographic* July 1988: 30-53.

Special Presentation...You're Invited; the Revival of Alexandria Library: a Unique Project of the 21st Century [flyer announcing 8 May 1991 meeting in New York City]. New York: National Online Meeting, 1991.

"Sphinx: Yale Student Spent 2 Years Crawling on Back of Great Statue." *New Haven Register* 1989.

Stanley, Jean-Daniel, Richard W. Carlson, Gus Van Beek, Thomas F. Jorstad, and Elizabeth A. Landau. "Alexandria, Egypt, Before Alexander the Great: A Multidisciplinary Approach Yields Rich Discoveries." *GSA Today* [Geological Society of America] 17:8 Aug. 2007: 4-10.

Stevenson, D. Alan. *World's Lighthouses Before 1820*. London: Oxford University Press, 1959.

Strabo. *Geography of Strabo*. 8 vols. Trans. Horace Leonard Jones. Cambridge, MA: Harvard University Press, 1967 [reprint; orig. pub. c. 1932].

"Submerged Monuments Tourism." *American Online*, 31 March 2007.

Thiersch, Hermann. *Pharos; Antike Islam und Occident; ein Beitrag zur Architecturgeschichte*. Leipzig and Berlin: Teubner, 1909.

Thompson, J. M. *Napoleon Bonaparte*. New York: Oxford University Press, 1952.

Thubron, Colin. *The Ancient Mariners* ["The Seafarers" series]. Alexandria, Virginia: Time-Life Books, 1981.

Walker, Charles. *Wonders of the Ancient World*. New York: Gallery Books, 1989.

Watterson, Barbara. *The Gods of Ancient Egypt*. New York: Facts on File, 1988 [reprint; orig. pub. c. 1984].

Wilcken, Ulrich. *Alexander the Great*. New York: W. W. Norton & Co., 1967 [reprint; orig. pub. 1931].

Williams, Daniel. "In Egypt, an Old Beacon of Tolerance Flickers: Fatal Stabbings Underline Growing Sectarian Tensions in Historic Port City of Alexandria." *The Washington Post* 13 May 2006: A10.

Williams, Kimberly. *Alexandria & the Sea; Maritime Origins and Underwater Exploration*. Tampa, FL: Sharp Books International, 2004.

Winkler, Erhard M. *Stone: Properties, Durability in Man's Environment*, 2nd revised ed. New York: Springer-Verlag, 1975.

INDEX

*[Pages in **bold** contain photos]*

Abbasids, 89
Abd el-Latif, 97
Abd el-Wahid Marrakuschi, 221
Abu Jasuf Jakud al-Mansur, sultan, 221
Abu Menas, 89
Abukir, 105-106, 163, 168-169, 175-176
Abul-Saadat, Kamel, 160, 164
Abusir, 6, 14-15, 82, 101, 128, 160
Abusir Tower, 128, **130**
acacia (wood), 67
Achillas, 77
Acro-Lochias, 32
Acropolis, 119
Adab (city), 61
Adamnanus, 70
Adams, William Henry, 69
Adler, Johann, 10, 12, 45, 48-49, 52-53, 57, 61-62, 64-65, 67-68, 73, 76, 78, 83, 92, 94-95, 97-98, 131, 215, 222-223
aerial photographs, **205**
Afghanistan, 9, 73, **74**, 132
Aga Khan Award for Architecture, 151
Agami Bay, 104
Agora, 26
Agricultural or Delta Road, 143
air pollution, 124, 147
air raid shelters, 36
Al-Abdari, 30
Al-Ahram Weekly, 147, 153, 172, 174, 176, 179
Albania, 106
Alexander Helios (Cleopatra's son), 79
Alexander the Great, **4**, 5, 8, 15, **16**, 19-23, 26-28, 32, 37-38, 40-41, 48, 71, 73, 115, 129, 162, 215
Alexandria Archaeological Society, 164

Alexandria breakwater, **158**
Alexandria Businessmen's Association, 171
Alexandria Declaration, 168
Alexandria Dive, 176
Alexandria harbor, **154**, **155**, 156, **158**, 181-182, **201**, 205, **210**, 223
Alexandria harbor floor, 176, 179-180
Alexandria illustrations, **108**, **109**, **110**, **111**, **112**, **113**, **114**, **117**
Alexandria market, **207**
Alexandria National Museum, 179
Alexandria planetarium, **200**
Alexandria Port Authority (APA), 154-155
Alexandria, Roman, **210**
Alexandria street signs, **206**
Alexandria Twentieth Century Project, 183
Alexandria University, 152, 167-169, 171, 175
Alexandria (Virginia), **197**, 222
Alexandria Wastewater System Expansion Phase I Project, 170-171
Alexandria Yacht Club, 170
Alexandrian Branch of the Nile, 33
Alexandrian illusionism, 65
Alexandrian War of 47 B.C., 77-78, 83
Al-Malik an-Nasir, 99
almonds, 80, 99
Al-Mu-izz, Khalif, 94
al-Nasir Muhammad b. Kalawun, 137
alphabets, 152, **202**
al-Shaikh, Ibn, 63
Amalric, 97
Amasis, 7
Amathus, 26
Amenemhet III, 214
American Historical Association, 106
Ammianus Marcellinus, 37, 82

Ammon-Ra or Ammon-Zeus, 19-22, 60
Ammonia harbor, 7
Ammonios, 53, 70, 83, 97-98
Amr, Abd-Allah ben, 70
Amr, Ibn al-'As, general, 91
Amrillah, Hakim bi, 72
Amun-Gereb, 176
amusement parks, 217
Anastasius I, emperor, 83
anchorages, 12
anchors, 44
Andrea Doria (ship), 162
Andreas, 85-86
Anfoushi, tombs of, 167
Anianus, 87
anniversaries, 88
Antiguo Matadero de Legazpi, Spain, 178
Antipater of Sidon, 215
Antirrhodos island, 32, 172
Antony, Mark, 33, 40, 79, 82, 116, 172
Apollonius of Tyana, 88
aquariums, 174
aqueducts, 11, 214
Aqueducts of Rome, 214
Arabian Gulf, 190
Aramco World Magazine, 184, **209**, **210**, **211**, **212**, 220-221
Arcadius, emperor, 89
archaeological museums, 169
Archaeological Society of Alexandria, 164
archaeologists, 10-11, 26, 35, 44, 60-61, 89, 95, 132, 134-135, 154, 159-163, 166-167, 171-176, 178-179, 181-182
archaeologists, underwater, 44, 159-164, **165**, 166-167, **168**, 171-176, 179
Archaeology magazine, 163, 172
arches, 36
Archimedes of Syracuse, 66, 71, 151, 218
architectural brinkmanship, 220
Architectural Digest, 192
architecture, 16-17, 47-48, 60, 151-152, 186, 189-190, 219
architraves, 61
Argos, 163
Arianism, 89
Aristeas, 85-87
Armani Hotel and Residences, 189
armies, 77, 104-105
Arrian, 19, 23, 26
Arsinoe, queen, **40**, 41
Artemis, 213
Artemision at Ephesus, 40
artists, 44, 106, **108**, **112**, 115
Asara Canal, 33-34
Ashurst, John, 122-123, 125
Asin y Palacios, Don Miguel, 62-63, 95-96, 215

assassinations, 40, 79
astronomers, 52
astronomical observatories, 62, 71, **211**
Aswan area, 60
Aswan Dam, 177
Aswan Declaration (library), 148-150
Aswan granite, 60, 159, 161, 166
Augusteum, 80
Augustus Caesar, 35, 79, 116, 134
Australia, 55
automatons, 65-66
avenues, 28-29
awards, 151

Babel, Tower of, 219
Babylon, 11, 22, 41, 48, 61-62, 213-214
Babylon, Walls of, 63, 214
Bagdad, 61
Baltimore Friends of the Bibliotheca Alexandria, 151, **204**
balustrades, 65
Bamiyan (Buddha statues), 216
bananas, 177
Banks, Edgar, 61, 70, 159
Barcelona report, 147
barges, 13
Bartholdi, Auguste, 221
basalt lava, 67
basements, 63
baths, 34
Battle of Abukir Bay, 105
Battle of the Nile, 105
Beaver, Patrick, 48, 59
Bedouin, 89, 101
Begram vase, 73, **74**, 132
Beibar el Gaschenkir, 98
Beibar, Zaher 98
Bellini (artist), **86**
bellows, 65
Benjamin of Tudela, 93
Berenice, 43-44
Berlin, Germany, 177-178
Bibliotheca Alexandrina, 148-152, 179, 181, **201**, **202**, **203**, **204**, 223
Bickerman, Elias, 87
Binnen Lake, 129
birds, 17, 21
Bismya, 61
Bithynia, 63
blocks, 59-60, 95, 124, 126, 152, 162-164, **165**, 166-167, 176
blocks, ID sheets **165**, 167, 175
Blunt, Henry, 36
Bodrum, Turkey, 44
Bolbitine branch of the Nile, 35
bombardments, 36, **117**, 124, 138

Bonaparte, Napoleon, 5, 28, **103**, 104-105, 138, 163
Bonn, Germany, 178
Borg El Arab, 144
Branson, Richard, 189
breakwaters, 118, **158**, 159, 162
bridgeheads, 11, 78
bridges, 11, 78, 152
bridges, sky bridges, 188
brinkmanship, 220
British, 59, **117**, 138, 160
British Museum, 74, 121, 134, 172
bronze, 61, 63-65, 116
Brucheion, 32
Brueys, Admiral, 104-105
buccines (trumpets), 131
Buddha statues of Bamiyan, 132, 216
Bull's Horn (rock), 42
Burj Dubai (skyscraper), 188-189, **194**, **195**
burning glass, 71

CGEA Onyx (company), 147
CN tower in Metro Center, Toronto, 186, 189
CNN television network, 147
Caesar Augustus, 35, 40, 79, 116, 134
Caesar, Julius, 35-36, 40, 77-79, 172
Caesarea Maritima, 134-135, **136**, 223
Caesarium, 80, 116
Cairo, 62, 94-95, 105, 118
Cairo Museum, 121
Calatrava, Santiago, 190-192, **193**
Callimachus of Cyrene, 215
Callisthenes, 129
Cambyses, 21, 116
camels, **20**, 89
camera obscura, 70-71
camouflage, 144
campanile at San Marco, Venice, 222
Canada, 186
Canal of Darius, 14
canals, 7, 12-14, 33-36, 89, 106
candlepower, 55-56
Canopic Branch of the Nile, 6-7, 13, 33-34, 101
Canopic Gate, 28, 30
Canopic Road, 28-29, 79
Canopus (city), 176, 179
Cape Eunostos, 138
Cape Hatteras Lighthouse, 55
Cape of Good Hope, 101
caravan trails, 20-21, 23, 89
caravans, 30
Cardin, Pierre, 181-182
cargo, 12
Carians, 8
Caroline, princess of Monaco, 150
Carroll, David, 49
Castor (god), 43

catacombs, 104, 129
catoptrics, 68, 71
cattle, 82
causeways, 11, 78
Cavafy, Constantine, 146
Cecil Hotel, 152
Cedrenus, Gregorius, 63
cemeteries, 30, 52, **88**
censorship, 151
Central Park, New York City, 64, 116, 125
Centre d'Etudes Alexandrines (CEA), 26, 36, 163, **165**
Centre National d'Art et de Technologie de Reims, 182
Chafetz, Gary, 21
chains, 10
Challans, Mary, 38, 40
Chamarya, 94
Champollion, Jean-Francois, 106
Changsha, China, **209**
Chephren, king, 121
Chersonesus, 26, 104
Chicago, 186, 189-192
Chicago "Illinois" (skyscraper), 188, 190
Chicago River, 191
Chicago Spire (skyscraper), 188, 190-192, **193**
Chicago Tribune, 186, 190
child labor, 156
China, 70, 187-188, **209**
Chirac, Jacques, 177
chlamys (cloak), 17
Chosroes, king, 91
Christian Science Monitor, 175
Chrysler Building, 185
churches, 62, 74, 222
cisterns, 34-36, 63
City of Silk (Kuwait), 188
Civil War, American, 115-116, 147
Clarie, Tom and Rosemary, **206**
Clayton, Peter, 37, 134, 223
Clement, 89
Cleomenes of Naukratis, 17, 27, 40
Cleopatra, 37, 77, **78**, 79, 82-83, 116, 172
Cleopatra Selene (Cleopatra's daughter), 79
Cleopatra's Needles, 64, 80, **112**, **113**, 115-116, 125
Cleopatra's palace, 171
cloaks, 17
clocks, 75-76
Closed or Royal Port, 32
Coat of arms, Alexandria, 24
coins, 57, 61, 65, 67, 69, 73, 75, 79, **128**, 130, **131**
College of Heliopolis, 33
colonists, 15
colonnades, 12, 33, 60, 160
Colossus of Rhodes, 41, 213, 221
columns (architecture), 35, 60, 97, 159, 162-163, 166
Commodus, emperor, 130-131, 134

conch-shells, 65
Conder, C. R., 135
Confederation Mondiale des Activities Subaquatiques, 163
Constantinople, 14, 91
Copenhagen, 62, **208**
Copts, 88, **90**, 134, 152
corn measures, 45
corn modius, 134
corn ships, 131
Corniche, 143, 146
cornucopia, 75
Corteggiani, Jean-Pierre, 166
Cosmos television series, **149**
cotton, 115, 142
Council of Europe, 182
Council on Tall Buildings and Urban Habitat, 189
crabs, glass, 63-65, 116, 220
Creek of the Marabou, 104
crenellations, 72, 74
crowns, 44, 79, 161
cruise ships, 155
Ctesibius, 66, 68
cults, 19
cuniforms, 61
cupolas, 98
curses, 86
Curtius, Ernst, 10
Curto, Paolo, 162
customs, 156
Cyprus, 82, 100
Cyrenaica, 7, 14, 61, 72, **74**, 90, 132
Cyrus the Great, 21, 116

Damietta branch of the Nile, 33
dams, 78, 177
Daniel, Suzanne, 87
Darb el Haj caravan route, 89
Dardanelles, 55
Darius Canal, 14
Darolles, Jacques, 182
Darwish, Ibrahim, 174
date-palms, 80
Davidovits, Joseph, 37-38, 59-60, 120
DeCamp, L. Sprague, 69
DeCosson, Anthony, 15, 34-35, 80, 89-91, 101, 137
dedications, 41, 47, 60, 155
Deep Sea Detectives, 51, 55, 161, 223
Delos, 47, 163
Delphi, 163
Delta Road, 143
Demetrius of Phalerum, 85-87
DeMille, Cecil B., 61
Denmark, 183
Der Spiegel magazine, 181
desalination, 167

desert, 19, **20**, 21, 23, 89-90, 144
Desert Gate, 30
Desert Road, 143-144
Dexiphanes, 48
Diabathra (gate), 10
Diamond Rock, 159
Dicasterium, 80
Didot papyrus, 41
Dinocrates of Rhodes, 17, 23, 32, 48
Diodorus Siculus, 21, 26
Dioscuri (gods), 43
diplomats, 47
disappearances, 21
diseases, 170
divers, 44, 92, 159-167, 171, 174-176, 179
docks, 12, 14, 32-33
Domitian, 69, 78-79, 130-131
Dragon Canal, 34
dreams, 8
drinking water, 35-36, 98
Drury, Allen, 32, 141, 146
Drusion lighthouse, 135
Dschahilija (Time of Awakening), 181
Dubai, United Arab Emirates, 188-190, **194**, **195**, 217
Dubailand amusement park, 217
Duke of Alba, 62
Dumas, Jacques, 163
Durrell, Lawrence, 148

earthquakes, 82-83, 94, 98, 137, 161, 175-176, 182, 187
Eastern Gate, 30
Eastern Harbor, 12, 97, 100, 118, 143, 173-176, 179, 181
Ebers, Georg, **4**, **20**, **27**, **40**, **52**, **78**, **90**, **98**, 101, **102**, **114**, 222
Ebstorfen, 98
Eddystone Lighthouse, 59
Egypt (or Progress) Carrying the Light to Asia, 221
Egyptian Labyrinth, 213
Egyptian Ministry of Antiquities, 163
Egyptian Navy, 160, 164
Egyptian Quarter, 32-33
Egyptian Supreme Council of Antiquities, 127, 130, 163, 166-167, 174-175, 181, 217
Ehrlach, Fischer von, 54
Eiffel Tower, 186
El Alamein, 143
El-Aref, Nevine, 174, 179
El-Bakri, Asma, 163, 175
El-Dekheila Port Authority, 154, 156
Electricite de France (EDF), 163
electrum, 115
Eleusinian road, 28
Eleusis (city), 174
el-Falaki, Mahmud Bey, 36, 172

El-Ghouri, sultan, 101
Ellis, William, 219
el-Magreb, Sahib, 63
el-Melik, Calif Walid ben, 71
El Mex, 169
El Mirador, 60
el-Moktadir, 63
el-Nabih, 36
El-Silsilah cape, 169, 173, 175
Emaar Properties, Inc., 188
Emir Buka ed-Din Baibars, 99
Empereur, Jean-Yves, 26, 35-36, 126, 163-164, **165**, 166-167
Empire State Building, 51, 55, 187-188
emporiums, 12
Enaton (town), 90
engineering, 217
entablatures, 61
epigrams, 41-42, 75
Epiphanius, bishop, 51-52, 82
Epoch of Martyrs, 89
Erasistratos, 66
erosion, 119-123, 125-127, 163, 171
Etesian winds, 15
Euclid, 33, 48, 66, 71, 151
Eunostos cape, 138
Eunostos harbor, 12, 106
EuroMed Transport, 156
excavations, 10, 26, 59, 163, 172
expatriates, 145
expeditions, 61
explorers, 135
Expo '98 World Fair, Lisbon, 182

fabric, 93
Faiyum oasis, 33
Falcon City of Wonders, 217
Farouq, king, 138
festivals, 41
figs, 5, 80
fire basin, 67
fireproof stone, 67
Fisher, David, 143-144
fleets, 7, 19, 104-105
flooding, 10, 15, 101, 106, 176-177
fluorescent lights, 182
Forster, E. M., 26, 41, 43, 48, 64, 70, 138-139, 153, 159, 218, 222
Fort Agame, 26
Fortress of the West, 7
forts, 100, 104
foundations, 63, 172-173, 182-183, 215, 217
founders, 14, 15, **16**, 22-23, 94, 160, 163, 174
fountains, 62, 98
Four Seasons Hotel Alexandria, 154
Fraser, A. Mackenzie, general, 106

Fraser, Peter, 9, 26, 42, 45, 47, 65, 73, 75, 130, 139, 218
Freedom Lights (New York City), 55
Freedom Tower (New York City), 190
French, 26, 104-105, 132, 167, 171, 190, 221
friends groups, 151
Frost, Honor, 44-45, 60, 159-160, **161**, 162, 164, 220
Fustat, 91

garbage, 147
gardens, 32, 34, 62, 129, 165
Gasr el-Lebia, 74
Gassir, Fouad, 26, 62, 69, 79, 100, 143, 146
Gate of St. Mark, 30
Gate of Spices, 30
Gate of the Catacombs, 104
Gate of the Moon, 30
Gate of the Sun, 30
gates, 10, 30, 61, 101, 104, 106
Gauri, K. Lal, 119, 121-122, 126
Gedrosian Desert, 20
gem portraits, **40**
gems, 74
General Union of Arab Archaeologists, 174
genius, 15-16
Genoa, 222
geographers, 11
Geological Society of America, 122, 125, 179
George Washington Masonic National Memorial in Alexandria, Virginia, **197**, 222
Gerasa, Palestine, 132
Germany, 144, 159, 177-178
Gerome, Jean-Leon (artist), **103**
Giraldo of Seville, 221
Giza, 94, 155
glass crabs, 63-65, 220
glass cups, 73
glass, mirrored, 182
glass tunnels, 175
glassworks, 82
global warming, 177
globe shape, 57, 65
Goddio, Franck, 126-127, 171, 173, 176-177, **178**, 179
gods and goddesses, 19-20, 22, 41, 43-45, 60, 133, 176
Gohar, general, 94
gold, 80, 219
Gold Plate of Perm, Hermitage Museum, 134
Golden Dome Dubai (skyscraper), 188
Goodchild, Richard, 61, 65, 69, 72-74, 132
Google satellite views, **205**
Gorringe, Henry, 64, 116
Graham, Bruce, 219, 222
grain, 13, 143
grain fleet, 134
granary, 12, 33, 45, 80
Grand Palais, Paris, 177, **178**

Grand Square, 30, **117**
granite, 60, 124, 152, 159, 161, 165-166
Grant, Michael, 29, 141
grapes, 5, 80
graves, 11, 21, 52, 79
Great Harbor, 12, 32, 35
Great Pyramid at Giza, 59, 119, 124
Greco-Roman Museum, 36, 167
Greek Bible, 85-87
Greek Quarter, 32
Greeks, 173
Green Gate, 30
Gregory of Tours, 63, 215
Grimsdale, Michael, **209, 210, 211**
Guatemala, 60
Guinness Book of World Records, 56
gypsum, 49, 59

Haag, Michael, 157
Habachi, Labib, 185
Hackin, Joseph, 132
Hadrian, emperor, 8, 19, 80
Hague, Douglas, 95-96, 134, 162, 218
hailstorms, 87
Hairy, Isabelle, 167
Halicarnassus, 44
Halicarnassus, Mausoleum at, 10, 213
Halliburton, Richard, **39, 46**
Hanging Gardens of Babylon, 62, 213
harpoonings, 159
Hartford, Connecticut, **198**
Hartford Courant, 186
Hatshepsut, queen, 185
haunting qualities, 157
Haven of Happy Return, 12
Hawass, Zahi, 124, 172, 174, 217
healing, 89
Heemskerck, Martin (artist), **64**
Helen of Troy, 8
Helepolis or City Taker, 40
Heliopolis, 116
Helios (god), 73-75, 132
heliostatic effects, 76, 182
Hellenic Institute for the Preservation of Nautical Tradition, 173
Hellenistic Age, 9
Hellenistic artifacts, 167
Hellenistic gods, 44-45
Hellenistic paintings, 10
Hellenistic tombs, 167
Hellenistic town planning, 28
hematite gem, 74
Hephaestion, 7, 9, 27, 40, 65
Hephaestion's tomb, 48
Heptastadium, 11-12, 36, 48, 78
Heracleion (city), 176-177, 179

Heracles, 176
Heracles Theater, Bithynia, 63
Heraclius, emperor, 91
Hercules, 176
Herod the Great, King of Judaea, 134-135
Herodotus, 21, 176, 213
Heron, 65, 68
Herschel telescope, 71
hieroglyphics, 106, 116, 152, 172, 182, **202**
Hilti AG (company), 173
Hilti Foundation, 172-173
Hippodamus of Miletus, 28
Hippodrome, 28
History Channel, 51, 55, 161, 185, 218, 223
Hobbs, A. Hoyt, 22, 145
Holum, Kenneth, 134-135, 223
Homer, 8
Horace, 82
horns, acoustic, 65
Horreya Avenue, 29
horses, 61, 63
Hosni, Farouk, 178
hotels, 154, 181
Hurlbert, William Henry, 115
hydraulics, 66
Hypatia, 89

Ibn Abd el-Hakam, 98
Ibn-al-Shaikh, Yusuf, 62, 95-96
Ibn Battuta, 99
Ibn Hordadbeh of Tunis, 94
Ibn Jubair, 97, 223
Ibn Sirapiun, 33
Ibn Tulun, Ahmed, 94
Idrisi, 53, 59, 69, 95
"Illinois" skyscraper, 188, 190
Illustrated London News, **39,** 117, **144**
India, 101
Indiana Jones, 61
Indians of North America, 191
inns, 15
inscriptions, 43-45, 47, 49
Institut Europeen d'Archaeologie Sous-Marine, 173
Institut Francais d'Archaeologie Orientale, 163
insurance policies, 178
International Monetary Fund (IMF), 170
intolerance, 152-153
invasions, 91-92, 94, 104-105
Iraq, 61
Irenaeus, 86
Irish, 80
iron clamps, 59, 124
Isis, 44, 60, 162, 164, 167, 172, 176, 179
Isis crowns, 44, 161
Isis Hathor, 161
Isis Pharia, 73, 129, 131, 160

Islamic fundamentalism, 153
Ismail Pasha, khedive, 52, 115-116, 221
Israel, 133-135
ivory, 219

Jacob's Well, 11
Japan, 56, 186
Jaqubi, Ibn Ali, 53
Jaqut, 97-98
Jaubert, Pierre, commissar, 105
Jennings-Bramly, Wilfred, 15
Jerusalem, 54
Jesuit College, Cairo, 36
Jesus, 144
jetties, 14
Jewish Quarter, 32
Jews, 28, 54, 85-87
Jin Mao Tower, 187
Jondet, Gaston, 159
Jordan, 63, 132
Josephus, Titus Flavius, 53-54, 68
Juan Carlos, king of Spain, 179
Juliopolis (city), 174
Julius Caesar, 35-36, 40, 77-79, 172
Jupiter-Serapis, 134
Justin, 17

Kadry, Ahmed, 163
Kalawun, sultan, 137
Kapisa (city), 132
Karm Abu Mina, 89
Karmon, Yehuda, 142
Kaufmann, Carl Maria, 89
kedan (stone), 59, 95
Keeley, Edmund, 146, 157
Keller, Walter, 122
Khafra, pharaoh, 121
khamsin (wind), 21
Kibotos basin, 13, 33-34
Kingdom of the Harpoon, 5
Kircheisen, Friedrich, 28, 104
Kitchener, H. H., 135
Kleber, Jean Baptiste, 104
Kneph-Ra, 19
Knidos, 48
Kom al-Nadura, 137
Kom El-Dekkah archaeological gardens, 165
Kom el Giza, 34
Kom-es-Shafur catacombs, 129
Kom Turuga, 34
Kourion, Cyprus, 82
Kraeling, Carl, 132
Kuala Lumpur, Malaysia, 187
kubba (prayer room), 99
Kuwait, 188
Labib, Subhi, 30, 35, 91-94, 97, 99

labyrinths, 63, 213
lamp-holders, 132
Las Vegas, 55, **199**
laser lights, 182
lava, 67, 11
Lawler, Andrew, 176-177
Lawton, John, 14, 220
Legend of the Seas, 155
legends, 8, 10, 17, 21-22, 37, 47, 49, 51-52, 55, 62-64, 69-72, 87, 91, 98-99, 115-116, 176
Lehner, Mark, 119, 121
Leo Africanus, 98
leucos lithos (stone), 59
Libeskind, Daniel, 190
Library of Alexandria, ancient, 27, 33, 85-87, 91, **149**
Library of Alexandria, modern, 148-152, 179, 181, **201, 202, 203, 204,** 223
Libya, 7, 14, 61, **74**, 129, 132
Liechtenstein, 173
Life magazine, 167
Lighthouse Hotel and Residence, Dubai, 189-190
Limber, T. Peter, **212**
limestone, 59-60, 120-121, 123-124
Lisbon, Portugal, 182
Lochias, cape, 12, 14, 32, 173-174
London, 115, 125
Loring, William, general, 116, 147
Los Angeles Times, 119
Lost Army of Cambyses, 21
Louisiana State Capitol Building, **196**
Louvre, The, 41
Lucian, 43, 48-49, 55, 60, 69, 215
Lunde, Paul, 97, 215, 218-219, 223
Luxor, 21, 151
Luxor Hotel, Las Vegas, 55
Luxor light, Las Vegas, **199**
Lynch, Kevin, 223
lynchings, 89

MSNBC television network, 177
M'Bow, Amadou-Mahtar, 149-150
machines, 218
Madinat al-Hareer, Kuwait, 188
Madrid, Spain, 178
magic, 144
Magreb, 30
Mahaffy, John Pentland, 80
Mahmudiya Canal, **34, 35**, 106
Majcherek, Grzegorz, 154
Malta, 104
Mamelukes, 93, 138
maps, **6**, 10, **13, 31, 81**, 98-99, **102**, 130, **142**, 171-172
Maqrizi, 15
Marabout Fort, 104
Marbioush the Greek, 47

marble, 9, 61, 124, 161, 187
marble, white, 59
Marcellinus, Ammianus, 37
Mare Eleusinium, 174
Marea Kingdom, 5
Marea town, 15, 82
Mareotic wine, 82
Mareotis Lake, 5-8, 12-15, 20, 33-34, 80, 82, 89-90, 101, 129, 169, 171
Mareotis town, 15
marine archaeology, 44, 135, 159-164, **165**, 166-168, 171-176, 179
Mariout, Lake, 169, 171
maritime museums, 175
Mark Antony, 33, 40, 79, 82, 116, 172
Marlowe, John, 61
Marmorica coast, 69
Marsa Matruh, 7
Martial (poet), 25
Martin-Gropius-Bau Museum, 177-178
Martyrium of St. Mark, 174
martyrs, 87, 89
Maryut Desert, 90
Maryut Lake, 6, 101, 129, 141
Maryut region, 80, 82
Maskelyne, Jasper, 143-144
Masonic National Monument, **197**, 222
masquad (prayer room), 99
Massachusetts Institute of Technology (M.I.T.), 223
Masudi, 45, 65, 71, 94-95, 215
Matheny, Ray, 60
Mauritanians, 63
Mausoleum at Halicarnassus, 10, 213
mausoleums, 10, 38
Mayans, 60
Mayne, Thom, 190
Mayor, Federico, 150
Mazaces, satrap, 7
McKinley, president, 61
Mediterranean, **6**, **7**, 14, 20, 25, 44, 147, 154, 156, 169-170, 177
Mediterranean Sea Protocol, 171
Medusa, 164
Mega Machines, 185, 218
Melikes-Saliher-Raziq, 97
Melorca, 221
Memphis, 7, 23, 38, 41, 48
Menelaus, 8
Menouthis (city), 176
merchants, 7
message towers, 26
Metropolitan Museum of Art, New York City, 64, 116
Mex, 101, 169
Miami Herald, 119, 152
Miglin-Beitler Developments Inc., 186
millennium, 182

Millenson, Michael, 190
minarets, 62, 184, 221-222
mines (explosives), 143
miracles, 21, 52, 63
mirrored glass, 182
mirrors, 55, 68-72, 220
Mitterrand, Francois, 150
Mobius Group, 92, 162
modius, 44, 134
Moeris Lake, 213
Mohammed (prophet), 91
Mohammed Ali Pasha, 35, 106, **108**, 138
monasteries, 34, 89-90, 144
Mongols, 92
monsoons, 15
Montazah, 143, 173-174, **206**
monuments, 60
moonlight, 92
mosaics, 61, 72, **74**, 132, **133**, 164
moschee (prayer room), 99, 221
mosques, 91, 94, 98, 139
Motewekki, Vezir, 99
motion pictures, 61
Mount Ararat, 61
Mount Nitria, 89-90
Mount of the Horns of the Earth, 7
Mount Vesuvius, 25
Mouseion, 33
Mqrisi, 45
Mubarak, Hosni, 150-151, 155, 177
Mubarak, Suzanne, 150-151
Museo Torlonia, 133
museums, 10, 33, 61, 116, 121, 132-133, 135, 151, 155, 167, 174-175, 177, 179
museums, archaeological, 169
museums, exhibitions, 167, 172, 177, **178**, 179
museums, maritime, 175
museums, underwater, 171
Mussulman, 95
mysteries, 21, 157
mythology, 116

Napoleon Bonaparte, 5, 28, **103**, 104-105, 138, 163
Nasser, Gamal Abdel, 145
National Centre for Art and Technology, Reims, 182
National Geographic, 59-60, 82, 92, 219
National Lighthouse Museum, 55
National Park Service, 55
natron (salt) lakes, 90
Natsios, Andrew, **170**
Naukratis, 7, 16, 34, 176
Naukratis canal, 89
Nautical Archaeology, 162
naval bases, 12
naval battles, 104-105
Navesink Twin Light, 55

navigation, 26
Nazareth, 63
Nazi bombers, 144
Nebuchadnezzar, 62
Necropolis, 28
necropolises, 30
Nelson, Rear Admiral Horatio, 104-105
Nesteroff, Vladimir, 160
New Seven Wonders Foundation, 215, 217
New Tokyo Tower, 186
New York City, 64, 116, 125, 186, 190, **200**
New York Harbor, 55
New York Times, 55, 62, **103**, 119, 140, 152, 154, 169-170
Nicium (town), 15
Nicopolis (city), 79, 174
Nile River, 5-7, 12-15, 33-35, 48, 80, 101, 106, 141, 176-177
Nilometer, 133
Nilus, 133
911 Tribute, New York City, **200**
Nitria, 90
Nitrian Desert, 82
Noah's Ark, 44, 61
noise, 146-147
Noor, queen of Jordan, 150
North American Indians, 191
NOVA television show, 126, 165-166
nummulite limestone, 59

oasis, 17, 19-21, **22**, 33
obelisks, 60, 64, 80, **112, 113**, 115-116, 125, 166-167, 182, 185
octagon shape, 57, 64
Octavian, 79
Odyssey, 8
oil, 142
oil flame, 67, 70
Oktokaidekaton, 90
Old Port of Pharos, 159
Old Testament, 85-87
Olive Land, 7
olives, 5, 7, 80
Olympia, 10, 213
Omar, caliph, 91
omens, 17
optics, 70-71
oracles, 17, 19, 21-22
Orient (ship), 104, 127, 163
Origen, 89
Osiris, 176
Osiris temple at Abusir, 44, 129, 160
Osor-hapi, 44
Ostia lighthouse, 133-134
Otero, Don Modesto Lopez, 62-63
Ottoman Empire, 101

Our Saviour's Church in Copenhagen, 62, **208**, 222
outposts, 7
Oxford Centre for Maritime Archaeology, 172-173
Oxford University, 172-173

Palace of the Ptolemies, 32
Palace Quarter, 32
Palestine, 28, 52, 132
Palm Deira, 189
Palm Jebel Ali, 189
Palm Jumeirah Island, 188, 189
Palm Tower, 188
Panaetius, 29
papyri, 41, 82
papyrologists, 14, 80, 88
Paraetonia, 20, 49
Paris, France, 115, 167, 177-178, 190
Parthenon, 124
Patriote (ship), 163
peace, 182
Pearson, William, 171
pedestrian bridges, 152
Pelli, Caesar, 186
Pelusium, 7
Pempton, 90
Pentateuch, 85-87
pepper trade, 99
perfumes, 142
Peter of Lusignan, 100
Peters, John Punnett, 10-11, 138
petroleum, 67, 70
Petronas Towers, 187
Phare (skyscraper), 190
Pharillon, 32
pharis (barge), 131
Pharos Old Port, 159
Phidias (sculptor), 213, 219
Philadelphia City Hall, 187
philanthropists, 115
Philip of Macedon, 22
Philo of Byzantium, 66, 86-87, 214
Philocrates, 85
Philostratus, 88
Phoenicians, 8, 23, 135
Picard, Charles, 65, 73, 134
Pierre Cardin International Foundation for Culture and Peace, 182
pilgrimage routes, 34, 45, 63, 89-90
pillars, 97-98
pink syenite (stone), 60
pirates, 8, 78
Pirate's Haven, 8
Pisa, 221
planetariums, 151, **200**
plaque, 45, 100
plaster, 49, 60, 82

platforms, 64
Plinthing (town), 15
Pliny the Edler, 25, 125
Pliny the Younger, 25, 47-48, 69
Plutarch, 7, 15, 17, 23, 172
pneumatics, 66
poets, 41-42, 146, 157, 219
Poliorketes, Demetrios, 41
Polish, 185
Polish-Egyptian Archaeology Mission, 154
pollution, 169-171
Pollux (god), 43
Pompey's Pillar, 98-99, **110**
Pontius Pilate, 134
Pope Shenouda, **170**
popes, 93, **170**
population, 147
porphyry, 80
Port of Safe Return, 12
Portugal, 182
Portus Magnus, 173, 179
Portus Mareotis, 33, 82
Poseideion or Temple of Neptune, 33
Poseideion channel, 25
Poseidon (god), 8, 73, **75**, 131
Posidippus of Pella, 41-42, 47, 75
pottery, 82
preservation, 163, 168
priests, 22, 38, 62
Princess Dudu (ship), 172
prismatic, 64
prisoners, 79
Proceedings of the British Academy, 62
Procopius of Gaza, 83
propaganda in stone, 218
prophets, 88
Proteus, 8, 41-42, 88
Psammetichus, 214
Pseudo-Aristeas, 86
Pseudo-Justin, 86
psychic research, 92, 146, 162
Ptolemaic Temple of Osiris, 129
Ptolemy I Soter, 33, 37-38, 40-41, 43-44, 48
Ptolemy II Philadelphus, 37, **40**, 41, 43, 47, 85, 164
Ptolemy IV, 13
Ptolemy IX, 40
Ptolemy XII, 171
Pyra of Hephaestion, 40, 65
pyramids, 37, 59, 119, 124, 213, 217
Pyrucheion, 32

Qaitbay Fort, 9, 36, **137**, **138**, **139**, 140, **158**, 160, 163, **164**, 165, 169-171, 175, 181, **205**, **207**, **212**
Qaitbay maritime museum, 165
Qaitbay, sultan, 138
Qazwini, 98

quarrying, 82
Quay of the Grands Couriers, 155
Queen Mary 2, 156
Quintilian, 25

Raban, Avner, 134
radar, 172
Radka, Larry, 55
railway stations, 155
rain, 21
ram horns, 22
Ramleh, 173
ramps, 61-62
Ramses II, 7
Rappoport, Angelo, 27-28, 33, 79-80
Ras-el-Tin palace and promontory, 9, 106, 138, 143, 159, 168
reconstructions, 106, **209**
Red Sea, 14
reefs, 26, 49, 51, 104
refugees, **144**
Regio Judaeorum, 32
reincarnation, 88
religion, 85-90
religious intolerance, 152-153
remote viewing (psychic research), 92, 162
Renault, Mary, 38, 40
renovations, 57, 70, 83, 94-95, 97-99, 121, 124, 138, 181
resorts, 15
Reuters wire service, 135
Rhacotis, 8, 12, 14-15, 32-35, 44, 179
Rhodes, 213
Ribbat (city), 221
rice, 177
riots, 77, 152
roads, 6, 20, 28-29
Roberts, David, 106, **108**, **112**, 115
Roberts, Emma, 115
Rockefeller, John D., 61
rocks, 12, 26, 49, 97, 159, 220
Rokn el din, 98
Roman Alexandria, **210**
Rome, 45, 54, 77, 80, 131, 214, 222
Rommel, Erwin, Field Marshal, 143
ropes, 61, 159
Rosetta Branch of the Nile, 33, 106
Rosetta Gate, 30, 104
Rosetta Stone, 106
Rosetta, town, 35
royal barge, 172
Royal Bark of Khufu, 59
Royal Fleet, 12
Royal Geographical Society, 132
Royal Harbor, 172
Royal Lodge, 79

Royal Palace Quarter, 12, 32-33, 169, 173
Royal Port, 32
Royal treasure, 79
Rudyerd, John, 59
Rue Rosette, 29
Rund Taarn tower, 62

sabbaka (swamp), 101
Sagan, Carl, **149**
Sahara Desert, 21
Said Pasha, 106
St. Ivo univesity chapel, 222
St. Mark the Evangelist, **86**, 87, 134, 174, 222
St. Mark's Basilica, Venice, 87
St. Mark's Zen Chapel, Venice, **133**, 134
St. Martin of Tours, 63
St. Menas, **84**, 89-90
St. Menas monastery, 90
St. Menaswas (city), 89
saints, 63, **84**, **86**, 89
sakhr (stone), 95
Saladin, 97
salt, 119-121, 123-124, 126-127, 165, 167
Samaritans, 11
Samians, 8
San Stefano Hotel, 154
sand dunes, 21
sandstone, 60
sandstorms, 20-21, 124
Santissima Trinidad (ship), 104
saqiehs, 36
Sarasins, 91
sarcophagi, 38, 40, 79
Sardinia, 104
Saudi Aramco World (magazine), 184, **209**, **210**, **211**, **212**, 220-221
Scetis, 89
Schedia, 34
Schwartz, Stephan, 92, 146-147, **162**
science fiction, 43
Science magazine, 176-177
Scipio, 29
Scotland, 55, **209**, 220
sculpture, 61, 163, 221
Sea Gate, 30
sea level, rising, 176-177
seals (mammals), 8, 41
Sears Tower, 186-187, 189
Sebasteum, 80
Sebastos Harbor, 134-135
Semiramis, 62
Septuagint, 85-87
Serapeum, 33, 45
Serapeum Hill, 160
Serapion Gardens, 160
Serapis (god), 33, 44-45, 87

Seth (brother of Osiris), 176
Seti I, 7
Seven Ancient Wonders of the World, 213, **214**, 215, 219
sewage, 162, 169-171
shafts, 61-62, 65, 70
Shaikh, Ibn al-, Yusuf, 62, 95-96
Shanghai, 187
Shanghai World Financial Centre, 188
Shelbourne Development Limited, 191-192
ships, 104, **154**, **155**, 156, 172
shipwrecks, 26, 101, 105, **168**
Shoshan, Boaz, 100-101
shrines, 38
sidewalks, 64
Sidon (city), 135
siege weapons, 40
silk trade, 93, 99
Silsilah, cape, 19, 173, 175
silt, 35, 101, 142
simoon (wind), 21
sister cities, 151
Siwa, 7, 17, 19-21, **22**
Skidmore, Owings & Merrill, 186, 189-190, 219
sky bridges, 188
skyscrapers, 185-187, **188**, 189-191, **193**, **194**, **195**, **196**, **197**, **198**, 218-219
Smith, Adrian, 189
Smithsonian Institution's National Museum of Natural History, 135, 176, 179-180
Smithsonian magazine, 215
Sodoros, captain, 71-72
Sofia, queen of Spain, 150, 179
Soma, 29, 32, 38, 79
Soren, David, 82
Sostratus, 41, 43-45, 47-49, 60, 62
Southern Gate, 30
Sozomen, 15
Spain, 178, 221
sphinxes, **103**, 105, 119, **120**, 121-122, 162, 166, 171, **199**
Spice Route, 14
spice trade, 99
spiral stairways, 61-62, 65, **208**
Sri Lanka, 183
stained glass, 187-188
stairways, 61-62, 65, 76, 98, 129, **208**
Stanley, Jean-Daniel, 176, 179-180
Statius, 69
Statue of Liberty, 220-221
Statue of Zeus by Phidias in Olympia, 213, 219
statues, 60, 65, 73-74, **75**, 131, 135, 159-162, 164-165, 179, 213, 216, 219-221
steeples, 62
Steganus Channel, 25
Stevenson, D. Alan, 54-56, 59, 68-71, 220

stone weathering, 119-127
Strabo, 11-12, 14, 43, 59, 69, 79, 213
Strato, king, 135
Stratonice, 174
Strato's Tower, 135
streets, 28
strengthening of light effect, 68
stucco, 60
Suard, Abbe, 159
submarine (underwater) archaeology, 160-164, **165**, 166-167, **168**, 171-176, 179
submarines, 175
subterranean canals, 36
Suetonius, 25, 133
Suez, 100
Suez Canal, 115, 142, 221
suicides, 54, 79
Sun god, 19
Sunnis, 91
surf breakers, 83, 97
surrender, 7
Susa, 40
suspended corridors, 48
Swain, John, 161
swamps, 101
Syene area, 60
syenite (stone), 60
symbols, 182, 213, 218-219, 221-224
Syncellus, 47
Syracuse, 71
Syrians, 92

Tacitus, 25
Taenia, 6
Taipei 101 (skyscraper), 187, 189
Taiwan, 187, 189
Taj Mahal, 119
Taliban, 132, 216
tall buildings, 185-191, **193, 194, 195, 196, 197, 198**, 218-219, 222
tamarisk (wood), 67
Tampa Tribune, 153
Taposiris (city), 174
Taposiris Magna, 6, 11, 14-15, 129, **130**, 172
Taposiris region, 82
Taurus channel, 25
telescopes, 70-71
Temple of Artemis at Ephesus, 213
Temple of Diana, 214
Temple of Jupiter Ammon, 19
Temple of Neptune, 33
Temple of Osiris at Abusir, 90, 129, 160
Temple of the Muses, 33
temples, 9, 19-22, 26, 33, 73, 80, 90, 160, 162, 176, 213-214
Terracina relief, Rome, 133

textile industry, 93
thagr (fortress), 100
Thames River, London, 115
Thasos, 26, 163
The Chest, 13
The Diamond, 9, 10,
The Great Door (port), 6
The Pinnacle, 188
Thebes, 19-21, 60, 80
Theodosius, emperor, 45
Thiersch, Hermann, 10-11, 41, 47-48, 52-53, 57, **58-59**, 62-65, 67, 70-71, 73, 75, 78-79, 92, **93**, 94-96, 98-99, 130-131, 133, 139, 165, 181, 220-222
thirst, 20-21
Thompson, James, 105, 148
Thonis (city), 176
Throckmorton, Peter, 44
Thubron, Colin, 12-13, 16, 32
tidal waves, 82
time capsules, 115
Time magazine, 167, 181
Time of Unknowing or Ignorance, 181
Times (London), 192
Timonium, 33, 79, 179
Tokyo, 186
Tomb of Stratonice, 174
tombs, 38, 48, 79, 129, 167, 172, 174, 176
tombs, painted, 10
Torah, 85-87
Toronto, 186
Toulon, Ahmed Ben, 62
tourism, 153, 155, 169, 175
Toussoun, Omar, 45
Tower of Babel, 219
towers, 186-189, 219, 222
trade, 5, 12-14, 16, 33, 80, 82, 93-94, 99-101, 129, 142, 156
translations, 85-87
trash, 147
travelers, 11, 14, 21, 29, 36, 62, 70, 82, 89, 95, 97-99, 101, 115, 135, 147, 176, 213
Traveler's Tower Hartford CT, **198**
treasure, 71
Treasures of the Sunken City, 166
Tripolitania, 61
tritons, 65, 131-132, 220
Troy (city), 8
Trump, Donald, 186, 189
Trump International Hotel and Tower, 192
Trump Plaza and Marina Residences, Dubai, 189
Trump Tower Dubai, 189
tsunamis, 82
Tunis, 94
tunnels, 172, 175, 213
Turks, 11, 101, 138
turra stone, 67

Tutankhamen, king, 121
Tuthmosis II, 115, 185
Twin Towers, New York City, 190-191
typhoons, 187
Tyre, 14, 23
Tzalas, Harry, 173-174

UNESCO (United Nations), 90, 122, 139, 148-151, 160, 167, 169, 174, 181-183, 217
UNICEF (United Nations), 156
underground buildings, 151
underground cisterns, 35
underground tunnels, 213
underwater archaeology, 44, 135, 160-164, **165**, 166-167, **168**, 171-176, 179
underwater associations, 163
underwater museums, 171, 174
underwater parks, 171
underwater tunnels, 174-175
U.S. Agency for Intl. Development (USAID), **170**, 171
University of Alexandria, 152, 167-169, 171, 175
University of Egypt, 33
University of Paris, 160

vacationers, 15
Vailati, Bruno, 162
Vanderbilt, William, 115
vases, 132
Veitmeyer, L. A., 67
Venice, 87, **133**, 134, 222
Vererabilis, Veda, 63
Vespasian, emperor, 79
Vesuvius, Mount, 25
Vezir Motewekki, 99
Vineyard of St. Menas, 89
violence, 152
Virginia, **197**, 222
Virginia Beach, **75**
Vitruvius, 15-16, 66, 125
Volney, Constantin-Francois, 101

Wadi el Natrun, 89, 144
Wales, 95
Walker, Charles, 27, 215
walls, 30, 187
Walls of Babylon, 63, 214
Warsaw University, 154
Warszawa radio mast, 185
Washington Post, 121, 152
water pollution, 169-171
water supply, 35
water table, 167
Watterson, Barbara, 45
weathering, 119
weathervanes, 75

Weber, Bernard, 215
Wedding Tent of Susa, 40
wells, 35
Western Gate, 30
Western Harbor, 12, 118, 143
wheat, 177
Wilcken, Ulrich, 14, 19, 27
Wilde, Oscar, 80
William of Tyre, 93
Williams, Daniel,
wind, 15, 21, 101, 104, 119-120, 156, 190
wind barriers, 120
windlasses, 61
wine, 82
Winkler, Erhard, 125
wonders of the world, 40-41, 62-63, 70-71, 129, 160, 174, 187, 213, **214**, 215, **216**, 217, 219-220
Woods Hole Oceanographic Institution, 164
World Bank, 177
World Confederation for Underwater Activities, 163
World Cultural Center, 190
World Heritage List (UNESCO), 90, 171, 183
World Islands, Dubai, 189
World Lighthouse Society, 183
World Monuments Fund, 125-127, 216-217
World Trade Center, New York City, 190-191
World War I, 26, 55
World War II, 36, 132, 143-144
Wright, Frank Lloyd, **188**, 190

Yaqut, Ibn-Abdullah al-Rumi al Hamawi, 92
Yokohama, Japan, 56

Zen Chapel of St. Mark, Venice, **133**, 134
Zeus-Ammon, 19-20, 22, 213
Zeus Soter, 42, 44, 73, 75, 132, 165

ILLUSTRATION CREDITS

Alexander laying out the city courtesy Andrew Chugg; Oasis of Siwa courtesy egypt.travel-photo.org; Poseidon at Virginia Beach courtesy Katie Kellert at Flikr.com; Abusir Tower courtesy Amicale Alexandrie Hier et Aujourd-hui www.aaha.ch; Caesarea courtesy Bukvoed at Wikimedia Commons; Stephen Schwartz psychic investigator courtesy Stephen Schwartz; Empereur teaching courtesy httpjdalbera.free.fr; Pharos block 1027 courtesy Kim Williams; Natsios and Pope Shenouda courtesy U.S.A.I.D.; Grand Palais Paris courtesy Patrick Debetencourt at pbase; Chicago Spire courtesy Shelbourne Development and Santiago Calatrava; Burj Dubai 160 floors courtesy Emaar Properties Inc.; Burj Dubai March 2008 courtesy Aheilner at Wikimedia Commons; Louisiana State Capitol courtesy Pattie Steib featurepics.com; Masonic National Memorial courtesy Ben Schumin c.Creative Commons; Traveler's Tower courtesy Flickr.com; Luxor light courtesy Wes Keller at pbase; 911 Tribute in Lights courtesy Denise Gould, U.S. Air Force; Alexandria planetarium courtesy p.vtourist.com; Bibliotheca Alexandrina dome courtesy Christian Richters, Aga Khan Trust for Culture; Bibliotheca Alexandrina letter wall courtesy Christian Richters, Aga Khan Trust for Culture; Bibliotheca Alexandrina from across harbor courtesy Christian Richters, Aga Khan Trust for Culture; logo of Baltimore Friends courtesy Baltimore Friends; Bibliotheca Alexandrina interior courtesy Christian Richters, Aga Khan Trust for Culture; Google satellite view courtesy Google; Our Saviour's Church courtesy Squirmelia at Flickr.com; Pharos Changsha, China courtesy Dawidbernard at Wikimedia Commons; Eilean Glas courtesy Michael Grimsdale *Saudi Aramco World*/PADIA; Pharos Harbor in Roman times courtesy Michael Grimsdale *Saudi Aramco World*/PADIA; Arab astronomers courtesy Michael Grimsdale *Saudi Aramco World*/PADIA; Fort Qaitbay surf courtesy T. Peter Limber *Saudi Aramco World*/PADIA; Seven Wonders certificate courtesy www.new7wonders.com.

ABOUT THE AUTHOR

TOM CLARIE holds a Master's Degree in History from the University of Connecticut and another Master's Degree in Library Science from Southern Connecticut State University, where he achieved the rank of full professor. He has researched this work on Egyptian and Alexandrian history since 1980, and visited Alexandria with his wife in 1988. He and his wife wrote the marine history, *Just Rye Harbor*, published in 2005. He also wrote two annotated bibliographies on parapsychology and occultism published in 1978 and 1984 by Scarecrow Press in Metuchen, New Jersey. In the 1990s, Clarie researched and designed 15 educational game decks published by U.S. Games Systems in Stamford, Connecticut. He is currently working on two detailed theater histories. For one of the theaters, he is transforming thousands of mildewed photos and newspaper articles into a multi-formatted archive.